CONSTRUCTING THE BLA[...]

M000287532

A John Hope Franklin Center Book

MAURICE O. WALLACE

Constructing the Black Masculine

Identity and Ideality in African American Men's

Literature and Culture, 1775–1995

Duke University Press   Durham and London 2002

© 2002 Duke University Press All rights reserved
Printed in the United States of America on acid-free paper ∞
Typeset in Carter & Cone Galliard by Keystone Typesetting, Inc.
Library of Congress Cataloging-in-Publication Data
appear on the last printed page of this book.

For Teddy, Johari, and Michael

And, not least, for Pam

CONTENTS

Although the high profile of race in the West has made the black male body into a stark palimpsest of the fears and fascinations possessing the cultural imagination, issues of gender and sexuality, on the other hand, have been so fully naturalized into our popular stories and stereotypes about maleness that the insufferable silence around these issues as constitutive elements in modern black male subject formation is too often mistaken for a sign of their discursive immateriality to black men's lives and letters. It is my hope that this book will go some distance to change that. For its aim is to illuminate the construction of black masculinity in a series of significant texts and contexts of black male subjecthood from 1775 to 1995 in order to adjudge how American preoccupations with gender and sexuality inflect not only the writerly record but the larger issue of the social ideal of black masculinity. I would be mistaken to imagine I could undertake so daunting a project alone, however. Those who have helped me achieve this work, therefore, deserve a greater thanks than these pages can convey. These acknowledgments are but the most public of my profound appreciation to so many.

As this book was seeing its very last revisions, my wife, Pam, was in the final days of her pregnancy with our second child. As I hurried to beat the deadline of her fast-approaching delivery, a deadline less sympathetic than my generous editor's, the irony of our coming to term together — her pregnancy, my book — did not once escape me. Not least because the book, like our unborn daughter, was much delayed in coming. Pam suffered bravely through more than two additional weeks of pregnancy than her obstetricians predicted. Although I belabored my work, for good and bad reasons, a much longer time than that, Pam was, of course, the more long-suffering. She bore both her pregnancy and my protracted isolation heroically. For her limitless patience and encouragement, I am thankful and blessed.

Others, too, deserve my grateful acknowledgment. From the first, Karla Holloway has been a selfless mentor, brilliant teacher, and precious friend. Her faith has sustained me. Cathy Davidson and Michael

Moon rescued me at a very critical time in my development. They, too, are models of intellectualism and trusted friends. Wahneema Lubiano, Houston Baker, Janice Radway, Eve Sedgwick, and Ken Surin also generously lent their genius to my efforts. Whatever sophistication may be found in these pages is due to their influence as well.

At Duke, I have also to thank Tom Ferraro, Ian Baucom, Barry Gaspar, Chouki El Hamel, Joseph Thompson, Stephane Robelin, Candice Jenkins, Rebecca Wanzo, Evie Shockley, Mendi Lewis, Michael Walrond, Julie Byrne, Nicole Waligora, Suzanne Schneider, Caleb Smith, Christian Campbell, Jaya Khasibhatla, David Woodard, Stanley Williams III, Jené Lee, Courtney Baker, Erica James, Alex Perez, Casey Young, and Jill Petty. Also Catherine Beavers, Edwina Newman, Clementine Smith, Cynthia Banks-Glover, and Pamela Montgomery. More recently, I have benefited from the extraordinary generosity of Priscilla Wald. In Priscilla I have found a wonderful new friend, colleague, and counselor.

The middle life of the book's composition was lived at Yale University. There, I had generous and wonderfully supportive colleagues in Robert Stepto, Hazel Carby, Vera Kutzinski, Gerald Jaynes, Rev. Frederick Streets, Elizabeth Alexander, Cathy Cohen, Judith Wilson, Wayne Koestenbaum, Laura Wexler, and Bryan Wolf. Tom Otten and Kelly Hagar did not only impress me with prodigious minds, but were great conversationalists and warm dinner companions when I needed them most. Geneva Melvin's inspiration, even today, has helped keep my work in order and perspective.

At Yale, I was also encouraged in this project by Richard Brodhead, Michael Thurston, Anthony Foy, Noelle Morrisette, Pearl James, Jayna Brown, Tauheedah Rashid, Jeaudine Bontemps, Nicholas Boggs, Elizabeth Hines, Teddy Miller, Suzanne Kim, Paula Campbell, Emily Raboteau, Jake Halperin, and Lorelei Williams. Many thanks too to Diane Repak.

This book has also benefited greatly from engaged responses to its ideas by Bill Maxwell, Dwight McBride, Carol Henderson, and two anonymous readers. Nellie McKay's quiet approval affirmed me when she did not know it. I hope *Constructing the Black Masculine* pleases her. Moreover, smart new books by José Muñoz, Jennifer Brody, and Sharon Holland inspired me to persevere in this project. I owe Faith Smith and E. Patrick Johnson significant debts too. Amy L. Wallace performed valuable research on short order, while my parents prayed their encouragement.

Finally, I have reserved my very deepest expressions of gratitude for Ken Wissoker, Leigh Anne Couch, Petra Dreiser, and Katie Courtland at Duke Press. Ken showed patience beyond words. With amiable nudgings when it was necessary, Ken made the experience of this first book painless. Katie was even gentler. Leigh Anne and Petra labored with me to the end. I owe each of them and Duke University Press a tremendous debt, which I hope desperately my contributions here can begin to repay.

I had institutional support in the preparation of this book as well. The A. Whitney Griswold Faculty Research Grant and Research Fund for Lesbian and Gay Studies at Yale afforded me the resources to secure and research James Baldwin's FBI records. The Andrew Mellon Dissertation-Year Fellowship at Duke University enabled this book's originary germination in the dissertation project I completed for my Ph.D. in 1995.

Earlier versions of chapters 2, 3, 5, and 6 have appeared, usually truncated, elsewhere. " 'Are We Men?': Prince Hall, Martin Delany, and the Masculine Ideal in Black Freemasonry, 1775–1853" first appeared in *American Literary History* (9, 3 [1997]: 398–424), copyright © The Johns Hopkins University Press. It appears here in significantly revised form. "Constructing the Black Masculine: Frederick Douglass, Booker T. Washington, and the Sublimits of African American Autobiography" was collected by Cathy Davidson and Michael Moon in *Subjects and Citizens: Nation, Race, and Gender from Oroonoko to Anita Hill* (Duke University Press, 1995, 245–70). It too has undergone substantial revision for publication here. " 'I'm Not Entirely What I Look Like': Richard Wright, James Baldwin and the Hegemony of Vision; Or, Jimmy's FBEye Blues" was published in *James Baldwin Now*, edited by Dwight McBride (New York University Press, 1999, 289–306). "The Autochoreography of an Ex-Snow Queen: Dance, Desire and the Black Masculine in Melvin Dixon's *Vanishing Rooms*" appeared in *Novel Gazing: Queer Readings in Fiction*, edited by Eve Kosofsky Sedgwick (Duke University Press, 1997, 379–400). I thank the editors of *America Literary History*, and the Duke, Johns Hopkins, and New York University Presses for permission to reprint these essays here.

Recently one of my colleagues in African-American Studies said to me that black women have succeeded in culturally "defining" themselves in their own terms and not those of the racial (or gender [*sic*]) Other. If he's right, then we have no choice but to conclude that black males have *not* done this quite as well as their female counterparts. As my friend, a gentle and scholarly man, put it: "People don't know who we are. Even *we* aren't sure who we are." — Charles Johnson, "A Phenomenology of the Black Body"

That modern American manhood is an affair "between men" is, by now, a familiar axiom. Eve Sedgwick's 1985 book *Between Men: English Literature and Male Homosocial Desire*, distilled from important works by René Girard, Gayle Rubin, and Sigmund Freud[1], advanced an early and ever more lucid theory of the homosocial structure of modern masculine life. Sedgwick's book helped pronounce, definitively, that, at its base, modern manhood was an endless rivalry for the power and privileges of patriarchy animated by the psychic discomfiture of men's mutual fears and desires for one another, often in sexually charged contexts. Of course, given the deeply psychic politics of race characterizing our (post)modern experience, there can be little question that our present conceptions of the masculine in the West owe as much to certain racial preoccupations as they do to the sexual ones that vex the very iteration "homosocial" itself.[2] Indicatively, in yet one more of her peerless essays, "Who Cuts the Borders: Some Readings on 'America,'" Hortense Spillers articulates the significance of race as a constituent factor — the very sine qua non — of the New World invention of the American man. According to Spillers, the "ideology of 'race' in the New World [con]text is founded upon the fundamental suspicion that one is not a 'man.'"[3] Although it may be argued that Spillers intends "man" to signify a universal subject without regard to sex, it should not be forgotten, as Robyn Wiegman notes, that "for African American female and male slaves [in the New World] the possibilities of escaping the category of the inhuman took shape under a bizarrely liberating figuration of gendered subjectivity—that to be *female* or to be *male* provided a rhetorical possibility for entering the determinations of modern social subjectivity."[4] It is not merely by a desperate repudiation of the feminine, in other words, that the New World American man was invented, but equally (if chronically understated) by the homosocial counterconstruction of black male savagery. At no point in the history of the New World, that is, has race *not* constituted a defining feature of our national manhood. Who, after all, can deny the endless and unspeakable power of so many desperate white schemes as American slavery, Jim Crow, the lynch mob, urban dispossession, and, most recently, the prison industrial complex to unman (read: dehumanize) the African American male? Yet, in spite of the historical saliency of race in the evolution of gender in the United States, the exact manner in which racial difference exacerbates an already contentious homosocial rivalry over patriarchal prerogatives (e.g. freedom, power, history, wealth) remains, for the most part, a mystery. Just how *black* masculine subjectivity constitutes itself relative to the masculine hegemony, in other words, or recognizes black masculine subjects as men, in opposition to the putative sociohistoric record noted by Spillers, is a feat of social and psychic wonder that has yet to be definitively named. *Constructing the Black Masculine* is a humble gesture in that direction.

Differently put, while the high profile of race in the West has created out of the black male body a walking palimpsest of the fears and fascinations possessing our cultural imagination, the body of scholarship foregrounding race as a significant text or subtext of masculinity studies remains ironically and inexplicably modest. Despite the burgeoning of recent cultural critical practices responsive to the deconstructive urgencies of race and sex in contemporary America, it remains, as Arthur Flannigan Saint-Aubin has written, that "scant attention if any is paid to the interarticulation between racial and sexual ideology"[5] in American masculinist discourse. As late as 1994, nearly a full decade following Sedgwick's *Between Men*, African American men, "if they [were] not elided altogether," as Saint-Aubin has observed, "[were] understood as a mere variance of European American, middle-class, heterosexual men. To place black men at the center as opposed to the margins of theories of masculinity [seemed] inconceivable."[6] Prior to the mid-nineties, not even a new wave of U.S. masculinity studies, a post–men's movement deconstructionism inspired by the continental work of Michel Foucault, Jacques Lacan, Juliet Mitchell, and other major poststructuralists, seemed capable of imagining black men paradigmatically "at the center" of its critical contemplations or of giving any more than the most peripheral acknowledgment to the racial contingencies of the American masculine ideal. Although the first wave of new masculinities scholarship had crystallized by the early 1980s after more than two decades of sustained feminist scholarship (and at least one decade of sustained black feminist scholarship),[7] not more than a scarce few of the monographs on men and masculinity published in the decade between 1984 and 1994 took up the particularities of African American manhood as a significant object of study, and none appear to have gained much from poststructuralist insights.[8] While such otherwise notable titles as *The Inward Gaze: Masculinity and Subjectivity in Modern Culture* (Middleton), *Male Subjectivity at the Margins* (Silverman), *Rediscovering Masculinity: Reason, Language and Sexuality* (Seidler), and *American Manhood: Transformations in Masculinity from the Revolution to the Modern Era* (Rotundo) comprise a vastly incomplete catalog of those first-wave texts (some British) that ruefully neglect the racial constitutiveness of the idealized man in America and Europe, the contemporaneous titles *Black Masculinity: The Black Male's Role in American Society* (Staples), *White Hero Black Beast: Racism, Sexism and the Mask of Masculinity* (Hoch), *Cool Pose: The Dilemmas of Black Manhood in America* (Majors and Mancini Billson), *Black Men: Obsolete, Single, Dangerous? Afrikan American Families in Transition: Essays in Discovery, Solution, and Hope* (Madhubuti), and *Black Macho and the Myth of the Superwoman* (Wallace), make up the virtual whole of a gaunt compendium of books published during the first wave that consider the social psychological paradoxes of black masculine experience overtly.[9] Not altogether accidentally, only Michele Wallace's essential *Black Macho* sustained its elucidative currency beyond the first wave as the emergent formations of black feminist knowledge exemplified by *Black Macho* had come, by then, to diminish the prosaic sociology of the other nearly "inconceivable" efforts to theorize the black masculine.

Significantly, 1994 witnessed a second wave in masculinity studies, one that transformed what was formerly unimaginable into the nearly realized. That year's watershed of publications on black masculinity including, but not limited to, Arthur Flannigan Saint-Aubin's psychoanalytic essay "Testeria: the Dis-ease of Black Men in White Supremacist, Patriarchal Culture," Kobena Mercer's politically engaged *Welcome to the Jungle: New Positions in Black Cultural Studies*, John Edgar Wideman's reflective *Fatheralong: A Meditation on Fathers and Sons, Race and Society*, and, crucially, Thelma Golden's curatorial tour de force *Black Male: Representations of Masculinity in Contemporary American Art*, actualized the erstwhile hope of situating black men "at the center as opposed to the margins" of a theory of masculinity, betraying the white mask of the previous first wave. These works, most notably, gave lie to the implied neutrality claims of so much white scholarship on men and masculinity, arguing powerfully for an explicit avowal of the inexorable conjunctiveness of race to sex and gender in masculine identity discourse and foregrounding what had been abandoned heretofore to the peripheries of sex and gender scholarship: the b(l)ackside of American masculinity studies.[10]

Since 1994 a number of other significant texts aimed at an ever deeper excavation of the character and construction of the black masculine in the United States has given rise to a yet inchoate but discernible subfield worthy of far greater text than the previous decade produced. Notable among them are monographs by Hazel Carby, Philip Brian Harper, Michael Awkward, Henry Louis Gates Jr., and Maggie Montesinos Sale;[11] and a small collection of edited works by Marcellus Blount and George Cunningham, Toni Morrison and Claudia Brodsky Lacour, Devon Carbado, and Don Belton.[12] This newest swell of committed interest in black men, masculinity, and the identity politics of African American subjecthood by the (traditionally white) academy has even given rise to a multidisciplinary journal singularly devoted to scholarly reflection on "the struggles and triumphs of African American men."[13] The founding of the *Journal of African American Men* (*JAAM*) in 1995, and the organization of any number of major conferences since then (including one convened in the same year on the profundities and provocations of the Whitney Museum's extraordinary *Black Male* exhibit), would seem to hint at a future for black masculinity studies that mirrors the present state of white masculinity studies as it is now depicted by Bryce Traister: "Judging from the sheer number of titles published, . . . papers solicited, and panels presented in the last ten years concerned with the analysis of masculine gender, it would appear that 'masculinity studies' [read: white] has emerged as a discipline unto itself. Masculinity, one might say without irony, is everywhere."[14] While institutional and publishing prejudices may never afford black or other diasporic masculinity studies the perceived ubiquity of white masculinity studies in the United States, the disciplinary evolution of black male matters may be, even at this early moment, irrevocable. However evolved, or still yet nascent, black masculinity studies may presently be, though, the urgency of a wider corpus of elucidative texts has grown significantly since the mid-1990s. The problematical politics of the Million Man March in 1995 dramatically evidenced that urgency.

An ambitious and unprecedented gathering of hundreds of thousands of African American men on the nation's capital, the Million Man March sought nobly to call African American men to "operational unity and [socio-political] solidarity."[15] While few persons of progressive black thought would dispute the political exigencies of "black operational unity," to cite Cornel West,[16] it was the march's none-too-apparent promotion of a narrow liberationist politics, one that perceives the crisis of black America phallocentrically as the consequence of an embattled black masculinity, that finally provoked rigorous dissent from African American feminists — women and men — black gay and lesbian voices, and radical democrats. That the legions of those who participated in the Million Man March, despite its ideological offences, outnumbered those who marched on Washington in 1963 to become the largest black political event in U.S. history, underscores the challenge of complexity and paradox, theory and praxis, still ahead of race, sex, and gender scholarship. That the O. J. Simpson verdict came only two weeks earlier meant that the urgency for greater critical analysis of black men's vexed lives was, by the time of the Million Man March, no longer a black urgency only, nor an invention of far-flung political radicalism, but a national and immediate problem deeply felt, however differently, by black and white Americans. Add to the Million Man March and the O. J. Simpson verdict the brutal sodomy of Haitian immigrant Abner Louima by a tiny mob of Brooklyn police officers in 1997, and the unforgivable 1999 murder of Amadou Diallo, an African immigrant shot nineteen times at the hands of four plainclothes New York officers who quite naturally — given this book's ocularcentric thesis — mistook the victim's wallet for a gun, and the attempt at any further justification of *Constructing the Black Masculine* seems downright pointless.

Schematically, then, *Constructing the Black Masculine* aspires to what social theorist Pierre Bourdieu calls "an outline of a theory of practice."[17] This project's objective is to elaborate a schema of generative modes by which African American men have historically survived the self-alienating disjunction of race and manhood in American culture.

Consisting of a discursive mix of literary theory, photography and the visual arts, race and ethnic studies, psychoanalysis, queer theory, feminist epistemology, and performance studies, *Constructing the Black Masculine* attempts to variously map the discrete metaphysics by which black masculine identity has sought its own ideological equilibrium of race and masculine subjecthood. More specifically, it seeks to understand the representation of masculinity in a series of significant texts and contexts of black male subjecthood from 1775, roughly, to 1995 in order to apprehend how social preoccupations with race, gender, and sexuality inflect not only the writerly record but the larger issue of the social ideal of black masculinity. All too aware of Traister's recent alert to the dangerously normativizing vagaries of the double-pronged crisis theory in contemporary masculinity studies, according to which masculinity seems always to emerge, predictably, *in* and *as* crisis, *Constructing the Black Masculine* nevertheless outlines another theory of gender angst. Its teleology, however, is not invested in reproducing another regulatory fiction so much as it is in bringing race to bear on a crisis theory in order precisely to deny the normativity of those erstwhile deployments.

Part 1 of this book, "Spectragraphia," posits the central problem of modern black male subjectivity. It argues that the trace of the black male body, its doubly spectral and spectacle perceptibility in the public eye, is an evolutionary consequence of the simultaneous "overabundance and . . . failure [*defaillance*] of the visible," as Jacques Derrida would have it, "the too-much and the much-too-little, the excess and the default [*faillite*]" of vision in (post)modernity.[18] Informed by recent reflections on modern photography (Barthes, Sontag, Silverman, Derrida), chapter 1, "On Dangers Seen and Unseen: Identity Politics and the Burden of Black Male Specularity," cites the monocularistic gaze of Western racialism as the signal menace to the coherence of the black masculine corporeal ego. Distinctive from *the look* which, following Kaja Silverman, I shall strive to keep strictly reserved for oculomotor activity (dioptrics),[19] *the gaze*, which is "the intrusion of the symbolic into the field of vision,"[20] offends by fixing or "enframing" (*das Gestell*) black male images narrowly within a restricted representational field Silverman calls "screens," Roland Barthes an "image repertoire," and Homi Bhabha "stereotype." These terms name a "rigid and limited grid of representations," as Kobena Mercer writes, "through which black male subjects become publicly visible . . . reproducing certain *idées fixes*"[21] about the nature of black male otherness.

Materialized in chapter 1 by a camerical metonymy that, owed to a suggestive constellation of mimetic and symbolic determinants, is also decidedly male, the racialist gaze (which by definition need not be a racist gaze) congeals black male bodies into statued rigidities, arresting representation at the threshold of human being. Differently put, as "camera lenses . . . sometimes look like guns or Cubist penises,"[22] in the way photography critic Alex Hirst has observed, cameras sometimes wield the same power of guns and penises to abase the Other (if not the cultural remembrance of them brandished at black men) to similarly reduce black male images to "crushing" Fanonian objecthood. Not unlike the ways photographic works of Robert Mapplethorpe (and Carl Van Vechten before him) once vexed black male representation, the camerical gaze of contemporary photographer Albert Watson self-consciously captures — that is, frames — the black masculine as a rigidity with results conveying a productive ambivalence toward the very project of metaphotography that a number of Watson's portraits realize. For, as my reading in chapter 1 of Richard Wright's *Native Son* illustrates in fiction, the metarepresentation of racial surveillance in photographic media too can cut a broad swath. At one end, the metaportrait allegorizes: Inasmuch as *Native Son* consistently reveals the protagonist's frustrated attempts at articulate self-expression to be only the most unfortunate consequence of a more extensive motor paralysis stammering speech and act coevally, Watson's portraits might well allegorize the indefensibly framed misrecognition of black male subjects under white eyes that Wright, specifically, and *Constructing the Black Masculine* generally, depict. Or conversely, because Bigger is a far more agile mind than the public image of him (i.e., his visual tracings in the fictional news accounts rendered in *Native Son*) portrays, Wright's aesthetic ambition in the novel (and Watson's visual endeavor) may be more precisely antiallegorical. As Bigger's attempts at articulate self-expression seem to grow, oddly, less urgent with him, his final withdrawal from speech in Book 3 of *Native Son* soon resembles the designs, not despair, of a kind of subaltern hero who most certainly *can* speak, but, following Gayatri Spivak's famous essay, tactically refuses to.[23] Whatever Bigger Thomas's fate, however, abjection or subversion (by novel's end, Bigger's life is indisputably doomed, but to the martyr-hero, some principles are worth dying for), in *Native Son* there's no contesting how profoundly reckless racial eyeballing can be on black male embodiment. Who's to say that the curious alienation one discerns in the looks of so many of Watson's black male subjects is not to be taken as a performance of refusal as well?

Because such reckless eyeballing as that which may provoke refusal *fixes*, or more preferably put, *frames* black men within phantasmagraphic screens of representation, chapter 1 establishes *enframement* as the ur-trope of black male specularity for this study. Chapter 1, then, is not only about black men's entrapment within professional photographic frames but about the concomitant angst produced by what Susan Sontag describes as the "photographic" vision of everyday life: a modern ethics of seeing the world, "a habit of . . . looking at reality as an array of potential photographs." "Photographic seeing, when one examines its claims," Sontag writes, "turns out to be mainly the practice of a kind of dissociative seeing, a subjective habit which is reinforced by the objective discrepancies between the way that the camera and the human eye focus and judge perspective."[24] As we are accustomed, moreover, to looking in our world (as much as looking at our world) through so many frames — "the frames of pictures, the frames of television screens, the frames and sub-frames of computer screens," Simon Unwin observes[25] — chapter 1 may be said to limn a theory of the frame(-up) upon which every subsequent chapter is predicated. An interpretive imposition on black men's being in public space, the frame (-up) restricts, if not altogether dooms, a black man's potential for transcending the chasmed otherness of race by establishing boundaries (screens, image repertoires, stereotypes), mental *parerga*, that thwart sameness. In much the same way colonial stereotype, in Bhabha's words, "impedes the circulation and articulation of the signifier 'race' as anything other than its *fixity* as racism,"[26] the *parergon* (lit., the frame, i.e. the ineradicable difference between the colonized and their colonizers) delimits the representational range of the "photo-graphed" (Lacan) black male by keeping him in his place. Of course, insofar as the parergon must labor, dam-like, against the weight of an irrepressible counterforce of associative identification poised to overflow it, it sometimes "creaks and cracks, breaks down and dislocates," as Derrida explains, "even as it cooperates in the production of the [framed] product."[27] Lying beyond the parergonal border, it is what he must not become, finally, that the fractured parergon strains to check.

But much more than representation threatens to undo a picture frame. For quite apart from the flat dimensions of height and width the picture frame so readily summons into view, a third and fourth dimension stand by to render both frame and subject "geometral." Opposed to the antiperspectivism of what Lacan describes as a metaphysics of "flat" optics, the picture frame's third dimension of "geometral" depth obtains by the frame's keyhole function. On the gallery wall, the easel, the mantelpiece crowded with bric-a-brac, the frame alienates all (even the admirer who would seem to be drawn to its picture). However alluring the picture's bidding, the frame authorizes but a single, fixed angle of vision that, like any keyhole view, enacts distance between the present world of the spectator and the picture world, thus distorting the picture's reality (what the reality of it must be like, in other words) by an anamorphic schema. The measure of the impassable space the frame insinuates between here and there, now and then, however — its geometral depth — "takes [the frame's] thickness into account [and] makes us see the picture from the side"[28] as to undermine flat photographic vision and keep living beings from being turned into things.

The frame's fourth dimension is time. Or rather, to put it more precisely, the frame's fourth dimension is history to which time, an indomitably living thing, pretends obeisance. While *Constructing the Black Masculine* announces a two-hundred-year history of black masculine self-expressivity from 1775 to 1995, this sweeping periodization functions as loosely as the running time of a film or video does. The running time of a filmic production does not record a measure of the duration of the continuous action that is called the film's plot so much as it records the sum total of time its discrete episodes accrue to render the film's accumulated meaning. *Constructing the Black Masculine* gets on, then, not according to the misimpression of a single and continuous historical frame extending from the late eighteenth century to the late twentieth century, but by a series of representative historical episodes that helps render black masculinity evolutionary, frame by frame. I have elected this strategy because, as the novelist Charles Johnson put it in his little-known essay "A Phenomenology of the Black Body": "We are . . . beings who must fashion *moment by moment* what meaning our lives will have. . . . [Thus] one can only achieve adequateness in describing the black male [by] . . . examining [him] as he . . . exhibits over time a series of profiles or disclosures of being."[29] Notwithstanding the chronological compass this book's subtitle announces, in *Con-*

structing the Black Masculine there is no pretense of periodization in 1775 and 1995. There are only the "profiles," the episodes, in between.

Chapter 2 is the earliest profile considered here. Giving emphasis to the long cultural history of African American Freemasonry, "'Are We Men?': Prince Hall, Martin Delany, and the Masculine Ideal in Black Freemasonry, 1775–1865" represents the first among three illustrations of black men's historical attempts to settle the spectragraphic predicament. Pursuing the impulse toward self-made manhood and black masculine ideality in the black American Masonic movement of the eighteenth and nineteenth centuries, chapter 2 describes a phenomenon that may be said, like Dana Nelson's theorization of "national manhood," to describe the formulation of "an ideology that has worked powerfully since the Constitutional era to link a fraternal articulation of . . . manhood to civic identity" in a specifically black new world context.[30] Emblematized by the race work of Prince Hall, founder and first Grand Master of African Lodge No. 1, and later by the Masonic writings of Martin Robison Delany, the nineteenth-century race man best known for the editorship of the *North Star* he shared with Frederick Douglass from 1847 to 1849, the historical African American Freemason sought to counter the spectragraphic frame-up through rituals and pictorial self-representations of disciplined, domesticated individualism and abstract disembodiment. While two widely circulated images of Hall and Delany, extraordinarily dignified and dressed nobly in full Masonic and military livery, picture them approximating a cultural ideal of black masculinity for the eighteenth and nineteenth centuries, their republican posings inversely highlight the pitfalls of pictorialization each man's picture seeks to resolve. For at precisely the moment the one or the other poses, he apprehends himself *as an image* and submits willy-nilly to the hegemony of camerical social vision that has previously abjected him and required his portraited self-display in the first place.

Following up on the problem of *spectragraphia*, chapter 2 puts itself to still another task. Inasmuch as the Masonic lodge-room has been, in mimetic form and function, an enduring sanctuary for the ritual (re)construction of black masculine identity, the lodge-room's austere architecture and uncompromising interiority have also figured to iconographically model the idealized masculine self, externalizing the internal impulse to ideality in wood and brick even as its externality, doubling back, helps the Mason internalize the lodge-as-self. It is precisely this nature of ritual work that Prince Hall Freemasonry has been quietly devoted to for over two hundred years. The oldest surviving organized body of black men in America, and, according to historian Loretta Williams, the only such group "able to date and document their existence from [the colonial period] to the present,"[31] Prince Hall Freemasonry is first in the historicization of the vague *edifice complex* animating black masculine consciousness that Part 2 of *Constructing the Black Masculine* calls critical attention to.

Relatedly, in chapter 3, "Constructing the Black Masculine: Frederick Douglass, Booker T. Washington, and the Sublimits of African American Autobiography," I explore the dialectics of desire and psychic disquiet in black masculine literary self-representation as the initial step toward delineating what I shall refer to, borrowing from Pierre Bourdieu, as the "habitus," or elemental structures, of black masculine consciousness where, to lift a more elegant phrase from James Baldwin, the price is paid for others' insecurities.[32] The psychic habits of racial and sexual repression which chapter 3 identifies by manifestations of acute ambivalence and panic in Douglass's *Narrative* of 1845 and Washington's *Up from Slavery*, are paradigmatic of the spectragraphic angst which forms, to no insignificant degree, the black masculine habitus materially realized by the austere architecture of the Masonic lodge-room in chapter 2 and the vast panoply of domestic architecture to come in chapter 4. Chapters 2, 3, and 4, then, coalesce loosely around *archi-textual* tropes, figurations of black vernacular architecture and craft in black cultural history and literature which, operating within the simultaneity of mimesis and metaphor, function as self-reflexive concretizations of the invisible anxieties of black masculinity. Where, in chapter 3, a crude broom closet offers the young, vulnerable Douglass a temporary safe place from his tormented witness of the racial (and inevitably sexual) violence unleashed on his Aunt Hester, chapter 4, "A Man's Place: Architecture, Identity, and Black Masculine Being," argues that a house (and its analogous architectures) is not only a hiding place from the overdetermined visibility of black maleness in the public sphere, but that it is an extrinsic, self-reflexive metaphor for the intrinsic "dispositions" of selfhood, those "structuring structures," as Bourdieu says,[33] that constitute the black masculine habitus. A figure, in other words, for black masculine self-possession, and not at all "in formal space of departure . . . [from] the confines of the [feminine] domestic,"[34] as separate-sphere ideology is wont to maintain, the house (and certain other architectures — the closet, the cabin, the cellar) achieves the image of the structure of black masculine consciousness and is among the principal objects, materially and metaphorically speaking, of African American men's literary and cultural figuration. Considered cumulatively, houses, huts, closets, cabins, and cellars constitute a unique class of archetypal constructions in black masculine expressivity intimately connected to the characteristic search and discovery of a cohesive black masculine self in black masculine life and letters.

Put more succinctly, chapter 4 reveals a reciprocal relation between the "socially constituted system of cognitive and motivating structures" that make up black masculine self-identity (habitus), and the "socially structured situation" in which desire or disquiet is manifested, as in Douglass and Washington.[35] In a manner congruent with Bourdieu's dialectic of the internalization of externality and the externalization of internality, the close reading of Jean Toomer's 1923 modernist classic *Cane* in chapter 4 reveals that the structuring structures of the black masculine — that is, the psychic topographies of desire and disquiet manifested by archi-textual metaphors that understand the black masculine to be at home (*das Heimliche*, according to Freud) or not (*das Unheimliche*) — reproduce themselves in constructions of space.[36] Not the least of these constructions, I hasten to add, is the imagined space of language articulated most forcefully by Eve Sedgwick's theorization of the homosexual closet as, at root, a speech act spatially — indeed architecturally — conceived. Not even in speech acts, however, is one entirely safe from the spectragraphic threat. Consequently, and because none of the early or historical efforts to elude the violence of monocularistic vision described in chapters 2, 3, and 4 ever fully escapes the briar patch of their fundamental reliance upon the very hegemony of vision that has framed black men from the first, these chapters comprise a section of their own. Together they make up Part 2 of *Constructing the Black Masculine*, "No Hiding Place."

Part 3 of *Constructing the Black Masculine*, "Looking B(l)ack," distinguishes itself from the previous sections by its concern to demonstrate black masculinity as a performative deformation of the black male body under (white, mostly male) objectification. Extending from what originally manifests itself in the resistant look of the subaltern subject, a manner of seeing that "has all along possessed the capacity to see otherwise from and even in contradiction to the gaze,"[37] the performative properties of the black masculine reappropriate the objectified body and, following the dialectical pathway forged in advance by the resistant look, "dramatically oppose the representational logic and material practices"[38] of enframement and arrestation. Part 3 is about the phenomenon of *debordement*, "a certain repeated dislocation" of the spectragraphic, "a regulated irrepressible dislocation, which," as Derrida's theory of the frame goes, "makes the frame in general crack, undoes it at the corners in its quoins and joints, turns its internal limit into an external limit . . . [and] makes us see the picture from the side of the canvas or the wood."[39] We are made to see black masculinity from new angles, new looks that powerfully revivify what would seem fossilized by the camera/gaze.

Chapter 5, "'I'm Not Entirely What I Look Like': Richard Wright, James Baldwin, and the Hegemony of Vision; or, Jimmy's FBEye Blues," returns in short order to the foundational insights of Wright's *Native Son* to highlight the irony of the near identical manipulations by the FBI (read FBEye) to "frame" Baldwin, visually and criminally, within a primitivistic image repertoire. Ironically, in his 1949 *Partisan Review* essay, "Everybody's Protest Novel," Baldwin excoriated *Native Son* for the calamity of Bigger Thomas's resignation to "the possibility of his being sub-human and feel[ing] constrained, therefore, to battle for his humanity according to those brutal criteria bequeathed him at his birth."[40] Baldwin's real-life trials as a native son of Harlem reveal more than the mere "possibility" of the state's panoptic power to render black men "sub-human"; Baldwin's peculiar specularity as a sexual minority to boot cinches a more certain intrusion of xenophobic fears and fixations upon the state's field of vision. While "Everybody's Protest Novel" hints at Bigger's powerlessness to wrest his humanity from the stubborn clutch of racial despair according to the "brutal criteria" of vision that first dispossessed him of it, Baldwin's fondness for the flash of cameras, his big-eyed, staring poses, and admittedly sly mien ("There's something misleading about my manner. I'm not entirely what I look like.") would seem to belie the basis of his attack on Wright, demonstrating how inescapable the struggle for racial honor is on any but the grounds "bequeathed [the striver] at his birth." More defiant than Bigger Thomas, however, Baldwin challenges the photographic predilections typical of Western ways of seeing with resistant looks out of eyes he discovered could serve him as weapons.

Similarly, chapter 6 points to another instance of specular defiance. "What Juba Knew: Dance and Desire in Melvin Dixon's *Vanishing*

Rooms" articulates the deformational potentiality of black masculine visibility in choreographic terms. It defines postmodern black masculinity as a proprioceptive improvisation on the spectragraphic themes of black masculine (mis)representation in the racist imaginary. Still more pointedly, chapter 6 argues that because postmodern black masculine identity tends to assert itself in a repertory of characteristically black male body stylizations that range from athletic to comedic to cool, the history, theory, and practice of black male performativity in dance, popular and performance, are especially suited to the task of uncovering (or perhaps only recovering) a hermeneutics of black masculinity that is neither heterocentric nor misogynistic but develops out of a uniquely male racial experience nonetheless. Highlighting Melvin Dixon's 1993 dance novel, *Vanishing Rooms*, and Bill T. Jones's 1995 memoirs, *Last Night on Earth*, I maintain that the improvisational capacities of dance offer critical recourse to another language for surveying alternate realities of liberated black masculine life. Recourse, I hasten to add, heretofore unexplored.

Finally, in the afterword to *Constructing the Black Masculine*, I show how Frantz Fanon's *Black Skin White Masks* performs not only a semi-autobiographical subversion of the racial gaze previously exploited by Baldwin, Dixon, and Jones, appropriating the discourse of theater to accomplish it, but equally how it deconstructs the inherent ocularcentrism of modern Western philosophy simultaneously. That is to say, besides depicting Fanon as acting up and acting out of predictably stereotypical frames of racial reference (a strategy and rhetoric which might be said in a sexualized context to bear an antecedental relation to contemporary gay and lesbian activism), *Black Skin White Masks* offers up an implicit critique of the ocularcentric philosophical traditions which have given us Heidegger, Nietzsche, Sartre, Foucault and, indeed, Fanon himself. Unlike the rest, however, Fanon unfixes the frame(-up).

Crucially, Fanon's supplementarity in this book on African American male identity also unhinges an additional frame that Derrida did not imagine, a frame particular to the schema of *Constructing the Black Masculine*. For the further aim of the afterword is to disturb the continental egoism of African Americanists and African American subjects localized within mainland U.S. cartographies. So who cuts the borders of African American masculinist identity? In *Constructing the Black Masculine* Fanon does, subverting the ocular frame(-up) by which

Western racialism succeeds while simultaneously disjointing the frame of U.S. narcissism. This coincidence of double and triple subversions in *Black Skin White Masks* affords the afterword a unique utility. Not only does the afterword now describe the deeply complex dialectics of a particularly masculinist anticolonial impulse. In the finality of the widening colonial landscape which Fanon's Martinique symbolizes in this study that impulse's shared, if understated, "Americaness" calls out for other, more deliberatively comparativist studies in black masculinity.

If *Constructing the Black Masculine* succeeds, then, it will do so not as a comparativist project so much as a project with a comparativist's vision by book's end. If it does not succeed, its vision will matter less than the failure it may mean, finally, to heed the cautionary wisdom of black male writer John Edgar Wideman whose metaphor of the "unfinished building" of the black masculine has helped to "frame" the scope and schema of this book: "Each generation approaches the task of becoming men as if no work has been accomplished before. Treats an unfinished building as if it's a decaying, useless building and feels compelled to tear it down, start over, instead of utilizing solid foundations bought and paid for with the ancestor's blood."[41] In this book so insistently wed to the tropological language and explanatory power of the arts and crafts of building design and construction, the introduction of new levels of thought, of discourse, of place and politics, like stories built upon a steady foundation, is the highest goal. That goal's fulfillment, however, cannot be purchased cheaply. For what I hope this book will reveal in the end, is that the structuring structure of the black masculine is neither a fully cohesive construction nor an entirely innocent one either. Much sooner than we may care to, we may have to not only abandon all references to a singular black masculine identity for an increasingly nuanced plurality of black masculine identities; but we may soon have to face up to the problem that even the most plural conception of masculine formations, to greater or lesser degrees, risks the reconstitution of masculinity into smaller, subtler regimes of heteronormativity and patriarchal prerogatives in black contexts. Only then will we know that we are, at long last, nearing completion of the building.

PART ONE

Spectragraphia

CHAPTER ONE

On Dangers Seen and Unseen

Identity Politics and the Burden of Black Male Specularity

There are said to be certain Buddhists whose ascetic practices enable them to see a whole landscape in a bean. — Roland Barthes, *S/Z*

Dateline: December 4, 1994. *The New York Times Magazine* features on its cover a reverse, full-color headshot of an unidentified black man. Earringed and hair closely cropped, the man's naked nape advertises the feature article in slim white superimposed letters: "The Black Man Is in Terrible Trouble. Whose Problem Is That?"[1] (fig. 1). Although the magazine's editors clearly intended the question of black male survivability raised by this title to address black men's *social* plight in contemporary America, the visual conditions of indeterminacy preserved by the anonymity of the man on the cover and his uncompromising rejection of the camera suggest that black men suffer the double jeopardy of a *social and representational* sort simultaneously. Taken by the much celebrated fashion and advertising photographer Albert Watson, who has been called "the greatest little-known photographer in the world," this dim portrait could scarcely have been any better suited to the public discourse going on around black masculine identity then and now. For few white photographers besides Watson—Van Vechten, Mapplethorpe, and Dureau notwithstanding—have lent so much racial relevancy to their photographic works.

Albert Watson's professional fitness for representing black men and black male matters, I admit, is not without its own troubles and problems. He is, after all, a middle-aged white man who's been blind in one eye since birth. (Since camera vision is of necessity monocular, the persistent difference race makes in the visual arts may be a greater bane than blindness to fair photography [i.e. to the just image over against the accident of just an image] of black male subjects by white men). Moreover, Watson's style is, as one critic put it, "brazenly fetishistic."[2]

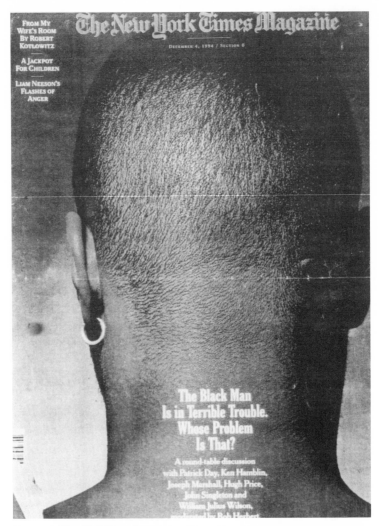

Figure 1. *New York Times Magazine*, Dec. 4, 1994

Since fetishism constitutes precisely the most egregious problem for representations of the black man in American public life, Watson's ways of picture taking would not seem to reflect an aesthetic manner suitable to any black masculinist project. But it is exactly Watson's signifying monocularity and the fetishistic photography he fancies that, counterintuitive as it may seem, suit his work well to contemplations of the "problem" of the black male. Both his person and work, then, his impaired vision and his portfolio of pictures, powerfully demonstrate the photographic ways white people tend to look at black people in racialist societies. In other words, the very issues that would provoke distrust about the race politics of Watson's photographs and their place, tangential as any magazine cover may seem, in American popular discourse, are, ironically, the precise ones that fit Watson for antiracist intellectual musings: His dozens of photographs of black men consistently reflect the face of black male identity not so much *as it is*, but *as it is prejudicially seen*. And Watson's cover for *The New York Times Magazine* is no exception. It is, like many more of its kind, what literary and cultural theorist W. J. T. Mitchell calls, in other words, a *metapicture*, "a representation of a representation."[3] Evincing the sort of hypericonization of cultural artifacts Mitchell has advanced in his two books, *Iconology* (1986) and *Picture Theory* (1994), Watson's cover portrait belongs to that class of pictures which, "in their strongest forms . . . don't merely serve as illustrations to theory; they picture theory."[4] As metapicture, Watson's cover for *The New York Times Magazine* pictures the nation picturing black men.

This is not Watson's first effort to frame the black male body for aesthetic effect. Among the identifiable subjects his camera has captured, heavyweight boxer Mike Tyson, bad-boy performer Bobby Brown, and the late rap artist/actor Tupac Shakur are more popularly known. In his framing of Tyson, Watson duplicates the technique and perspective of the *New York Times Magazine* cover (fig. 2). Only one's vague familiarity with Tyson's conspicuous profile rescues him from the anonymity of Watson's other model. His 1992 portrait of Bobby Brown is similarly seen (fig. 3).

Differently approached, Watson's portrait of Tupac Shakur was part of the collection of images that promoted the 1992 film, *Juice*, in which Shakur played a lead role. Given Watson's penchant for shooting black men from behind, as we have seen, it is interesting to compare this picture of Shakur, facing the camera and looking deeply, directly into its lens (fig. 4). Shakur's stare appears to counter the camerical gaze depersonalizing Brown, Tyson, and the nameless Other. But in truth Shakur's counterlook fails. For the veil of the heavy black hood lying sinisterly over Shakur's head diminishes his power to resist the camera's gaze, not least because it villainizes, dresses Shakur in a fiendish garb. His stare threatens, then, with an ocular bravado but never meaningfully challenges the gaze of the white male artist because any significant subversion of it is always already contained — framed — by the subtextual work of black male stereotype. To add insult to pictorial injury, the would-be resistance in Shakur's eyes is mocked, finally, by the

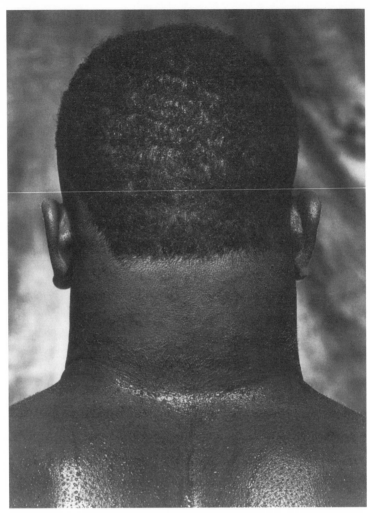

Figure 2. Albert Watson, "Iron" Mike Tyson

signifying phallicism of his short, blunt pistol. Shakur might just as well have been photographed from behind too, since his is a comparably abject pose. The picture remains, however, uniquely instructive. As it illustrates most vividly, Watson's many images of young, black men are, finally, photographic studies in fetishism. These black male models are photographed not as men, but "as specimens."[5] "These are primarily photographs about the power of fetish," James Truman writes in the introduction to Watson's published collection, *Cyclops*, "testify[ing] to the photographer's enthusiastic complicity in the process."[6] Watson's artistic indulgence in the black masculine, like his fascination with

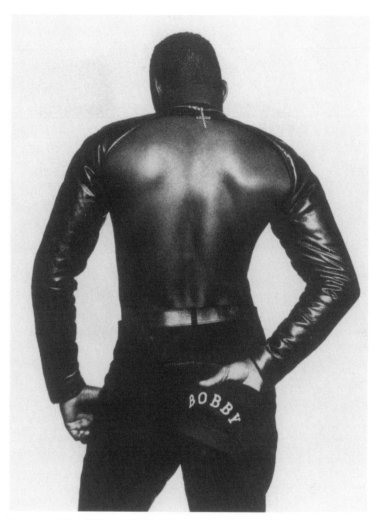

Figure 3. Albert Watson, Bobby Brown

rock stars, fashion models, and other American cultural totems, is "pushed to an almost unnatural degree." But not without design: "At first glance, many of these photographs might appear hostile, alienated; their taut surfaces bristle with an unrelieved tension. This isn't just technical effect — or, rather, it is technical effect in the service of something more profound."[7] (Just sentences later, Truman deconstructs his own defense of Watson by comparing the photographer's approach to the fetish-subject to "Livingston setting sail for Africa.") Whether or not cultural theorists with slightly less investment in the more strictly technical dimensions of photography (and particularly African Ameri-

Figure 4. Albert Watson, Tupac Shakur

can cultural theorists who might fall in this lot) will agree that Watson's photographs are a "service" to the problems and politics of race and gender in America, it is finally more productive, as Homi Bhabha has noted, to comprehend "the *processes of subjectification* [or, here, *objectification*] made possible (and plausible) through stereotypical discourse."[8] Rather than judge the work a service or an injury to black visual respectability in advance (*I* see ethical value in the practice of late judgement), the project of exposing its ideological substructure, its "regime of truth," is an urgency of the first order. "Only then," as

Bhabha argues, "does it become possible to understand the . . . ambivalence" of the object of the fetish fixation, to apprehend its power to be "at once an object of desire and derision."[9]

Therefore, like Truman, I want to resist censuring Watson's black male fetishism. Unlike Truman, however, I want to do so on grounds that have little to do with "technical effect." Instead, I argue—as Kobena Mercer has in two compelling essays devoted to race, homoeroticism, and identity politics in the controversial works of Robert Mapplethorpe—[10] that to take Watson's picture of the shadowy subject America finds menacing as uniquely the projection of the photographer's personal aims and intentions is to err significantly from the productive path forged by Bhabha. While certainly every photographer brings a perspective profoundly personal to his or her work and lenses colored by individual biases and alibis, still a coterie of editors, publicists, and technicians—to say nothing of both imagined and real consumers—complicates an easy calculus of influence. I can put this another way. When we define the photograph as belonging to the photographer, this does not mean that it is made outside of a very wide field of desires, interests, and tastes which contract with the photographer for its production. At bottom, then, the public photograph (the magazine cover, the book jacket, the news photo, the billboard, the exhibit portrait, even the criminal mug shot) is always also a messy assembly-line construction. As an artifact of the culture of its production and circulation, Albert Watson's black man on the *New York Times Magazine* cover realizes this vital point made by Kobena Mercer which I take for a fundamental premise of this study: "Black masculinity is not merely a social identity in crisis. It is also a key site of [ideology and] ideological representation" where a major "contest of competing . . . forces is played out"[11] both within the frame and beyond it.

Within the frame, Watson's picture accedes to the photographic equivalency of the "blank darkness" that emanates from those "silent black bodies . . . in American literature" on which Toni Morrison said the nation's "historical, moral, metaphysical, and social fears [and] problems . . . [were once] articulated."[12] The visual conditions of anonymity, alienation, and stereotype racialists require for what Morrison calls "playing in the dark," and Philip Brian Harper, in a slightly different but no less relevant sense terms "trade," are eidetically reconstructed here to reveal at the etiological roots of racial misrepresentation an archaic manner of seeing, a vestigial optics belonging properly to nineteenth-century technologies of vision. The racial gaze, that is, would seem to be a survival of the *camera obscura*'s mechanical age.

THE CAMERICAL ROOTS OF RACIAL REPRESENTATION

Sometime in 1936 Walter Benjamin, the German-Jewish philosopher, wrote: "During long periods of history, the mode of human sense perception changes with humanity's entire mode of existence. The manner in which human sense perception is organized, the medium in which it is accomplished, is determined not only by nature but by historical circumstances as well."[13] To be sure, the nineteenth-century advent of photography was the sign of an historical transformation in process. The unprecedented productions of new scientific and technological knowledge, and their contemporaneity with what Benjamin called "the growing proletarianization of modern man" demanded not merely a democratization of the art of image-making disallowed by the bourgeois predilections of painting, but, far more fundamentally, the new culture of modernity, hungry for still more knowledge production, demanded greater visual information about the changing world. Writes Robert Hirsch in *Seizing the Light: A History of Photography*: "People wanted to know what their world looked like, and the photographic image arrived at the right moment with the type of proof people had been prepared [by the change of history] to accept."[14] Inaugurated by the scientism of the camera lucida, that photographic moment has endured, despite the coming of film, the full span of the twentieth century. Its anachronicity today, however, in the face of an extraordinary diffusion of cybernetic and digital technologies of vision production escaping referentiality in the visible world, has had woeful consequences upon black masculine visibility.

Despite the narrowly titular homage Roland Barthes's paid to it in his 1980 reflections on photography, *Camera Lucida*, the history of the camera lucida is little known to us in the twentieth century. Invented in 1807 by William Hyde Wollaston, a gentleman scientist of England, the camera lucida was a "highly portable and beguilingly simple little device" for the accurate reproduction of images by hand.[15] Predating the daguerreotype and calotype by thirty years, the camera lucida was not, in fact, a camera per se (at least not in the modern sense) but "an optical instrument" that, more nearly than the camera obscura before it, prefigured the camera.[16] Although Jonathan Crary's brilliant speculative history of modern vision, *Techniques of the Observer: On Vision and Modernity in the Nineteenth Century*, argues for the paradigmatic place of the camera obscura and stereoscope in the study of modern visual and perception knowledge, in this book I prefer to give the camera lucida that place. I do not believe Crary is incorrect exactly to posit either camera obscura or stereoscope as a concretization of optical principles that extend from the sixteenth to the nineteenth century. Nevertheless, where it concerns our modern manner of seeing racial subjects, the camera lucida surpasses both camera obscura and stereoscope in its simulation of the modern habits of looking, spectacularizing black male bodiliness. This is not least the case because the camera lucida represents a presaging rupture in the history of early camera vision—that premodern apprehension of the external world through visual perception ever increasingly determined by seeing devices.

The difference in the design construction of the camera obscura and the camera lucida vividly highlights the significance of the rupture of history of vision reflected by the invention of the camera lucida. Where the earliest constructions of the camera obscura were small dark buildings that artists entered to capture and trace an image which the light from a small hole in one of its walls had inversely projected onto an opposite wall, the originary portability of the camera lucida, "a glass prism held at eye level by a brass rod attached to a flat, portable drawing board," signaled the achievement of a hegemony of camera vision.[17] In the substitution of camera lucida for camera obscura, Western man went from operating inside the device to having the device, or more properly its technology, operate inside him.[18] Even when Johannes Keppler made improvements on the camera obscura in 1611 that made it equally portable as the camera lucida, the camera lucida still formalized, nay, regularized a new fully internalized variety of camera vision.

According to art historian John Schaaf, the camera lucida "perfectly transmitted perspective and forms."[19] Its failure to "translate [indefinite forms] into visions," however, made the device "a devilish frustration for anyone who lacked understanding of how to digest complex visual information for presentation into a two-dimensional medium."[20] It was just such a frustration that led Wollaston's fellow Englishman, William Henry Fox Talbot, to devise a few years later the negative-positive process on which modern photographic development is based. Talbot had tried to grasp the technique of the camera lucida in which the artist holds the prism above a sheet of paper and, seeing a reflected image of what is before him, traces its outline. Rankled by the awkwardness of its use, Talbot went on in 1833 to "think out a plan for fixing the images he had seen,"[21] for *arresting representation* on chemically treated, light-sensitive paper. If William Hyde Wollaston was the harbinger of a new modern ocularity in the nineteenth century, then Henry Fox Talbot was first to harness it in proto-photography.

Two centuries later, Wollaston and Talbot are still worth mention. For Albert Watson's *New York Times Magazine* portrait, to make the case one way, would seem to owe as much to Wollastonian perspectivism as to Fox Talbot's more formal contributions to modern photographic techniques. Watson's work for the *New York Times Magazine* shares with the science of Wollaston's camera lucida a reminiscently Platonic valorization of "forms" over "vision" ("form" being the originary thing "which presents itself to vision"),[22] an aesthetic posture which, being indifferent to "complex visual detail," is content to merely trace outlines of the image under view, a task performed after the manner of Watson's Cyclopean way with "one eye on the model"![23] Furthermore, the form of the camera lucida's chief part, "a four-sided reflecting prism,"[24] mimics not only its own capacity, but Watson's, to enframe (*gestalten*, lit. "to set in place") its subject. On this point rests the considerable weight of the argument the whole of *Constructing the Black Masculine* is devoted to, an extended argument about spectacle, fetish, and the chronic foreclosure of realist representation in black male visual contexts. Enframement is this argument's ur-trope.[25] As the first stratagem of the conditioned reflexes of modern racial vision, enframement is tropologically indispensable to the second-level meaning of Watson's black male photographs. As an interpretive key to making full sense of the metadiscourses of Watson's work, enframement conveys the black masculine predicament forcefully. It is a trope for then and now.

PICTURE FRAMING

In his essay, "The Age of the World Picture," Martin Heidegger distinguishes the modern era from earlier epochs by the hegemony of the image, the represented idea, in philosophy. According to Heidegger, whatever exists from the vantage point of modern metaphysics is comprehensible only to "the extent to which it lets itself be put at the disposal of representation."[26] "Whatever is," in other words, is already always set up as a picturable object of representation. And "only that which becomes object in this way . . . is considered [in the modern age] to be in being."[27] To enframe a subject, then, is to objectify it "in such a way that man who calculates can be sure, and that means be certain" in his own picture-prone mind, for his own comfort "of that [object's] being."[28]

In "The Age of the World Picture," Heidegger is critical of the ready submission of ideas to the image. For Heidegger, as Watson's photographs cannot avoid illustrating, the picture is always subject to reproducing blind spots that tell more about the scopic criminality of the one who enframes than that of the enframed one. However illuminative I believe Heidegger to be, I want to argue, somewhat differently from him, that it is not the picture per se that tricks the (mind's) eye, but the picture *frame* that fools.

Perhaps the most far-reaching reflections on the phenomenological function of the picture frame are not in photographic theory but in a theory of painting, once photography's rival idiom. In his 1987 work on Kantian aesthetics, *The Truth in Painting*, Jacques Derrida advances a theory of the frame, the *parergon*, as "neither [the] work (*ergon*) nor [the] outside [of] the work (*hors d'oeuvre*)" but that which, not merely surrounding the painting, "*gives rise*" to it.[29] The parergon fools by its extraneous look when it is actually "called up and gathered together" as an analytic, not mere adornment, for judging the true subject of a work. Notwithstanding the pretext of a title or tradition, the subject, "which [simply] cannot be determined, localized, situated, *arrested* inside or outside *before the framing*, is simultaneously . . . both *product* and *production* of the frame," its yield and unique labor.[30] The parergonal truth in painting Derrida describes, I take for the truth of photography as well since, as Barthes surmises, "The first man who saw the first photograph . . . must have thought it was a painting: same framing."[31] Is it too much to claim a parergonal function, then, in the sociovisual production of the black body as fetish by the modern racial gaze? If Jamaican art historian Petrine Archer-Straw is correct to locate the formal roots of modern black fetishization in the co-opting of African artifacts by European avant-garde painters at the turn of the century to signify their transgressive ideas of modernism,[32] then there can be little debate that some concept of the frame is as necessary to the fetish function of the racial gaze as to the painting or the photograph since framing the man of color (in both optic and juridical senses), like framing the artistic image, also formalizes a delimited two-dimensional vision of black men in (white) America.

As a phenomenological survival of the scientism of the camera lucida, the framework of the racialist gaze succeeds by a camerical trompe l'oeil. Just as the image received through the camera lucida "is not 'real,'" in the way that the projected image of the camera obscura is (in actuality the image projected by the camera lucida is a prismatic illusion), what racialists see gazing at the black male body, is a *"virtual image,"*[33] at once seen and unseen, spectacular and spectral, to their socially conditioned eyes. Theirs is a vision that sees only "a simulacrum of sensible visibility,"[34] the effect of a "peculiar disposition of the eyes" as Ralph Ellison put it, that compels racialists "to see only . . . themselves, or figments of their imagination."[35] Ellison expresses the consequential condition of black male virtuality brilliantly in his 1952 magnum opus *Invisible Man* when his hero declares:

> I am an invisible man. No, I am not a spook like those who haunted Edgar Allan Poe; nor am I one of your Hollywood-movie ectoplasms. I am a man of substance, of flesh and bone, fiber and liquids. . . . Like the bodiless heads you see sometimes in circus sideshows, it is as though I have been surrounded by mirrors of hard, distorting glass. . . . [When you're invisible] you're constantly being bumped against by those of poor vision. . . . you often doubt if you really exist. You wonder whether you aren't simply a phantom in other people's minds. Say, a figure in a nightmare which the sleeper tries with all his strength to destroy. (3–4)

It is the constant projection of just this sort of public *méconnaissance*, this framing of the black male visually reduplicated in the bodiless head of the metapicture on the cover of *The New York Times Magazine*, that I wish to call, heuristically, *spectragraphia*.[36] Into this term, which names a chronic syndrome of inscripted misrepresentation, I mean to collapse not only the iconic simultaneity of the spectral and the spectacular in racialist representations of black men, but a somewhat greater family of arrestive signifiers which share etymological roots in the Latin *specere* (to look or regard): *specimen, speculum, specious, suspect* — all signifiers of an optically inflected framing of black men within the rigid representational repertoire of each term's disreputable and diminishing significations.

Spectragraphia implies imperfect—indeed, illusory—cultural vision. One sees through a dark "distorting glass" a virtual image of black masculinity, one trusted so devoutly as to realize the proverbialism of *blind faith*. For all that it purports to see symbolically in the black masculine form, the spectragraphic gaze, like that which is commanded by the frame in Derrida, remains a vision of what the racial solipsistic among us will not, cannot see: their own self-serving blindnesses. These are not primarily ophthalmological defects, however, so much as they reflect a stubbornness of the will to see (*voir*), and thus, to know (*apercevoir, savoir*) the black masculine intersubjectively. Since, as Derrida goes on to say, "the whole history, the whole semantics of the European *idea*, in its Greek genealogy . . . relates seeing to knowing,"[37] the spectragraphic impulse, as a willful blindness, protects the bemused from *ever having to know*. After the manner of *Invisible Man*, contemporary black novelist and philosopher Charles Johnson narrativizes this peculiar habit of racialists in the essay "A Phenomenology of the Black Body." In it, Johnson relates this academic experience:

> I walk down the hallway at the university and pass a professor I know well. He glances up quickly, yet does not acknowledge that he knows me. He has seen a black, a body, that remains for him always in the background. . . . Passing, he sees me as he sees the fire extinguisher to my left, that chair outside the door. I have been seen, yet not seen; acknowledged as present to him but in a peculiar way.[38]

Nearly seen as a picture by his professor, "a black, a body, that remains . . . always in the background," Johnson realizes in his skin that which in photographic film development is called the "opaque pigment."[39] It is the opaque pigment that carries the "blocking-out material," preventing light from passing through designated parts of a filmic negative. In Johnson's narrative, black skin, in his professor's race-charmed eyes, would seem to carry a similarly blocking material. For the light that illuminates the corridor in Johnson's memory does not illuminate for the heedless professor Johnson's subjective presence. Inasmuch as seeing bears on perceiving and knowing, it is obvious, then, why the professor "does not acknowledge that he knows" his student. Johnson's black skin, amalgamated into the institutional decor, is a sign of his spectrality as a social subject, "seen, and yet not seen," sensed as a thing in the room, but a thing no more significant than a poster affixed on the hallway kiosk. More than that, Johnson embodies the curious duality of a picture *as* a frame, *as* a parergon, insofar as he also delimits and fixes the inner and outer border of the symbolic intellectual space to which he, as supplement to the *ergon* (the foregrounded figure of the professor ambling down the corridor), does not, in his professor's mind, properly belong. He is but partially present there, a spectacle not so much by a condition of hypervisibility as by Ellisonian virtuality.

Johnson's experience of spectragraphic misrecognition only instantiates a part of the theoretical enterprise I derive from the pictorial profundity of Albert Watson's most important image, however. As much a speculum as a specimen of the framed black male subject, what we have in Watson's *New York Times Magazine* cover is not just a second-level portrait of black maledom but, from the vantage point of W. J. T. Mitchell, "a portrait of the artist" — Watson — "holding up a seductive mirror" before him.[40] Refracted in that mirror is "a beholder," an observer who is at once the photographer, the sovereign camera, and the racialist spectator who, for fear of having to face himself in black men's eyes, would rather not see what trouble the black man is in. Put this way, Watson's photography reflects two blindnesses simultaneously: a natural one unique to Watson, and a willful one shared by those subscribers who would prefer not to see — those, in other words, who do not want to know. In this light, the reasons for Watson's model being so fully turned away from the camera's view are ever clearer. Such a posture reconstructs the necessary anonymity of black male subjects that the white imaginary requires to guarantee black men's distance as Others. From this perspective, the impossibility of a reciprocal gaze to disrupt the machinations of alterity by force of what Kaja Silverman has referred to as "heteropathic identification" provides the white reader of the magazine the ability to safely and imaginatively explore what he religiously believes is not the self without having to witness what grief, affliction, or rage such experiments countenance.

Like the Africanist personae Morrison theorized in American fiction of the nineteenth century, Watson's visual, to recapitulate, is an ideograph for the American propensity to see black men half-blindly as a blank/black page onto which the identity theme of American whiteness, with its distinguishing terrors and longings, imprints itself as onto a photographic negative. Black men come to embody the inverse picture necessary for the positive self-portrait of white identity. Thusly does the feature figure of *The New York Times Magazine* come to stand for the dark faceless specter who at one and the same time possesses and protects the popular American imagination. As James Baldwin ventriloquistically wrote in this connection in 1951:

> When [the black face] has become [by our blind ambition] blank, the past as thoroughly washed from [it] as it has been from ours, our guilt [as Americans] will be finished — at least it will have ceased to be visible, which we imagine to be much the same thing. But paradoxically, it is we who prevent this from happening; since it is we, who, every hour that we live, reinvest the black face with our guilt; and we do this . . . helplessly, passionately, out of an unrealized need to suffer absolution.[41]

It is by a commensurate purging onto the blank darkness photographed under Watson's eye that a more recent whiteness justifies itself, one divested of the alibi of fixed difference powerfully reinforced at midcentury by the legal sanction of Jim Crow and its architectures. As a consequence of this helpless, passionate will to virtual whiteness (as against the materiality of its former expression in segregated schools, theaters, housing, and public toilets, to say nothing of the belief in it as a flesh-and-blood reality), racialist reflexes suffer the fictions of black male otherness, fictions that are owed at root to white fixations about alterity and entitlement, to be taken for fact.[42] Clearly, the perceived fiction of black men's illegitimacy as proper American men is preferred above the truth of such a perception as a self-legitimating projection of bourgeois white male arrogance.

To put the matter yet another way, it is by an abiding bankruptcy of vision that black male bodies in public spheres go phantasmatically misrecognized. Since, as Lauren Berlant has written, "the *white*, male body is the relay to legitimation . . . [and] the power to suppress that body, to cover its tracks and its traces, is the sign of real authority, according to constitutional fashion,"[43] it is precisely the ineradicable afterimage of the black male body in the white mind — or, to follow Berlant more closely, what Freud called the "permanent traces" of perception (in other words, "memory-traces" that are not so much left *after* memory but *after perception* in preconscious deposits before memory) — that forestalls the achievement of "real authority" black men, under patriarchy, might otherwise freely gain.[44] It is the insufferability of the inescapable afterimage of the absent black antecedent that would seem to worry the effort, at least in the white imagination, to "cover [one's] tracks and traces." For the traces of black male visibility are retained in the white unconscious "permanently";[45] they defy cover.

But the problem of the black masculine extends beyond its historical possession of the (white) American mind. While it is irrefutably true, following Kobena Mercer, that "the nation's crisis comes to be dramatized, demonized and dealt with"[46] most starkly through black men (Ellison said, "On the moral level I propose that we view the whole of American life as a drama acted out upon the body of a Negro giant who lying trussed up like Gulliver, forms the stage and the scene upon which and within which the action unfolds"),[47] I believe it is also true that the public dispute over the symbolics of nationhood and culture is also sufficiently replicated within black male subjects of all stripes (homosexual, heterosexual, poor, monied, middle-class, working-class, disabled, etc.) as to bear out Baldwin's further thesis that "the American image of the [black man] lies also in the [black man's] heart; and when he has surrendered to this image life has no other possible reality. Then he, like the white enemy with whom he will be locked one day in mortal struggle, has no means save this of asserting his identity."[48]

Until now, the formal touchstones for this study have been almost entirely photographic. But pictorialization belongs no less to narrative prose than to photography. *Ekphrasis*, in fact, names the narrative and poetic form of the pictorial project I have described to this point in photographic terms.[49] While this book will span a range of narrative prose works by African American men, from Frederick Douglass's 1845 *Narrative* to Melvin Dixon's 1992 novel *Vanishing Rooms*, it is Richard Wright's 1940 *Native Son* that I want to put forward just now as the urtext for the ekphrastic threat to black male representation and the private life of the black masculine.[50] But first a proem. For if *Native Son* is the locus classicus of the problem of black male spectacularity in American prose, then the prologue to Ellison's *Invisible Man* is a prolegomenon, albeit postscripted, for Wright's portrayal of that condition. There, Ellison abstracts the mundane experience of black male hypervisibility and enframent in Wright with an inimitable modernist power.

"One night I accidentally bumped into a man," recounts Ellison's hero, "and perhaps because of the near darkness he saw me and called me an insulting name" (4). That the invisible protagonist is seen *because* of the near darkness, not in spite of it, reveals something significant, I believe, about black masculine virtuality, or what I have found necessary to call, sometimes with inescapable awkwardness, spectragraphia. Here, black masculine virtuality obtains in the affective power of shadows. For, as the Invisible Man explains, "the man had not *seen* [him], actually" (or "seen him *actually*," I might have said), but a shadow cast "beneath the lamplight in the deserted street" (4; emphasis Ellison's). Snatching the man by his coat and battering him to the ground in a rage of humiliation and anger, the Invisible Man only then comprehends his virtual personhood: "In my outrage I got out my knife and prepared to slit his throat . . . when it occurred to me that the man had not *seen* me, actually; that he, as far as he knew, was in the midst of a walking nightmare! . . . Something in this man's thick head had sprung out and beaten him within an inch of his life" (4–5). Although the next day's *Daily News* reports that the assaulted man had been "mugged," who can doubt, given the visual stimulus for the man's aspersions ("he saw me and called me an insulting name"; "he looked insolently out of his blue eyes and cursed me"), that the Invisible Man had been "mugged" too, camerically framed by a lucidanal look? The scene of sciamachy externalizes the psychology of race, spectacle, and camera vision quietly underwriting the plot of Richard Wright's naturalist tome *Native Son*. Preceding Ellison by a dozen years, *Native Son* realistically portrays the problem of spectragraphical misrepresentation. Exploiting the metaphorics of blindness, *Native Son* dramatizes, with naturalistic flair, the overdetermined consequences of a virtuality of black masculine being that is simulatively photographic.

BLIND AMBITIONS

Perhaps *Native Son*'s most important revelation on black male visibility lies in the paradox that Bigger Thomas's overdetermined shadings in the novel obtain both because and in spite of the representative blindness of Mrs. Dalton, Bigger's wealthy if charitable employer. Mrs. Dalton's physical blindness renders Bigger a fiction to her; and yet it is because of a far more catholic blindness, less peculiar than pandemic, that Bigger, in mounting the dim backwing stairwell to Mary Dalton's bedroom, her soft, white, inebriated body caught in his arms, "felt strange, possessed," as if, *because of the near darkness*, "he were acting upon a stage in front of a crowd of people."[51] When, moments later, Bigger finds himself defenseless in a corner of the room near Mary's bed, Mrs. Dalton groping at the bedroom door, it is the in-grained memory-trace of "the last colored man who worked for [the Daltons]" (62), Green, that Bigger cannot ever conceal himself from. (How telling that Mrs. Dalton, ten years blind, seems to have lost her sight at exactly the time Green comes to work for her family! All the more because the liberal earnestness with which she backed Green's improvement, her noblesse oblige, is also blind: "Mrs. Dalton *made* him go to night school" [62; emphasis added]). To Mrs. Dalton's darkened mind, then, the inconceivability of Bigger having a good reason for skulking around Mary's bed is not a wit different from the inconceivability of finding Green there. Uncovered, either would dash Mrs. Dalton's best hopes for them by the readiness of an all-too-vivid screen of sexual trespass peremptorily incriminating both. The tor-ment, then, of Mrs. Dalton's blindness at the door where Bigger has se-creted Mary to bed lies in its paradoxical function. For Mrs. Dalton's blindness extends from an "overabundance and . . . failure [*défaillance*] of the visible," at once. Hers follows from "the too-much and the much-too-little, the excess and the default [*faillite*]"[52] of a visuality Bigger knows will ultimately betray him, ultimately frame him.

This, of course, explains why even though Bigger "knew Mrs. Dal-ton could not [actually] see him," he was nevertheless certain "that if Mary spoke, she would come to the side of the bed and discover him" (97) with a sharper faculty. If Bigger trusts Mrs. Dalton's "stony" eyes not to expose him, in other words, he distrusts the duplicity of that honed sixth sense Ellison conceived in *Invisible Man* as a phenomenon of the "*inner* eyes, those eyes with which [racialists] look through their physical eyes upon reality" (3). Bigger's burden of spectacularity does not require Mrs. Dalton to see him in any physical way at all. She has "inner eyes" that photograph and enframe according to what Sontag describes as a modern ethics of "dissociative seeing": "A habit of look-ing at reality as an array of potential photographs."[53] From the begin-ning, Bigger has had the feeling "that [Mrs. Dalton] could see him even though he knew that she was blind. . . . Her face was still, tilted, waiting" like the face of an old-fashioned studio camera (68). Mrs. Dalton's look arrests Bigger dead in his spectragraphic tracks. Cornered in the white girl's bedroom, Bigger is twice trapped by architecture and image, the latter irreversibly transforming the former from the place of sleep into the place of sex. In a doubly photographic and criminological sense, Mrs. Dalton's gaze (for that is certainly what her look has, in an instant, become) frames Bigger and arrests him in body and being well before the Chicago police take him into their custody. *Arrestation*, now, becomes one more keyword in this study's effort to locate and name the consequences of the spectragraphical condition in *Native Son*.

The scene of Mary's murder depicts the fictional phenomenologies of arrestation paradigmatically. Having lingered too long already over the young heiress's nubile body before Mrs. Dalton calls, Bigger is suddenly "seized" by the "white blur . . . standing at the door, silent, ghostlike." Mrs. Dalton's unexpected appearance, itself spectral but still innocently "white," "gripped his body." Transfixed beside the bed, "he waited tensely, afraid to move for fear of bumping into something in the dark and betraying his presence" (97). Inasmuch, however, as the gloom of Mary's bedroom reconstructs the darkness of Mrs. Dalton's vision, Bigger is (always) already betrayed. For presumably the whole scene has been acted out beforehand in the darkness of Mrs. Dalton's mind and the minds of those blinded others her character is calculated to symbolize. Consequently, Mrs. Dalton's visitation at Mary's door, one realizes soon enough, is hardly what it appears. Only superficially one of her routine calls on Mary, Mrs. Dalton's haunting of the scene stands more profoundly for an inescapable indictment against black men as consummate sexual outlaws. It stands but to reason then that the "hysterical terror" Bigger experiences in the dark remove of Mary's bedroom should be rendered in classically castratory terms.

As if caught under Medusa's sinister stare, Bigger "stiffened" (97) at the sight of Mrs. Dalton. Stone giving way to metal, he "clenched his teeth and held his breath, intimidated to the core by the awesome white blur floating toward him. His muscles flexed taut as steel . . . so taut they ached" (98). The mythological parallel is vital here. For Freud wrote revealingly,

> The sight of [Medusa] . . . makes the spectator stiff with terror, turns him to stone. Observe that we have here . . . the same origin from the castration complex and the same transformation of affect! For becoming stiff (*das Starrwerden*) means an erection. Thus in the original situation it offers consolation to the spectator: he is still in possession of a penis, and the stiffening reassures him of the fact.[54]

Far and above just the "stiffening," Bigger's "taut" body, "clamped" teeth, and "clenched" fist (99) are a masturbatory affirmation that, despite the possibility of his being lynched should Mrs. Dalton discover him lurking about her daughter's room (and having his member mutilated as part of that unspeakable ritual), he is, for the present at least, "still in possession of [his] penis." But that, in the racist imaginary, had often been the problem all along.

However much the castrative menace of Mrs. Dalton may recall that of the mythic Gorgon Medusa, it is not Mrs. Dalton's gaze Bigger dreads most. He fears her hands more. He fears her "touch." If Mary would speak, Mrs. Dalton would no doubt "discover him, touch him" (97) crouched by the bedside of Sleeping Beauty. That she can not see him with her natural eye, he seems to know, is inconsequential. Finding him there by touch, she would "see" perfectly, corroborate what the seeing inevitably visualize in the black male body: a sexual brute, a hungry rapist, a bad nigger. In touching Bigger, though, Mrs. Dalton would not be touching *him* at all, but his virtual image, a flesh-and-blood fiction of the white imagination, that embodied "brew of darkness, otherness, alarm, and desire,"[55] as Morrison writes, so vivid to the white mind's eye.

So, in spite of herself, Mrs. Dalton virtually sees. And her touch is probative if not also electrically conductive, which is to say, a relay, a medium of neuropathic transfer. Bigger's guarded maneuverings in the shadows stage a contagion terror: "With each of her movements toward the bed his body made a movement to match hers. Away from her, his feet not lifting themselves from the floor, but sliding softly and silently over the smooth deep rug" (98). To be touched by Mrs. Dalton, his dance intimates, is to run the risk of acquiring her blindness, as in a game of blindman's buff, say, or hide-and-seek. Hedging her touch, Bigger fears blindness, fears being "it" because being "it" is a resignation to seeing oneself, as Du Bois said it memorably, "always . . . through the eyes of others."[56] Being "it" is being-for-others, here a condition constraining Bigger to become his own penumbral other.

The anoptic peril, however, goes further than even that. Beyond just otherness, the added danger of acquiring blindness and its self-alienating consequences lies in Derrida's more particular conclusion about the deeper structures of meaning reflected by an anoptic alterity. According to Derrida, any blind man (to say nothing of the blind man who is also black) is "a figure of castration." Not only that, he is "a sort of phalloid image" too,

38   Constructing the Black Masculine

an unveiled sex from head to toe, vaguely obscene and disturb-
ing. . . . More naked than others, a blind man *virtually* becomes his
own sex, he becomes indistinguishable from it because he does not
see it, and not seeing himself exposed to the other's gaze, it is as if he
had lost even his sense of modesty. . . . Following this analogy
between the eye and the sex, can it not be said that the eye of the
blind man, the blind man himself, derives its strange familiarity, its
disquieting strangeness, from being more naked? From being exposed naked without knowing it? Indifferent to its nakedness, and
thus at once less naked and more naked than others as a result?[57]

Like a modern Perseus under the pornographic and castrative threat
of Medusa's direct stare, Bigger plays the cagey part. He keeps his
head "cocked at an angle" (97), watching Mrs. Dalton's movements obliquely so as to avoid getting blindsided/blindsighted by her.
Though fearful of not only exposure in Mary's bedroom, but overexposure, being made "more naked" by Mrs. Dalton's groping, Bigger
can't escape the sexual screen.[58] Before her, "he grew tight and full, as
though about to explode" (97). His reflex is, of course, not a miscegenatory wish but a masturbatory reassurance that, despite the emascula-
tive threat, he is still a man. Bigger's relief that both he and his member
have survived Mrs. Dalton's menace once her "awesome white blur"
quits the room where she has had Bigger holed up, Wright depicts in
unmistakably postonanistic imagery: "Bigger relaxed and sank to the
floor, his breath going in a long gasp. He was weak and wet with sweat.
He stayed crouched and bent, hearing the sound of his breathing filling
the darkness. Gradually, the intensity of his sensation subsided and he
was aware of the room. He felt that he had been in the grip of a weird
spell and was now free" (99). Even as Bigger is "in the grip" of
Mrs. Dalton's "weird spell," between the lines above is a different grip-
ping event, one which is not holding Bigger so much as he has been
holding it. This and other masturbatory allusions in Book One of *Native Son* underscore the castration fixation (the "weird spell"?) haunting (largely heterosexual) black male self-identity which such blind
(white) regard for black masculine being as Mrs. Dalton's tends to
induce.

In Book II, Bigger attempts a futile flight. Betrayed by the sort of
trace Silverman, following Freud, describes more exactly as a "flow of
perception across the psyche" which, "far from providing a registration

of the 'real,'" gets "worked over in all kinds of ways by censorship and fantasy,"[59] Bigger is tracked down in Book II by the Chicago police department and charged with the rape and murder of Mary Dalton. The protagonist's criminal arrest, I want to point out however, is only a formalization of his fetishistic enframement as spectacle and specter in white eyes prior to and following this moment. His bodily capture by police, in other words, merely repeats the scopic function under racialist regimes. While the structural influences on Bigger's ruined life in *Native Son* are well-documented, the irreducibly corporeal burden of visibility he bears ought not to be neglected.[60] Although the most vital scenes supporting a materially inflected version of the spectragraphic argument are in Books II and III, their foundations, as I shall turn again briefly to Book I to show, are laid much earlier on.

Very near *Native Son*'s opening, the meaning of black spectacularity to white eyes is revealed to Bigger filmically, and it is the revelation of *Trader Horn* that is his inescapable torment from the novel's beginning to its nihilistic end. Just pages into Book I, an idle Bigger and his best buddy Jack find a late-morning diversion at the movies. In all but the recently restored, unexpurgated edition of *Native Son*, the novel highlights two posters hanging in the lobby of the Regal theater announcing the day's showings: "One, *The Gay Woman*, was pictured on the posters in images of white men and white women lolling on beaches, swimming, and dancing in the night clubs; the other, *Trader Horn*, was shown on the posters in terms of black men and black women dancing against a wild background of barbaric jungle."[61] Inside the theater, Bigger and Jack watch *The Gay Woman* curiously, enviously. Before long, its scenes of white wealth, "cocktail drinking, dancing, golfing, swimming, and spinning roulette wheels,"[62] fade to black and *Trader Horn*'s "pictures of naked black men and women whirling in wild dances" (36) unfold messily on the screen. As the novel's original moment of white spectatorship, the showing of *Trader Horn*, "the roll of the tom-toms and the screams of black men and women dancing free and wild" (37), frames Bigger's public potential within a primitivist image repertoire from the first ("Kill that black ape!" a mob will be heard to say later on). *Trader Horn* is a moving metapicture of white spectation in *Native Son*.

When much later in Book II detectives uncover the ashes of Mary Dalton's charred body smoldering in the blazing furnace of the Dalton mansion, it is as much the dread of a similar scopic arrestation as it is the fear of criminal arrest Bigger cannot bear: "He could not stay here now. At any moment they would begin to suspect him," and *suspect* him in the strictest etymological sense (*su* + *specere*) with a camerical look that "would hold him . . . even if they were not certain whether he had done it or not" (253). If Bigger believes, in fleeing the basement scene of the discovery of Mary Dalton's incinerated body, that his physical absence is enough to dissociate himself from the savagery of *Trader Horn* representationalism, "a small picture" (258) of him in the *Chicago Tribune* and the next day's headline, "REPORTERS FIND DALTON GIRL'S BONES IN FURNACE. NEGRO CHAUFFEUR DISAPPEARS. . . . AUTHORITIES HINT SEX CRIME" (281), promptly disabuses him of that delusion. For the paper's "hint" at a sexual crime calls up and, to use Silverman's terms again, "work[s] over . . . by censorship and fantasy" the memory-trace left by the previous day's picture of Bigger to frame him within a visual narrative of black carnality like *Trader Horn*. If Bigger himself does not understand the visual machinations underlying the fundamental certitude that "to hint that he had committed a sex crime was to pronounce the death sentence" (282), Wright will not permit the reader to fail to see that it is not Bigger's person so much as his trace-image that incriminates black men in white minds.[63]

Much has been made by Wright scholars of Bigger's inability to articulate the absurdity of his life in Book III of *Native Son*. But few seem to have discerned Bigger's linguistic frustrations in "Fate" causally as the corporeally arresting consequence of a kind of picture-taking racial gaze that fixes (settles and swindles simultaneously) or enframes within a rigid and limited grid of representational possibilities (among which the depraved criminal image is especially salient) black male being. It is not simply that Bigger, once captured, "is deserted by [all] linguistic facility" before his accusers, to paraphrase a typical reading of Book III.[64] More than that, their gazes are bodily "paralyzing" (318), and in *Native Son* the tongue is simply another immobilized muscle. Aligned in Book III with the implicitly male look of the mechanical camera which "has for over a century and a half," Silverman recently wrote, "provided the gaze with its primary metaphor,"[65] the racial gaze in *Native Son* congeals Bigger's body into a Medusan rigidity, arresting his representational potential before white eyes within a bestial frame-up. The narrator consistently observes in "Fate" that Bigger "held very still" (324) under his persecutors' looks; his "black face rested in his hands and he did not move" (329). "Bigger was paralyzed with shame"

(348). "[He] sat very still" (326). Little wonder, then, that when he "tried to move his tongue" (320), it lay languid and "swollen" in its place. Smaller wonder, absent the agencies of self-assertion, he faints at Mary Dalton's inquest, losing (self-) consciousness.

"NEGRO RAPIST FAINTS AT INQUEST" reads another edition of the Chicago paper. The story that follows discloses the simultaneity of a visual and criminal frame-up of black male bodiliness:

> Overwhelmed by the sight of his accusers, Bigger Thomas, Negro sex-slayer, fainted dramatically this morning at the inquest of Mary Dalton, millionaire Chicago heiress. Emerging from a stupor for the first time since his capture last Monday night, the black killer sat cowed and fearful as hundreds sought to get a glimpse of him.
>
> "He looks exactly like an ape!" exclaimed a terrified young white girl who watched the black slayer being loaded onto a stretcher after he fainted.
>
> Though the Negro killer's body does not seem compactly built, he gives the impression of possessing abnormal physical strength. He is about five feet, nine inches tall and his skin is exceedingly black. (322)

Literally, Wright seems to want us to understand, Bigger cannot bear the *sight* of his accusers. He faints not because he sees them, but because they, a "compact array of white faces and . . . flashing . . . bulbs," see him, their "eyes gazing at him with calm conviction" (318). The article's anonymous reporter displaces the public (sexual) terror onto "a terrified young white girl," reconstructing her anthropoidal image of Bigger with paternalistic precision. As the article describes more of Bigger's physical features—his protruding lower jaw, his long "dangling" arms, and his "huge, muscular" shoulders (322)—each outline, each apish appearance, is consistently attended by its cathexis in the white imaginary. Bigger's jaw, for example, "protrudes obnoxiously, *reminding one of a jungle beast*" (322; emphasis added). Looking at his arms "dangling . . . to his knees," the article goes, "*it is easy to imagine how this man, in the grip of a brain-numbing sex passion, overpowered little Mary Dalton*" (323; emphasis added). His shoulders "he keeps . . . hunched, *as if about to spring upon you at any moment*" (322; emphasis added). The effect of this brutish picture of Bigger is to make the black male body available for white public fantasies of wild "brain-numbing sex" ("hundreds sought to get a glimpse of him"). Like King Kong kept at the safe remove of the movie screen, Bigger, securely contained—framed—visually and criminally in the article between the "two policemen to whom he was handcuffed" (386), is less the linguistically constituted subject of the article as the visual "figment of that black world which they," the real subjects, the white spectators, "feared and were anxious to keep under control" (318).

The newspaper now, as ekphrastic text, arrests representation as s(ec)urely as the racial gaze. Symbolically, the narrator states, Bigger "lowered the paper. . . . He held very still" (324). Paralyzed, indeed mortified, by the threat of "newspapermen ready with their bulbs"[66] (388), Bigger tries "to feel the texture of his own feelings . . . to tell what they meant" (404), but, "twice trapped" (422), succumbs to their image of him—succumbs, in effect, to his death:

> Listlessly, he talked. He traced his every action. He paused at each
> question [State's Attorney] Buckley asked him and wondered how
> he could link up his bare actions with what he had felt; but his words
> came out flat and dull. White men were looking at him, waiting for
> his words, and all the feelings of his body vanished, just as they had
> when he was in the car [framed] between Jan and Mary. When he
> was through, he felt more lost and undone than when he was cap-
> tured. Buckley stood up; the other white man rose and held out
> the papers for him to sign. He took the pen in hand. Well, why
> shouldn't he sign? He was guilty. He was lost. They were going to
> kill him. Nobody could help him. They were standing in front of
> him, bending over him, looking at him, waiting. His hand shook.
> He signed. (358)

Although his Communist party attorney, Max, hopes to "represent" (335) a hopelessly framed man—"Just sit and say nothing," he counsels (336)—Bigger's representation is a *fait accompli*: "How can I," Max begs the court, "make the picture of what has happened to this boy show plain and powerful upon a screen of sober reason, when a thousand newspaper and magazine artists have already drawn it in lurid ink upon a million sheets of public print?" (446). In few other places in African American literature is the ekphrastic menace to black male subjecthood more plainly revealed. Even Max's desire to "make a picture . . . show . . . upon a screen," whatever good it aims to do, cannot help, finally, but to deliver Bigger to peril. One might argue, then, that it is precisely this representational crisis in public life and letters to which the particularity of black masculinist writing in the United States, emblematized in *Native Son*, responds: "[Bigger] hated this; if anything could be done in his behalf, he himself wanted to do it; not others. The more he saw others exerting themselves, the emptier he felt" (338). Perhaps more explicitly, the black male writer is to be seen in the frenetic "Negro" professor, "turning and twisting in the white men's [manipulating] hands" while "trying desperately to free himself" (396) from their arrestive hold. Pitched into a cell with Bigger, he cries through the steel bars, "'Give me *my* papers'" (396; emphasis added), recalling not only those earlier papers—the newspaper, the signed confession—which were rather *their* papers, but, dialectically, the violence of the parergonal frame(-up) as it "twists the proper articulations" of the frame's contents (here, black self-expression) "out of shape."[67] And, effectively, out of view. Consequently, one comes not to see black life realistically, but blindly, relenting in that misrecognition to the seduction of representational *oversight*, a socially conditioned outlook that typically sees in black men more (*over*sight) or less (oversight), but rarely what's there. Such anoptic indulgences create in the blank/black divide between overembodiment (i.e. Bigger as ape) and invisibility (i.e. Bigger as any black man with a shared look) what Ed Guerrero calls "a vast, *empty space in representation*."[68] Where the detailed features of the black male face would be, Albert Watson, for another example, projects just such a space onto the empty, nondescript profile of his model's near bald head.

BACK TRACKING

To be good, to be bad are merely variants of the primordial condition that either presupposes: to be *in camera*.—D. A. Miller, "Secret Subjects, Open Secrets"

Since the public struggle to reconcile the nation's anxieties on black male bodies is also replicated within black men privately as the angst of enframement, the private will to survive the visually inflected problematics of race and manhood in American culture can ill afford to cease discussion here, since Bigger Thomas, ostensibly, is no model for survival. Baldwin lamented Bigger's surrender to virtuality famously in 1951, imputing Bigger's tragedy to "a perverse and powerful desire to force into the arena of the actual those fantastic crimes of which [he had] been accused . . . [and thereby] making the nightmare real."[69] What *Native Son* most significantly fails to illuminate, according to Baldwin, is "the paradoxical adjustment which is perpetually made" by the twelve million or more who all "have [their] private Bigger Thomas living in the skull."[70] Baldwin does not recognize in *Native Son* "the 'private life' " that Barthes defines as "that zone of space, of time, where" a man is "not an image, an object." And "it is [one's] *political* right," Barthes goes on to declare, "to be a subject which [one] must protect."[71] It is exactly this "political" defense articulated by Barthes and unrecognized by Baldwin that I want to now back track in my own argument and call attention to in *Native Son*. As Mercer proved by a revisionary reading of Mapplethorpe's troublesome black male nudes, a second reading compelled to wrestle with the political consequences of reading racial fetishism in Mapplethorpe according to a prior political posture, some images insist upon their own ambivalence.

Admittedly, my earlier claims about Bigger's near silence in Book III of *Native Son*, for example, and the scopic causality I ascribed to it, all proceeded out of an assumption that silence follows from an abject condition. But that doesn't always hold. For read differently, Bigger's silence in Book III specifically may actually subvert the scopic regime, being hardly an abject state, but the preferred muteness of a subaltern hero who most certainly *can* speak, but, following Gayatri Spivak's famous essay, tactically refuses to. That is, if Bigger is impotent to meaningfully break into the linguistic fray of affairs in Books I and II, then in Book III he is at least afforded nominal space to speak to Max. Max offers Bigger opportunity enough: "What's on your mind, Bigger?" (400); "Now Bigger I want you to tell me all about yourself" (400); "What you say is in strictest confidence" (402); "Bigger, the State's Attorney gave me a copy of your confession. Now, tell me, did you tell him the truth?" (403). Even when "Max had evoked again in him that urge to talk, to tell, to try to make his feelings known" (403), however, Bigger consistently forgoes his chance, away from the public eye. "Mr. Max, it ain't no use" is Bigger's near refrain. Such locution betrays a presumption widely held that Bigger *cannot* speak. Like the subaltern theorized by Spivak whose voicelessness is a "witholding" of "a secret that may not be a secret but cannot be unlocked"[72] except by the subaltern, Bigger refuses to talk (twenty-five years before Miranda, no less), showing a more keen resistance to the discursive structures of American sociality chronically misrepresenting him than a great many critics of Wright, including Baldwin, have granted Bigger. In a word, Bigger's silence before Max *poses*. By this tactic, Bigger disables not only a primitivist discourse ("Kill that black ape!" [314]), but the mad scopophilial logic that the racial discourse in the novel cannot ever seem to escape. In Book III, I aver, Bigger "disidentifies" with the scopic regime. His "disidentification," a "survival strategy the minority subject practices in order to negotiate a phobic majoritarian public sphere that continuously elides or punishes the existence of subjects who do not conform to phantasms of normative citizenship,"[73] may well be reflected in Watson's *New York Times Magazine* cover too.

As I have already said, Watson's photograph evokes the awkward look of racialists on black male bodies. But a look, I hasten to add, is no less a particularized body posture, a proprioceptive display of the "representationally inflected body"[74] in time and space, than it is a manner of seeing. In another sense, a look is a pose too. Instead of serving to reflect a public vision of the black masculine, therefore, one might make out in Watson's cover a more willful posturing of the featured body, a corporeal intentionality not to face forward because to face the camera/gaze would be to surrender oneself—one's image, really—to the composite police sketch or the criminal mug shot. Facing the camera/gaze conjures an irreducible exteriority into existence that cannot be tolerated in the pursuit of the private life. Perhaps what Watson has captured, to recapitulate, is not a reflection of racial monocularity or willful blindness so much as a subversive mimicry of the photographic gaze realized in a self-protective "cool pose."

In their book *Cool Pose: The Dilemmas of Black Manhood in America*, Richard Majors and Janet Mancini Billson define the "cool pose" as "the presentation of self many black males use to establish their male identity. . . . [including] physical posturing, impression management, and carefully crafted performances" intended to "offset an externally imposed 'zero' image."[75] Insofar as the cool pose, then, names virtually any expressive strategy of bodily self-presentation peculiar to black masculine identity, the about-face of Watson's subject may constitute a cool pose too. And since any pose in front of the camera, cool or otherwise, is itself "photographic in nature" and, from a certain point of view, "imitative of [the arrestive function of] photography,[76] the cool pose of a black man under the photographic gaze might very well mimic the photographic ritual itself and, thus, mockingly, diminish the power of the camerical look to successfully enframe it. (One has only to recall the exaggerated cool poses of the rap artists of the 1980s — arms folded shoulder to shoulder, head tilted to a defiant angle, eyes challenging — to get my point.) Barthes expresses this mimicry in the following way: "I lend myself to the social game, I pose, I know I am posing, I want you to know I am posing, but (to square the circle) this additional message . . . in no way alter[s] the precious essence of my individuality."[77] Rather, it reasserts identity, transforming it by a *dis*-identificatory means. In *Disidentifications: Queers of Color and the Performance of Politics*, José Muñoz explains disidentification:

> Disidentification is about recycling and rethinking encoded meaning. The process of disidentification scrambles and reconstructs the encoded message of a cultural text in a fashion that both exposes the encoded message's universalizing and exclusionary machinations and recircuits its workings to account for, include, and empower minority identities and identifications. Thus, disidentification is a step further than cracking open the code of the majority; it proceeds to use this code as raw material for representing a disempowered politics of positionality that has been rendered unthinkable by the dominant culture.[78]

That cool poses *in camera* (Miller) disidentify is clear. They "recycle" the ocular technologies that would otherwise objectify and frame a man by deconstructing ("cracking open" encoded meaning) and reconstituting the self (i.e., "recircuiting" encoded meaning) theatrically as to explode the frame.

The cool pose is not without its pitfalls, however. The figure who poses, for example, "once [he feels himself] observed by the lens . . . instantaneously makes another body for [himself]."[79] He apprehends himself as an image in advance of the shutter's click. In this, he experiences himself as not-me, but some other (me). "Each time I am (or let myself be) photographed," Barthes observes, "I invariably suffer from a sensation of inauthenticity, sometimes of imposture."[80] The pose, then, risks "a cunning dissociation of [first-person] consciousness from identity"[81] creating a certain paradox in the (cool) pose: To the extent that it projects one more image, however oppositional to an enframed one, the (cool) pose submits to the hegemony of photographic vision in modern racialism. And while the posing subject "transforms the space around the body,"[82] as Silverman says, such space is nevertheless inapprehensible apart from the delimitation of a frame of some kind. A deformation of an objectified body is not, finally, decolonization. Mimicry, I submit, is not necessarily mastery.

If the point of Albert Watson's photograph is in the pose rather than the camerical look provoking it, then the portrait may actually testify to the "blind aspiration"[83] of black men to approximate an ideal image, one which renders the black male present but manfully impenetrable to the fetishistically colonizing predilections of the camera/gaze. As the English photographic critic Alex Hirst writes in the introduction to Rotimi Fani-Kayode's provocative images *Black Male/White Male*, "Camera lenses may sometimes look like guns or Cubist penises, even when they're pointed at males. But in spite of 'shooting' pictures, cameras epitomise [*sic*] receptivity."[84] Inasmuch as the visual pleasures of racial fetishism in Watson rely upon the framed and receptive black body to endure what Lee Edelman calls "a symbolic inscription corresponding to that of the [penetrated] female body,"[85] the counterpose, which is but a symbolic enactment of the black male pursuit of masculine ideality, is often also a gynophobic, and quite probably homophobic, expression of manly inviolability "insofar as the penetrated body is construed as acting . . . to . . . delegitimate the male body as such."[86] This, of course, is the impossible paradox of black male subjectivity in the West. For as Hortense Spillers writes, "the ideology of 'race' in the New World [con]text *is founded upon the fundamental suspicion that one is not a 'man.'*"[87]

Conceivably, then, both Bigger Thomas's silence and the posterior perspective on Albert Watson's several black male subjects seek a repudiation deeper than that of the gaze. A repudiation of the receptive "feminine" is their shared outcome, if it has not been a shared ambition all along. But what if the gaze is not male as E. Ann Kaplan wondered? Or white, as Jane Gaines and Jackie Bobo have considered?[88] What if the gaze is female? Black? Loving? Passionate? Clearly none of these can reasonably describe the gaze in *Native Son*. And if the possibilities are too difficult to imagine looking at the *New York Times Magazine*, I propose the similarly preserved posteriority of Lyle Ashton Harris's *For Cleopatra* for a succinct and final contemplation of this chapter's concern with race, sex, and the scopic drive in everyday black (male) life (fig. 5).

Harris's 1994 photograph would seem to extend from, perhaps signify on, the aesthetic sensibility of Watson. As with so many of Watson's images, the subject is photographed from behind. In contrast to

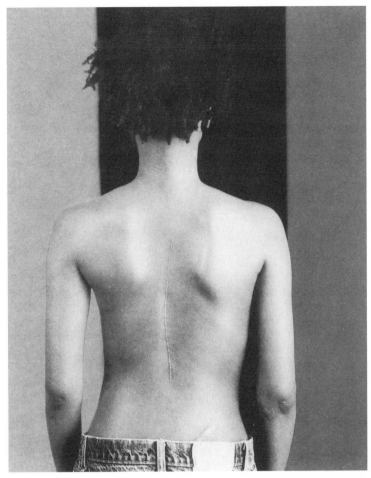

Figure 5. Lyle Ashton Harris, *For Cleopatra*

Watson's most important image, however, the anonymity of Harris's subject is a more complicated anonymity. In the first place, "the anonymity of the person with scarifications, dreadlocked hair, and [a scoliotic pose before] black nationalist tricolors" observed art critic Richard Powell, ambiguates gender by a representative blackness that Powell describes as "soft, mercurial, nonexclusionary."[89] Read backwards onto previous images of the same perspective by Watson, *For Cleopatra* challenges the presumption of the maleness of them all, to say nothing of the maleness of masculinity studies per se since we know now, thanks to Judith Halberstam's wonderful book, that female masculinity is no longer an unimaginable identic formation.[90] Notwithstanding the gender question, however, in Harris the anonymity of the

On Dangers Seen and Unseen   49

subject would seem to be undercut by a back tracking of a more violent sort than reckless racial eyeballing. On the back of the black subject, potentially another palimpsest of white fears and fancies, a story is en(s)crypted, a peculiar narrative written in flesh (and almost certainly in blood). Here *someone's* story is recorded. But what class of story, exactly, cannot be settled. Just as earnestly as it may repudiate an antagonistic gaze, *For Cleopatra*, the product of a gay black photographer, may well call for a spectatorship, may, in fact, offer an unspeakable witness to the consequential hazards of a "too-much and . . . much-too-little" blackness, and in so doing undermine, in last analysis, all facile notions of a single position or politics of scopic indulgence.

While the final chapter of this book will take up the problem of the gaze in just this sort of way, those leading up to it shall have to contend with the black male presumption of scopic malice. It has been precisely this presumption that has vexed African American male self-representation for generations and catalyzed an historic pursuit of masculine ideality in the cultural history and literary production of African American manhood beginning in 1775. While the present chapter has foregrounded certain twentieth-century manifestations of the spectragraphical conundrum, it is a problem that is at least centuries old.

PART TWO

No Hiding Place

CHAPTER TWO

"Are We Men?"

Prince Hall, Martin Delany, and the

Masculine Ideal in Black Freemasonry, 1775–1865

Are we MEN!!—I ask you, O my brethren! are we MEN?—David Walker,
"Appeal to the Coloured Citizens of the World"

We profess to be both men and Masons; and challenge the world to try us,
prove us, and disprove us, if they can.—Martin Delany, *The Origins and
Objects of Ancient Freemasonry*

There is hardly a more original experiment in the social (re)production of the black masculine ideal than in the ritual formalizations
of identity and ideality in African American Freemasonry. Probably
no other cultural movement before the Civil Rights campaigns of the
twentieth century has been more emblematic of the social and psychic
drama of black masculinity in the American cultural context. And yet
very little about the historical and cultural impact of black Freemasonry
has been the subject of scholarly attention. Even though black Freemasonry offered the African American male "his first opportunity to
find himself," as one early historian phrased it, academic neglect of this
historical and cultural phenomenon has gone virtually unchallenged.
This in spite of the fact that scores of notable black men—including
distinguished eighteenth- and nineteenth-century figures like David
Walker, William Wells Brown, Josiah Henson, John Marrant, Richard
Allen, and Booker T. Washington—have traveled the Masonic "road to
self-hood" for over two centuries.[1] In this chapter, I therefore seek to
map the course along which the African American male discovered the
"road to self-hood" in Freemasonry in 1775. More specifically, I delineate how black Freemasonry in the colonial and Victorian eras helped
invent the black masculine ideal philosophically and, perhaps more

importantly to this book's design, pictorially. Two elegant full-body portraits of Prince Hall and Martin R. Delany, both eminent Masons, at last offered African American men in 1903 and 1865 respectively, visual models of the sort of "disciplinary individualism" and black masculine perfectibility the earliest Masons purposed to preserve ritualistically.[2] Inasmuch as these two portraits represented Hall and Delany as models of black exceptionalism to be emulated by other black Masons and respectable African American men, Hall and Delany were to be taken as "typical" African American men. By "typical," I do not mean, following Mark Seltzer, "the idea of the typical [African] American," so much as, "the idea of the [African] American *as* the typical — of [African American men] as typical, general and reproducible."[3] As representative men, Hall and Delany owe no modest debt to the culturally reproductive forms and functions of masculine identity institutionally prescribed within black American Freemasonry.

THE BIRTH OF BLACK FREEMASONRY IN AMERICA

The history of black Freemasonry in the United States is an uncommon one. Few studies of black American fraternalism exist, and the volume of text devoted to it in studies of white American fraternalism, where it is seldom even mentioned, is meager indeed. But of the small number of extant histories of black Freemasonry, the most reliable of them date the origins of the black American Masonic movement in the United States to 6 March 1775. On that day, just weeks before the official onset of the American Revolution, Prince Hall of Boston, a free black artisan, and fourteen other free black men of Boston entered a British encampment at Massachusetts's Bunker Hill. There, an outfit of Irish Freemasons belonging to a British regiment initiated the fifteen men into Army Lodge No. 441.[4] For a payment of 25 guineas each, Hall and his companions entered into the Ancient and Accepted Order of Freemasons, a historic fraternal order reputed to have been already several centuries old. Immediately, the new Masons organized a "coloured" lodge of their own, Provisional African Lodge No. 1. This original lodge of black Freemasons in the United States made Hall its first Grand Master.

To legitimate their formation, Hall and his fellow founders required a charter from an American Grand Lodge, one of several confederated bodies of local units of Freemasons. According to William Muraskin,

Hall "repeatedly attempted to obtain a warrant from the white Masons of Massachusetts," but had no success.[5] Provisional African Lodge No. 1, impotent to overcome white Masonic racism, remained in institutional limbo as a provisional unit for almost ten years following. Their provisional status restricted what Masonic activities they could perform under official auspices. Finally, on 29 September 1784, after nine fruitless years of petitioning white American lodges from all across the colonies, Grand Master Hall obtained a charter for Provisional African Lodge No. 1 from the more brotherly Grand Lodge of England.[6] The new charter redesignated Provisional African Lodge No. 1 African Lodge No. 459. However vain his first trials to gain recognized legitimacy from U.S. lodges, Hall's early struggles were nevertheless significant because they tacitly challenged the inflated rhetoric of white American Freemasonry as an "association of good men" allied, they claimed, "without regard to religion, nationality, or class."[7] Hall's repeated appeals forced the white Masonic lie by pluck and persistence.

Just as importantly, Hall's agitation also militated against the racial exclusivity of the U.S. Continental Army. Only three months after his Bunker Hill initiation, and at the very time he was making his first appeals to the white Masons of Boston, Hall, in an extraordinary balancing act of early American progressivism, lobbied Joseph Warren and John Hancock, leading members of the Committee of Safety (and, technically, brothers in Masonry), for the right of black men, free and enslaved, to enlist.[8] Wary, however, of Hall's proposition, the Committee of Safety rejected the idea of black enlistment, fearing it masked black insurrectionary designs. Later, in December of 1775, General George Washington, newly in command of the Continental Armies, reconsidered Hall's petitions. Still concerned with the potential for insurgency by armed slaves, on the one hand, but threatened, on the other, by the increasing success of the British to recruit African Americans into its forces, Washington issued a compromise: "As the general is informed that numbers of free Negroes are desirous of enlisting," he announced, "he gives leave to the recruiting officers to enlist them."[9] Although Washington's concession to Hall's campaign did not permit slaves to take up arms, his directive meant that as free men, Hall and the Freemasons of African Lodge No. 459 were eligible to enlist at long last. Whether Hall or any of his fraters did or not is difficult to ascertain. The evidence remains sketchy, but enough has survived to convince many historians that Hall, at least, exercised his hard-won right. Sidney

Kaplan, for example, discovered that "military records of the time reveal at least six black Prince Halls of Massachusetts in the army and navy of the revolution. It is probable," Kaplan concludes, "that [our Prince Hall, Grand Master of African Lodge No. 459] was one of these."[10]

A tireless abolitionist and leader of Boston's free black community, Hall, it seems, was intent upon securing New England's enslaved and free men of color a meaningful place in two of the most crucial spheres of masculine authentication in colonial American culture, Freemasonry and the military. In these two crucial subcultures, "the social and cultural technologies for 'the making of men,'" as Mark Seltzer writes, thrived.[11] Hall's efforts point up the single-minded earnest with which African American men in the colonial period aimed to prove and link their manliness to the building of nationhood. Among the first black public men in America, Hall deserves primus inter pares status in the cultural history of African American manhood. At his death in 1807, the fraters of the first African Grand Lodge renamed their body Prince Hall Grand Lodge to honor the leadership of this remarkable figure in constructing what historian Loretta Williams distinguished as "the only body of black men in America able to date and document their [sic] existence as an organized body from 1775 to the present."[12]

Because Hall remains so central to the corporate identity of black Freemasons nearly two centuries after his demise, I want to turn now to the paradox of his apotheosis into a "typical [African] American," in that ironically extra-ordinary sense of the phrase advanced by Seltzer. For both within Prince Hall Freemasonry and outside of it, Hall's life and career have served to standardize African American manliness by a photographic investment in the simultaneous idealization and imagined imitability of his (black) life. Although precious little scholarship has attended to either the facts or fiction of Prince Hall since his death, his obscurity in early American historiography belies his profound iconicity as the talismanic hero of African American Masonic history and the earliest productions of typical African American manhood in the United States.

PRINCE HALL AS REPRESENTATIVE BROTHER(MAN)

Regrettably, little about Prince Hall's early life is actually known, so full of "lore and legend" are the accounts his birth and boyhood.[13] But with nothing in the way of an autobiography, memoir, or early biography to guide a proper telling of his life story, Hall's fabulation would seem to have been both necessary and unavoidable. Although a recent sketch of Hall's life and place in American literary culture avers that "if Prince Hall had not actually lived, he . . . would have been invented,"[14] I argue differently that Hall's life, insofar as we know anything about it, *was* an invention in spite of his having "actually lived." One need only consider that the first published sketch of Hall's life did not appear until 1903, more than 125 years after his death, to see why his fabulation could hardly be helped.

Notably, William Grimshaw's *Official History of Freemasonry among the Colored People in North America* identified Hall as "a Mason and a preacher in the seventeenth [*sic*] century [who] was lifted to a lofty position by events for which there is no reasonable accounting in accordance with anything that is allied to the law of nature."[15] Grimshaw portrayed Hall romantically, ultimately metamorphosing him into an abstract ideal:

> Prince Hall was born September 12th, 1748, at Bridgetown, Barbados, British West Indies. His father, Thomas Prince Hall, was an Englishman, and his mother a free woman of French descent. . . . When twelve years old young Hall was placed as an apprentice to a leather worker. He made rapid progress in the trade. His greatest desire, however, was to visit America. When he confided this wish to his parents they gave him no encouragement, but he was determined to seize the first opportunity offered to accomplish his desire. With eager eyes he watched every sail that entered the harbor in the hope that he might hear the words "bound for America." . . . One morning in February 1765, young Prince heard the glad tidings that there was a vessel in port bound for America. . . . The vessel arrived in Boston, Mass., in March, 1765. When he stepped upon the shores of New England he was seventeen years of age, small in stature, but his slight frame was surmounted with a shapely head, adorned with refined features, bright and piercing eyes, aquiline nose, mouth and chin firm and spiritual. He was in a strange land without friends or education, but [he was] determined to fight his own way.[16]

Later, in 1922, Carter G. Woodson recapitulated Grimshaw's version of Hall's biography in *The Negro in Our History*. From that year forward, it was repeated so regularly under Masonic auspices that it came to con-

stitute a reflex of African American Masonic expressivity and identification. By the time Grimshaw's embroideries were finally debunked in
Sidney Kaplan's 1973 *Black Presence in the Era of the American Revolution*
and Charles Wesley's 1977 biography *Prince Hall: Life and Legacy*,
Grimshaw's narrative was already writ large in the black Masonic mind,
and secure. If Kaplan and Wesley proved to be more meticulous re-
searchers than Grimshaw, clearly few Prince Hall followers cared.

Among other variances, Kaplan and Wesley discovered that neither
Hall's parentage nor his *pays de nationalité* could be verified by Grimshaw's own methods and sources. According to Kaplan, Hall's name
first appears in the official record during the 1740s, not the 1760s, as the
slave of William Hall of Boston. If, indeed, *our* Prince Hall was a slave
in 1765 and not the freeborn bootstraps hero Grimshaw painted, then
the certainty according to which Grimshaw offers Hall's date of birth,
"September 12th, 1748," is also necessarily questionable, especially
since no birth record of any Prince Hall of the period appears to be, or
have been, extant. Where it concerns Hall's birth, then, all that Grimshaw could say in 1922 with any certainty whatever, Wesley in 1977 said
best: "[Hall] was born somewhere and on some date."[17] Parroting
Booker T. Washington on his own obscure birth ("I suspect I must
have been born somewhere and at sometime"),[18] Wesley's words, however unsuited to the trained historian, at least bespeak an important
theoretical point not lost on the contemporary producers of black cultural critique. Namely, that the unknown facts of Hall's birth hint at a
greater problem of racial being and nothingness wrought by the natally
alienating conditions of slavery, a socioexistential dilemma of black
virtuality, according to which the familiar existentialist axiom "I think;
therefore, I am" comes to be replaced by the more simply put, vexing
expression of black being, "I think I am." It has been precisely this
dilemma of black virtuality, in fact, that has compelled so much of the
effort to reconstruct black cultural history to have to rely, in greater or
lesser degrees, on fiction for its methodology. Consequently, black cultural history, as novelist Charles Johnson has observed, "begins to
appear . . . as partly a product of imagination, a plastic and malleable
thing freighted with ambiguity."[19] Possibly for this reason, Wesley's
opinion of Grimshaw's historical method was, for all its sharp crit-
icisms, conciliatory in its conclusion: "Grimshaw's book may have
weaknesses," he granted, "but this account became alive while clothing
historical errors so that the author is a maker of a kind of history,"

nevertheless.[20] Grimshaw's "kind of history," I wish to point out here, is conspicuous not simply for its fictive aspect, however. Grimshaw's *Official History of Freemasonry among the Colored People in North America*, and, more specifically, his romanticization of Hall, are also driven by pictorial imperatives that, however much they may idealize their objects of view, nevertheless betray a hegemony of racial vision which neither Hall nor Grimshaw could ever hope, under the circumstances of the Grimshaw's methodology, to finally escape.

Among the dozen or more other significant portraits accompanying the text of Grimshaw's *Official History* is a full-length photoengraving of Hall that is his book's frontispiece. The image of Hall in the familiar powdered wig and knee breeches of colonial gentility does not fail to reflect the "slight frame," "shapely head," or "refined features" first and fastidiously detailed in an 1884 public lecture by George Washington Williams, the avowed father of U.S. black history. Not coincidentally (for Grimshaw only popularized Hall's story), Williams described Hall exactly as Grimshaw was to: "We may see Prince Hall now, a man small in stature. His slight frame is mounted by a shapely head, adorned with refined features; his eyes are bright and piercing; his nose aquiline; his mouth and chin, firm and spiritual. He wears a powdered wig, a black velvet suit, an immaculate shirt with ruffles. He carries a cane in one hand, and a roll of documents in the other."[21] Grimshaw's visual portrait of Hall faithfully reconstructs Williams's description (fig. 6). Some seventy years later, however, the picture was discovered to be "a clumsy forgery,"[22] one of many such fabrications attributed to Grimshaw. A second portrait, one ostensibly depicting Nero Prince, another free black Bostonian and Hall's successor as Grand Master of African Lodge No. 459, was exposed as counterfeit too. It turned out not to be a portrait of Prince at all, only an inexpensive copy of a steel engraving of Thomas Smith Webb — according to Wesley, a white Mason, U.S. Army major, and orchestra conductor — below which Grimshaw deceptively appended Nero Prince's name. Thus, the very same likeness appears in the "photographic" record of the revolutionary era for two persons[23]: Nero Prince, an African American, and Thomas Smith Webb, a white American. Wesley speculates that Hall's image in *Official History* was similarly simulated. Unfortunately, he concludes, "it was a Grimshaw fabrication which most Prince Hall Masons have looked upon with admiration and respect and carried . . . in their memories in worshipful ways. It may be that Grimshaw was well-intentioned when

Figure 6. Prince Hall

he is said to have made and used this picture. He must have reasoned that having no picture of Prince Hall, therefore, we will make one of him."[24] While Wesley's unearthing of Grimshaw's forgeries cannot but shock the scholarly sensibility, from another angle altogether, Grimshaw's imitation should hardly surprise given Seltzer's limnings of a pervasive fascination with imitation and reproduction at the turn of the twentieth century, a part of the more general obsession with the artifactual making of persons and things in turn-of-the-century American culture. If, as Seltzer goes further to show, the cultural logic of the late nineteenth and early twentieth centuries supposed that individuals were productively "made" (think of the concept of the "self-made" man) and Americanness itself was "artifactual and reproducible,"[25] then Grimshaw's 1903 portraits of Prince Hall and Nero Prince may not be forgeries, strictly speaking, so much as they may be worthy copies of masculine ideality, models valorized as heroic examples of American manhood. Setting out to portray Hall as a revolutionary hero and representative man, Grimshaw's picture of Hall, to put the matter another way, might just as well be the illustration of a model (and therefore imitable) black man, a type of man, a copy of an at once military and Masonic masculinism for the reproduction of black manhood in Masonic contexts.

Because this governing "system of flotation" between exceptional and typical individualism hinges upon an individual body's (Hall's) assimilability into the corporative body of the nation, race, lodge, or regiment (and vice versa), Grimshaw's portrait of Hall argues for the selfsame "privilege of abstraction" according to which the original framers of Constitutional identity transformed themselves from propertied white male particulars into a republican abstract.[26] Distinguished in every physical aspect from the racist images of arguably *the most typical* (i.e. common) representations of black men in eighteenth-century runaway slave advertisements, Hall, with "a roll of [republicanizing] documents" in hand, is depicted by Grimshaw as a doubly Constitutional and Masonic citizen, his body abstracted by a look, a pose of republican representativeness ("mouth and chin, firm and spiritual," "a powdered wig, a black velvet suit, an immaculate shirt with ruffles"). Hall's image resituates black masculinity no longer outside of the letter of Constitutionality (as slave or a fractional man), but squarely (that is, directly and, as a "photograph," geometrically) within it. It implicitly opposes the image of the fugitive body—that which is inapprehensible (in the literal sense of *apprehendere*, to seize) to republican logic.[27]

As I have said, eighteenth-century fugitive slave advertisements likely offered the most typical (i.e., standard, reproduced, imitated, copied) representations of black maleness in colonial American culture. According to the late historian Lorenzo Johnston Greene, between 1704, when the *Boston News-Letter* became the first regular newspaper of the colonies, and 1784, a span just twenty years shy of a full century,

"nearly every issue of a New England newspaper . . . carried advertisements for fugitive slaves."[28] In the mid-Atlantic states, too, the *Pennsylvania Gazette* alone published 1,324 announcements for runaway slaves
between 1728 and 1790, of which 91 percent described males.[29]

Perhaps more crucial than the raw data supporting the pervasiveness
of the fugitive image, Greene described the problems of representation
that characterized these advertisements, misrepresentations of the black
masculine which Hall conspicuously counterposed. Because fugitive
slave announcements, indifferent to complex visual detail, only broadly
outlined the runaway's physical features, they were, in Greene's words,
"seldom precise." The distinguishing details of height, weight, and
color, were mostly "vague." Of the sixty-two advertisements Greene
examined, "only five masters attempted to portray the features of their
fugitives. And even these paid little attention to the color of the eyes, the
shape of the nose or the size and shape of the mouth."[30] If, as it is said,
the proof of every rule is an exception, the contrast obtaining in one
slave's "very thick lips" and another's "curled head of hair"[31] proved by
their minstrel ludicrousness the normative sketchiness of black male
imaging in early America. But even if the specific exceptions of "thick
lips" and "curled . . . hair" challenged rather than supported the rule of
the nondescript, clearly none of the advertisements discussed by Greene
approximated the visual particulars of Hall's "bright and piercing eyes"
or "aquiline nose." Moreover, Grimshaw's Hall, "shapely," "refined,"
and "immaculate," bears little trace of the "moles, scars, brands . . .
impaired vision and loss of limb"[32] that betray the fugitive's irremedia-
ble embodiment as against the requisite disembodiment of Constitutional citizenship. Whereas the fugitive body is imagined as disfigured,
Hall's is disciplined and dignified, armed acceptably with words, not, as
Warren and Hancock feared, weapons.[33] In Grimshaw the picture of
the black male as an outlaw to Constitutional identity, one arrested in
representation even when his body remained at large, is substituted by a
radically different image: the black male as disciplinary individual and
model citizen. He is the master('s) copy of ideal manhood.

Grimshaw's picture of Hall's "disciplinary individualism," however,
may not finally be capable of realizing Hall's paradigmatic potential at
all. For the irony of disciplinary individualism, in Seltzer "the replace-
ment of the individual and organic body by the collective body of the
organization,"[34] is that it puts the very condition of subjecthood it

would putatively confer upon Hall's republican posing in jeopardy. Where the disciplinary individual submits his body, Pauline fashion, to the will and muscles of the corporate body, the "individuality of [that] individual" becomes "uncertain," keeping "steadily visible the tension between self-possession and self-discipline, between the particular" — Hall as black masculine standard — "and the generic" — Hall as a standard black male.[35] In this way, Grimshaw's treatment of Hall threatens to remand the black masculine to symbolic slave status as a self-*dis*possessed identity even as it attempts to reconstruct eighteenth-century black male representation from a position of black masculine/ Masonic self-ownership.

The Masonic ideology of masculine manufacture and (re)production, articulated in the rite of the Third Degree, "the *Making* of the Master Mason,"[36] encourages a conception of persons and bodies as artifacts that, like Grimshaw's biography of Hall, can be made (up) and remade. Since its reconstitution in London in the early 1700s, modern Freemasonry has promoted an artifactual process, vaguely mechanical, for the science of what Mark Seltzer calls simply "producing men."[37] It stands to reason that Grimshaw, once Grand Master of a Prince Hall lodge in Washington, D.C., would, having no image of Hall extant, produce — indeed, mass-produce — one artifactually as a forgery (a copy) of a "photograph" reproduced in and by a book, copying not merely the first copy, but every subsequent one in the book ad nauseum.

It is not at all surprising, then, given Seltzer's characterization of the cultural logic of turn-of-the-century America as obsessively manufactural, that Grimshaw, a dedicated Freemason, would be so brazen a forgerer. Why Hall, himself an artisan and expert tanner, was drawn so forcefully to the Masonic movement seems equally, if differently, evident. His willingness to go to the great lengths he and his peers did to pursue Masonic privileges, I want to suggest, was only to be expected.

THE ARTISAN HERO

In her book *Constructing Brotherhood: Class, Gender, and Fraternalism*, Mary Ann Clawson argues persuasively that "in the case of Masonic fraternalism . . . the image of one particular social actor, the artisan, dominated the reality-defining drama/discourse of fraternal ritual."[38] By the time of Freemasonry's flowering in the United States, the artisan had emerged definitively as a national figure for republican citizenship. Deeply esteemed, he personified values of muscular labor, capitalist productivity, economic independence, and masculine self-sufficiency in direct response to the social and economic imperatives of early modern proprietorial culture. Although many of the more aristocratic enthusiasts of European Freemasonry promoted the architect as the fittest idol of Masonic identity, American Freemasonry championed the artisan from the first. In becoming a Mason in America, in fact, a man became a figurative craftsman, whatever his actual trade or office. When he took up the distinctive paraphernalia of compass, square, plumb line, and leather apron, he was, in Clawson's words, "express[ing] a[n] . . . awareness of craft labor's contributions to . . . the success of commerce and manufacture . . . implicitly acknowledg[ing] the moral worth of economically productive activity."[39] It is no wonder then that hundreds of thousands of black men in America, Europe, and the Caribbean yearned so earnestly to belong to Masonry's symbolic ranks.[40] From an iconographic view alone, Freemasonry was well suited to the economic and political ambitions of early race men like Prince Hall, who also, importantly, tended to share with one another a labor history a century or more old.

While an accurate count of black craftsmen since Jamestown 1619 may be impossible to determine, no calculus can deny that African American men claim a long and unique artisanal history in the United States. According to Booker T. Washington's 1909 *The Story of the Negro: The Rise of the Race from Slavery*, the black crafts tradition preceded even Jamestown: "Although the slaves that were first imported from Africa were, as a rule, rude and unskilled in the industrial arts of the white man, yet the native African was not wholly without skill in the crafts, and it was not very long before some of the dark-skinned strangers had mastered the trades."[41] Washington's genuflection to "the industrial arts of the white man" notwithstanding, *The Story of the Negro* stands as one of the first efforts to historicize African American labor and crafts beyond crude generalizations about slavery. It was not, however, the first such attempt. In *The Negro Artisan*, published seven years before Washington's *The Story of the Negro*, W. E. B. Du Bois averred that "the Negro slave was the artisan of the South before the war."[42] As an ex-slave named J. D. Smith, one of the interviewees for Du Bois's study, recalled, "On every large plantation you could find the Negro carpenter, blacksmith, brick and stone mason."[43] Through slavery and for some time afterwards the African American artisan, Du Bois would go on to show, held "undisputed sway" in American crafts and trades.[44]

Prince Hall fraternalism's appeal, then, drew not only upon the gendered identity of the artisan (following Clawson) but equally on the historical relevance and respectability of the artisan as a racialized identity. And it is within the symbolic grammar of black craft activity and artisanship that such independent ideological and cultural formations of African American manhood as formalized in Prince Hall ritualism are to be found. A uniquely black male subculture often overlooked, African American Freemasonry illustrates, in microcosm, the broader dialectics of African American male identity construction.

MASONRY, MANHOOD, AND THE LABOR OF CONSTRUCTION

I don't like to work—no man does—but I like what is in the work—the chance to find yourself, our own reality—for yourself—not for others— what no other man can ever know. They only see the mere show and never can tell what it really means. — Joseph Conrad, *Heart of Darkness*

For the descendants of slaves work . . . signifies servitude, misery, and subordination. Artistic expression, expanded beyond recognition from the grudging gifts offered by the masters as a token substitute for freedom from bondage, therefore, becomes the means towards both individual self-fashioning and communal liberation. — Paul Gilroy, *The Black Atlantic: Modernity and Double Consciousness*

Ritualistically, the work that Prince Hall Freemasonry undertakes to transform black men into symbolic artisans, and thus members of the masculine body politic, discloses a dialectic of identity development that Paul Gilroy has described as a "social self-creation through labour [*sic*]."[45] Although the white Freemason comes to be according to the same dialectic, the black Freemason is of a unique cast because his indoctrination into artisanal consciousness has been anticipated by an earlier consciousness of structure and design that the history of black artisanal labor has previously formed. By this latter consciousness and its aesthetic expressions beneath the mundane and mechanical exercise of work, aesthetic expressions "expanded beyond recognition," that is, black men in America have self-reflexively constructed the black masculine into their labor as men and Masons. The 1849 slave narrative of

Rev. J. W. C. Pennington, "the fugitive blacksmith," for instance, records Pennington's resolve "to do…[his] work with dispatch and skill" and "a high degree of mechanical pride," in spite of the toil of it:

> I sought to distinguish myself in the finer branches of the business by invention and finish; I frequently tried my hand at making guns and pistols, putting blades in penknives, making fancy hammers, hatchets, sword-canes &c, &c. Besides I used to assist my father at night in making straw-hats and willow-baskets by which means we supplied our family with little articles of food, clothing and luxury, which slaves in the mildest forms of the system never get from the master.[46]

Pennington is only one among many others who evidence the extraordinary aptitude of African American craftsmen, slave and free, to craftily transform the perfunctory, labor-intensive practices of everyday black life into self-affirming, self-expressive exercises of freedom and identity. In this transformation from *animal laborans* to *homo faber*, from begrudged slave laborer to self-fashioning craftsman, lies the subterfuge of *la perruque*, "the worker's own work," as Michel de Certeau theorizes, "disguised as work for his employer."[47]

In *The Practice of Everyday Life*, de Certeau further explains that "the worker who indulges in *la perruque* . . . cunningly takes pleasure in finding a way to create . . . products whose sole purpose is to signify his own capabilities through his work."[48] For de Certeau *la perruque* names an "artisan-like inventiveness," to state the matter baldly.[49] Such inventiveness as defines *la perruque* has enabled African American men like Pennington to transform a labor event which, following Arendt, discloses little to nothing of "the subjective attitude or activity of the laborer,"[50] into self-reflective work, including the ritualistic work of Freemasonry.[51] That Prince Hall Freemasons regard their rites as work (not labor) in the idiom of the wider fraternity of Masons, black and white, and moreover know Freemasonry itself as "the Craft," is indicative of the equally self-creational potential of the artisanal fetish in Freemasonry. But this observation alone is inadequate to highlight the fetish function of the artisan among Prince Hall fraters. For the greater insights are discernible through a "realist tautology" in Masonic logic. What Seltzer defines as "the circular relations between interior states and material conditions (between psychology and sociology)" is everywhere encouraged in Masonic symbology.[52]

Since Freemasonry involves the symbolic application of architectural principles to the construction of male subjects as edifices, it is the Master Mason of the Prince Hall Craft who possesses the full knowledge of how to properly construct the black masculine. That is, the Master Mason alone knows which secrets of the Craft cohere the man, like a building, "in one enduring and connected mass."[53] Consequently, the singular consciousness of "one enduring and connected mass" of selfhood would appear to be the ultimate dreamwish of the conflicted born-somewhere-and-on-some-date black male subject, whom Du Bois named in *The Souls of Black Folk* a "seventh son" afforded "no true self-consciousness."[54] The interior adjustment of the fractured life of black manhood to the promise of cohesiveness represented by buildings is fundamentally, then, the surplus-producing work Prince Hall Freemasonry seeks to perform, expressing itself, idealized, in the blueprint iconicity of the Masonic lodge-room as much as in the artisan.

According to the eminent Masonic chronicler Albert Mackey, the construction of lodge-rooms across the world has obeyed a fairly consistent set of design principles since at least the seventeenth century. Mackey explains, for instance, that a lodge-room must approach a rectangle and "should always, if possible, be situated due East and West," an orientation meant to evoke, in part, a now ancient conception of the earth's shape and form. In Mackey's words, "any other form but that of an *oblong square* [is] eminently incorrect and unMasonic."[55] Given this form's hint at a cherishable, if mythologized, pre-Columbian past, it is no wonder that generations of African American men, geographically and temporally distant from their Afro-genesis, would find the lodge-room an agreeable locus for self-creation. As Muraskin has conjectured, the lodge-room's geometrical symbolism "has presented the black man with a worldview that has aided in his creation of self-respect by supplying him with a history that is radically different from the traditional one associated with his people": it "has erased from the mind of the black Mason his actual descent from slaves" and offered an alternative old world ancestry hearkening back afrocentrically to "the days of the Pyramids . . . the earliest beginnings of the [Masonic] Order."[56] In the Prince Hall lodge-room, "the fact of . . . [a Mason's] former condition as [slave], or that of his parents [has] no bearing whatever on him"; the nothingness of slave being is overcome by the lodge-room's architectural insistence on a transcendent cultural memory.[57]

Although both black and white Freemasons have shared certain narratives of Masonic history for centuries, some versions of these narratives differ markedly between groups. While white Freemasons have claimed descent from ancient Egyptian stock and style as consistently as their black counterparts, only those histories authored by black Freemasons record the ancestral Egyptians as black. And not only the Egyptians. In the Prince Hall typology, "Solomon, the builder of the Great Temple . . . upon which Masonry the world over stands . . . was a black man" too.[58] For Prince Hall Freemasons, then, it is "out of Egypt *and through the black man*," that Freemasonry's special knowledge "of arts, sciences and [other] forms of culture" first dawned.[59] No such racialized genealogy has ever come to be espoused by white Freemasons, however. That fact hardly matters to their Prince Hall fraters, however, who hold that white Freemasons owe their Masonic inheritance to the genius of the black man as well—this is the Prince Hall myth of pride.

Significantly, the black Freemasons' embrace of this gloriously gendered and racialized narrative of the Masonic genesis is directly attributable to the prolific writings and decided influence of Martin Robison Delany, "journalist, editor, doctor, scientist, judge, soldier, inventor, customs inspector, orator, politician and novelist."[60] Co-editor with Frederick Douglass of the *North Star* paper from 1847 to 1849, Delany is perhaps better remembered for his treatise *The Condition, Elevation, Emigration and Destiny of the Colored People of the United States Politically Considered* (1852) and for having organized the first scientific expedition from the West to the African continent in 1859 (Delany was seeking to develop cotton production in West Africa). What is much less known about Delany is the distinction he holds as the first Freemason in America to publish a history of the Prince Hall Craft. Worshipful Grand Master of the St. Cyprian Lodge of Pittsburgh in 1852, Delany published a thin but exceptional tract entitled *The Origins and Objects of Ancient Freemasonry: Its Introduction into the United States, and Legitimacy among Colored Men* (1853), documenting his ethnologically derived conclusions that the first flowering of all Masonic wisdom occurred in black Africa. Anticipating his later *Principia of Ethnology: The Origins of Races with an Archaeological Compendium of Ethiopian and Egyptian Civilization* (1880), *The Origins and Objects of Ancient Freemasonry* asked rhetorically, "From whence sprung Masonry, but from Ethiopia, Egypt, and Assyria—all settled and peopled by the children of Ham?" and argued passionately that to deny the black Freemason this venerable history was "to deny a child the lineage of its parentage."[61] Undoubtedly, such a heritage was among the chief appeals of Freemasonry to Delany, a passionate race man on par with Douglass, David Walker, Henry Highland Garnett, and Alexander Crummell. Although not all of the most notable race men of Delany's time were Prince Hall followers (Douglass, for example), still, for many distinguished others, like Crummell, Freemasonry had power enough to comprehend the historical discontinuities of black masculine life and to reconcile them acceptably. Freemasonry's success for bringing about historical and iconic congruity has been owed from the first to the lodge-room's topoanalytical capacity to evoke the ameliorative, if romaticized, black past portrayed in Delany's *Origins and Objects*.

However, as the Masonic lure for African American men seems to have been preeminently iconic (i.e., in the symbolism of the artisan and the lodge-room), and only secondarily historical, Delany was most likely drawn into the order by its artisanal appeal. Even if, among the vast inventory of vocations cited above by Gilroy, no mention of the trades appears, Delany nevertheless shared in the history and consciousness of the black trades and craft tradition as an inventor (much more a theorist of structure and design than a practitioner).[62] Early in 1852, on learning that the Pennsylvania Railroad was extending its tracks over the Alleghenies towards Pittsburgh, Delany devised a more efficient means for locomotive travel over the mountainous terrain. He carried his plans for a self-powered steam engine capable of greater degrees of ascent and descent to a New York lawyer for patenting. After several weeks of correspondence between his lawyer and the Patents Office in Washington, Delany's drawings were returned to him with apologies; his application had been rejected. Only full-fledged U.S. citizens, the Patents Office maintained, were eligible to hold patents on their inventions. Although Delany took great pride in his free black standing, that pride would not alter the political reality that, however unenslaved he was, in 1852 he, nor any African American, was then a full-fledged Constitutional citizen. Despite later improvements upon the steam engine by others, his mechanical innovation went cast aside into a vast dustbin of other discarded designs on Patent Office floors never to see materialization that year.

Perhaps if it is true, though, as Mark Seltzer has posited relatedly in *Bodies and Machines*, that the "crisis of agency and its appeals" were, by the second half of the nineteenth century, "most evident in the figure of the railway locomotive,"[63] then the symbolism of Delany's steam engine,

at least, clearly survived its official disregard. For, under Seltzer's reading, the Patent Office's rejection of Delany's application was, at root, a
more resounding rejection of the socially motile, self-determinative —
even phallic — aspirations Delany's mountain-crossing locomotive almost certainly represented. Delany's drafting of *Condition, Elevation,
and Emigration* during the weeks of waiting to hear from Washington
seems to have anticipated the Patent Office's response on precisely these
grounds. The first significant political analysis of its kind, *Condition,
Elevation, and Emigration* bemoaned black disenfranchisement and, unexpectedly discordant with the abolitionist agenda, favored an emigrationist politics that encouraged black colonization of Central and South
America. Unfortunately, the book was beset with enough "misspelled
names, wrong dates, [and] awkward passages" to betray its hastiness.[64]
As a result, it garnered little public notice. Few thought *Condition,
Elevation, and Emigration* worthy even of mention in abolitionist and
uplift circles. The only substantial commentary voiced on it at the time
came from the prominent abolitionist William Lloyd Garrison. Though
he differed with Delany's emigrationist politics, Garrison nevertheless
described the work favorably as replete with "valuable facts and cogent
appeals." His further flattery of the author as "a vigorous writer . . . full of
energy and enterprise" depicted Delany in very nearly the same commercial language of mechanical advance ("vigorous . . . full of energy")
Delany's locomotive symbolized.[65] True to the form of such symbolism,
Delany had traveled throughout Europe and across western Africa
within seven years of *Condition, Elevation, and Emigration*, pursuing, in
the end, an emigrationist course to Canada, family in tow. Settling in
Chatham, Ontario, where one-third of the population of 4,000 had
arrived as fugitives from slavery, Delany chose emigration to Canada as
the lived sign of his unassimability into the American body politic.[66]

More interestingly, though, Delany was a striking if "familiar sight"
in Chatham.[67] To see him at the town hall, at church, or other public
venues clad in the traditional shocoto pants and dashiki of West Africa
was not especially unusual, according to biographer Dorothy Sterling.
Although his sartorial tastes were calculated, in part, to counter stereotypes of African primitivism (according to Sterling and others, he also
frequently wore a long dark hued robe with scrolls of fabric wrapping
the neck like a collar, an attire he claimed was the ceremonial dress of
an African chief), his dress was primarily a visibly material reflection
of the surplus of signification black male bodies, mostly denied the

(white, male) privilege of abstract disembodiment, inspire as outlaws to Constitutional representation under racialism. For a time Delany reveled in his "outlaw" image. But with the hope of the Civil War to fulfill black ambitions of social and political parity, his attitude towards black American enfranchisement and, just as significantly, his dress, changed dramatically.[68] The potential of a war won by antislavery Union forces revived in Delany a hope for black American uplift and equality under the law. Eager to volunteer but well beyond the age of enlistment, Delany left Chatham and returned to the United States in 1863 to help raise black troops for the Union cause. In a correspondence to then-Secretary of War E. M. Stanton, Delany offered his energies, convinced, he wrote, that black enlistment was "one of the measures in which the claims of the Black Man may be officially recognized, without seemingly infringing upon those of other citizens."[69] Insofar as the persistent phallocentrisms of Delany's African dress (the long dark robe of the tribal chief), locomotive design (the train mounting, penetrating the Alleghenies), and history of Freemasonry (its Solomonic lineage) disclose manliness itself to be the most fundamental of "the claims of the Black Man" ("I AM A MAN," 1960s Civil Rights protesters shouted), that claim stood to be settled by the wide visibility of black men in uniform. Seemingly, Delany knew then what critic Michael Hatt has only recently made clear about the iconization of soldiering: by the middle of the nineteenth century, "[m]asculinity defined and was defined by the soldier's task . . . the soldier's rough and rugged lifestyle; his determination and endurance; and by his physical control . . . [demonstrated] not least in the military requirement for discipline."[70] Delany's efforts would prove by a singular gesture the terminological, to say nothing at all of the social, congruities of black masculinity. In Delany's letter to Stanton, however, was an implicit avowal that black masculinity only cohered in a white context. Judging "the measures" of black men, in other words, "was a question of negotiating between sameness and difference," as Hatt explains, allowing black men manhood, but without disrupting the differentials of power, position, or property accorded by race on the social or political claims of (white male) others.[71]

With an acute sense of the continuities obtaining between nationhood, citizenship, and masculinity which soldiering naturally evokes, Delany took to recruiting ardently. For his earnest and tactical brilliance in proposing to raise African American Union troops on both sides of the Mason-Dixon, Secretary Stanton commissioned him a major in the Union Army on 26 February 1865. Swearing solemnly by the Constitution to fulfill the duties of his charge as the United States' first black field officer, Delany was transformed instantly from Constitutional cipher and political nonconformist to disciplinary individual and model (black) citizen. As a testament to this achievement, *The Weekly Anglo-African* advertised a dignified postcard portrait of the black major—like Prince Hall extraordinary in one sense, but necessarily "typical" in another. The portrait, made by the well-known New York portrait photographer Abraham Bogardus depicted Delany fully uniformed with magisterial mien: "Price per copy, 25 cents."[72]

Once shunning conventions of Western dress, Delany assumed the air of a thoroughly disciplined and regimented subject in his exquisite regalia (an image of corporal asceticism prefiguring the military formalism of Marcus Garvey a half-century later). No longer a menace to the representational integrity of the body politic, as soldier Delany became its willfully governed subject and defender—roles one could hardly have imagined for so insurgent a figure as Delany had he not been, we recall, also a Freemason. For what Freemasonry and the military both required was, above everything, a disciplined and reproducible masculinism. The image-object of a photographic revolution launched by the Frenchman André Adolphe Eugène Disdéri in 1854 toward cheaper, faster, and more portable portrait-making, *The Weekly Anglo-African's* promotion of Delany, his image and its commodification in the *carte de visite*, realized just such an ideal.

Not long after Disdéri introduced the carte de visite portrait in France, "cartomania" swept the United States. The new 2½" x 4" format, a small photographic portrait mounted upon durable cardstock, first appeared in the United States in 1859, democratizing photography, in a sense, by opening up the market in photographic portraiture to mass consumption for the first time. Inexpensive, portable, easily reproduced, and a fashionable curiosity, these *cartes* effected such a boon in the United States that by 1860 they were a flourishing industry unto themselves. And the Civil War, not a few years later, secured the industry's American success. "The outbreak of the Civil War, with the calls for volunteers to serve in the military, separated hundreds of thousands of young men from their families. Every hometown photographer made portraits of its sons in uniform while they were on leave or upon mustering out. . . . Millions of these soldier portraits were produced."[73] Although the affordability of the carte de visite permitted the soldier portrait the widest market imaginable — virtually every Union soldier posed for one, and often many times over — portraits of venerated officers and esteemed statesmen were particularly saleable. These, in fact, comprised the largest class of carte de visite portraits between 1861 and the end of the war. Notably, photographic historian William Darrah has listed the Bogardus studio among the most prominent U.S. publishers of the military portrait in the nineteenth century.[74] A distinguished Broadway studio photographer with a historic portrait of twenty-third U.S. President Benjamin Harrison to his credit as well, Bogardus achieved as much in the (re)production of Delany's officer's portrait as Delany's career had for the idealizing project of early African American masculinity and republicanism.[75]

While the 25 cents *The Weekly Anglo-African* set for Delany's portrait is alone enough to prove its carte de visite format (throughout the 1860s, the average price for cartes de visite ranged from $1.50 to $3.50 per dozen), Bogardus's was reproduced from a considerably larger handcolored lithograph of 20⁹⁄₁₆" x 17¼", held today by the Smithsonian Institute National Portrait Gallery (fig. 7). Despite the National Portrait Gallery's uncertainties about the lithograph's creator ("Unidentified Artist," it says) and its year of composition ("Circa 1860–1864," the gallery surmises), it is very likely that, since there were many drawings and paintings, "including many of American origin . . . dated 1859 to 1865," uniquely created for reproduction in carte format, the lithograph Bogardus copied was his own.[76] Whoever the lithographer, though, the lithograph's age is no longer a question. In light of the documented fact that Delany's commission as major was not issued until February 1865, his image appearing in *The Weekly Anglo-African* just weeks later, can there be any doubt, even with the National Portrait Gallery, about the lithograph's 1865 origin? I suggest not. Of course, while the origins of the Delany carte de visite may be fairly determined this way, there would seem to be no possibility of identifying an original photograph, a template for the guarantee of realist reproduction, to assure us, as photographs are called upon to do, that the subject actually existed this way. Already a copy, an imitation of the prevailing photorealism of Civil War cartes de visite, Bogardus's first reproduction of the Delany lithograph projected "pure semblance," to use Slavoj Žižek's term, from the start, an artificial mimesis of sturdy black masculine ideality retouched to abstraction, in the place of the "real" Delany, who

Figure 7. Abraham Bogardus, Martin Robison Delany

at fifty-three years old in 1865 was "large [and] heavy set, with a bald, sleek head which shines like a newly polished boot."[77]

Delany's portrait was also a sharp contrast to the more familiar iconography of mid-century African American male excess depicted in the antebellum black male mug shot, in the pornography of biologist Louis Agassiz's 1850 South Carolina slave daguerreotypes ("America's first, scientifically-sanctioned, Black 'nudie shots,'" I knew a graduate student to call them once),[78] and in the disfiguring details of the popular antislavery carte "The Scourged Back," showing a vast spider's web of scar tissue on the lashed back of a much-abused Louisiana slave in 1863. The Bogardus carte of Delany presented the black major in the most visually disembodied and abstracting light imaginable.[79]

Bogardus did more than simply idealize Delany, however. He standardized Delany's idealization, pronounced its typicality, ironically enough, by posing Delany according to Disdérian protocols. Setting the international standard for carte style and technique, Disdéri promoted conventions of portraiture designed to systematize poses according to the profession or the position of the subject. As a result, his and other studios produced thousands of nearly identical Civil War images. Delany's pose, repeating the solemn stateliness of the myriad other soldier subjects photographed between 1860 and 1870, therefore belied his career's exceptionalism. It inherently diminished the singular achievements of Masonry and military distinction that had earned his carte marketability in the first place. Owing to the redoubled effect of standardization created by Delany's dress and pose and the potential, implicit in the announcement of *The Weekly Anglo-African*, for the serial reproduction of the Bogardus carte in perpetuity, the Delany portrait came to portray not an exceptional man but a typical one, general and reproducible by others. The carte distilled broad, black masculine ambition into a single image and helped to shape a specific form of black masculine ideality. The appeal of black regimentalism, however, could be seen just as conspicuously in Masonic displays of masculine self-fashioning as in Civil War cartes de visite. In fact, a glance at Bogardus's image of Delany may well confuse it with one of the period's somewhat rarer Masonic *carte* portraits. But the double identity of army major and Freemason a glance might confuse in the Bogardus carte, a close study, I argue, will see conflated in Delany's own art: namely, his ambitious 1861 fiction *Blake; or, the Huts of America*.

Given Delany's importance to the cultural history of African American Freemasonry, and the fraternity's reciprocal influence on his life and career, a critical search for Masonic arcana cached between the lines of *Blake* would seem to be expected in Delany scholarship. And yet only the very fewest scholars have undertaken such a project. Perhaps, though, it is wise that only very few have. For to mine *Blake* thoroughly in this way is to risk erring in the direction of much American anti-Masonic paranoia, from Yale College president Timothy Dwight in

1798, to Nation of Islam spokesman Louis Farrakhan in 1995.[80] Such a gamble notwithstanding, let me propose the Grand Official Council in Part 2 of *Blake* as not so much a Masonic assembly—for there are women in this body—but as a depiction of at once Masonic and cabalist secrecy.

With its insurrectionary and black nationalist designs on the proverbial table, the Grand Council depicted in chapters 60, 61, 69, 70, and 74 of *Blake*, a Talented Tenth of self-proclaimed "seclusionists," meet in the isolated "southwest corner of [Madame Cordora's] mansion in an airy attic room, reserved for the purpose."[81] Mimicking the gender politics and poetics of space that characterize the Masonic lodge-room, the doubly closeted meeting of the Grand Council not only recasts Masonic architecture as cabal command post, but usurps its female ownership for wholly patriarchal programmatic ends. That is to say, as Robert Levine emphasizes, "that although [the hero] Blake early on affirms his desire to work with male and female leaders," and is content to indulge Madame Cordora's protests of the council's occasional lapses into religious and ethnic essentializing, "he mostly seeks out black males for assistance in organizing his [revolutionary] plot."[82] This prejudice, and the guard who keeps post outside the council doors permitting no one entry without the "closest possible inspection," to say nothing of the familiarly Masonic affectations of titles and hierarchy that pronounce Blake "Commander in Chief of the Army of Emancipation" (256), all coalesce into a decidedly "Masonic, Pan-Africanist vision" of racial rescue imagined by Delany.[83] There may be more, of course, to *Blake*'s Masonic sublimations than the lodge-room seclusion of the Grand Council's attic chamber alone. For the Masonic lodge-room, if not the attic chamber, models an exemplary selfhood of Pauline equivalency between buildings and bodies as well.

While the lodge-room layout strives to reconstruct an ancient cosmogony long since disappeared, it should be clear that the structure's metaphoricity moves in two directions. Although the primary dimensions of the lodge-room seek to mimic a cartography of the ages, the lodge-room's structural austerity helps the Mason to imagine the lodge-as-self. In other words, the spatial concentration defining the strict carceral framing of the lodge-room actualizes a unified Masonic consciousness, an ideal Masonic-I. Clearly, too, the recommendation that the "lodge-room should also be isolated where it is practicable, from all surrounding buildings" conveys a self-referential design.[84] Still more suggestively, Mackey enjoins:

> There should be two entrances to the room, which should be situated in the West. . . . The one on [the] right hand is for the introduction of visitors and . . . leading from the Tiler's room is called the Tiler's, or the *outer door*; the other, on [the] left, leading from the preparation room [where candidates await initiation], is known as the *inner door*, and sometimes called the *northwest door*.[85]

Implicitly, this unalterable topography posits a public (outer) and private (inner) conveyance into the lodge-as-self nearly homologous with Raymond Williams's formulations of the *material sign* — the "outer door" — of public representation and the *inner sign* — the "inner door" — entering into the private negotiations of Masonry and manhood.[86] (Surely it is not a coincidence that the two auxiliary rooms into which the inner door and outer door enter and exit are also called "secret . . . closets" by Mackey.)[87] This public/private dichotomy of representation suggested by lodge-room architecture, however, is not unique to the gendered identity of Freemasonry. For it is as crucial to the Du Boisian notion of racial double consciousness as it is to Masonic identity. Perhaps no less important than the black/white, African/European binarisms that typically characterize the twoness of black American identity, the public/private dialectic has never been altogether alien to Prince Hall Freemasons. They, too, are among those whom Lawrence Levine has described as a "people who have walked through American history with their cultural lanterns obscured from the unknowing and unseeing eye of outside observers."[88] Levine's depiction of black cultural life imaginatively highlights the concord of strategic dissimulations in public culture that African Americans have privately engineered for their survival. As a mimetic reproduction of a familiar structure of consciousness, then, the lodge-room must have been, and must remain, especially signifying for Prince Hall Freemasons.

INTERIOR DESIGNS

Given the many prohibitions restricting African American sociability in eighteenth- and nineteenth-century America north and south, it is a feat of modern history that Prince Hall Freemasonry survived its first century. In 1770s Massachusetts, for example, a 9 pm curfew imposed upon its free black population probably curtailed the work of fledgling Provisional African Lodge No. 1 and jeopardized the secrecy of its initiations.[89] Later, states such as South Carolina went even further, outlawing any assembly of slaves or free blacks "in a confined or secret place" altogether.[90] A vast range of other repressive measures between those of Massachusetts, at one extreme, and South Carolina, at the other, were also enacted elsewhere, from Connecticut to Tennessee and Georgia. Nevertheless, by 1865, the year Delany made U.S. military history, Prince Hall lodges had been securely established in fourteen states including Maryland, Kentucky, Louisiana, and South Carolina.[91] That Prince Hall fraternalism thrived despite black codes in virtually all parts of the governed country is a testament to the covertness and cunning by which black masculine identity has kept itself hidden from the arrestive encroachments of public inspection. And it bears repeating that this will to secrecy and silence has been historically reflected in, among other sites, the uncompromising insularity of the lodge-as-self. In form and function, the Prince Hall lodge-room has been an enduring sanctuary for black masculine subject formation for over two centuries (fig. 8). Its integrity as a refuge from the objectifying specularity of the black male in public culture is guaranteed by the architectural imperative of "lofty walls" to "preclude the possibility of being overlooked by cowans or eavesdroppers."[92] Whatever else Masonic authorities intended "lofty walls" to signify, in the context of black male specularity and the madness engendered by racist over-sight, they cannot escape casting the Masonic lodge-room as an asylum, structural as much as social, for the black Mason's most essential self-interests.

As to the interior layout and furnishings of the lodge-room, Mackey's *Encyclopedia* provides the following blueprint:

> In a Lodge-room the dais should be elevated on three steps, and provided with a pedestal for the Master. . . . The pedestal for the Senior Warden in the West should be elevated on two steps, and that of the Junior Warden in the South on one. . . . The tabernacle also forms an essential part of the Chapter room. This is sometimes erected in the center of the room. . . . There are some other arrangements required in the construction of a [lodge-]room, of which is unnecessary to speak.[93]

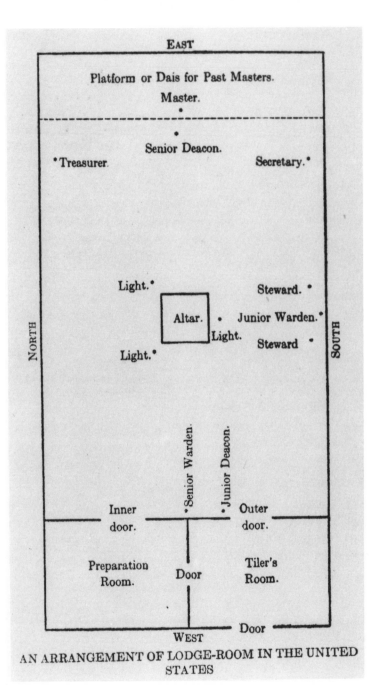

Figure 8. Arrangement for Masonic lodge-room in the United States

By limning only the most fundamental features of this blueprint, forsaking "unnecessary" details, Mackey implicitly underscores how essential the posts of Master, Senior Warden, and Junior Warden actually are. In each post's symbolism lie the gender and sexual subtexts of American Masonic appeal.

As Mackey explains in *The Symbolism of Freemasonry*, "The Master and Wardens are symbols of the sun, the lodge-room of the universe, or world."[94] As his text further reveals, the sun and universe hold still deeper significations as symbols of the generative power of the phallus or *membrum virile*, and of the cteis or female "receptacle," respectively.[95] Differently put, the sun and universe, phallus and cteis, represent "the two different forms of the generative principle," male and female, which "perfect the circle of generation" in the natural world.[96] A projection of the belief that the productive powers of dual sexes may exist in the same individual, the union of phallus and cteis, realized by the material design of the lodge-room, speaks for an androgynous subjectivity intent upon displacing women from the generative process of masculine self-creation by recourse to an alternative practice at once artifactual and male—*Freemasonry*. While the lodge-room as cteis—as womb, one may say—bears a conspicuously uterine character (it is within the protection of the lodge-room, recall, that initiates are said to be "born again" into the light of Masonic truth),[97] the triumph of the androgynous ideal upsets the conventional female-uterine relation. In an act of what Seltzer calls the "confiscation of the generative function," the Master Mason enacts "a compensatory male response to [an ostensibly] threatening female productivity."[98] Disbarring women from among its ranks, the lodge is mother enough for the Freemason. And its members men enough to make "real" men out of those especially whom slavery's insistence upon *partus sequitur ventrem* (the mother's condition forever following "all her remotest posterity") has made, in a manner of speaking, mama's boys.

To pursue Prince Hall fraternalism, then, is inevitably to take up the mantle of an embattled black masculinity and to take on an ameliorative structure of consciousness which, reconstituting this imperiled identity, conceives of the lodge-as-self. In consonance with Pierre Bourdieu's dialectic of the internalization of externality and the externalization of internality, the architectonics of the lodge-room replicate externally and reinforce internally the organization of the Prince Hall Masonic mind, establishing the preconditions for a historical *edifice complex* shared by black Masons and black non-Masons alike. While few examples besides the lodge-room and few other institutions beside Prince Hall Freemasonry illustrate so lucidly how the black masculine is "made in America," still fewer individuals make a better study of man-made masculinity in historic African American contexts than Frederick Douglass and Booker T. Washington. I turn now to precisely their predicaments, sexually inflected, of spectacle and respectability in Douglass's *Narrative* of 1845 and Washington's *Up from Slavery* of 1901.

CHAPTER THREE

Constructing the Black Masculine

Frederick Douglass, Booker T. Washington, and

the Sublimits of African American Autobiography

I suspect I must have been born somewhere and at sometime.
— Booker T. Washington, *Up from Slavery*

By now, I hope it is clear why I have chosen to identify this book
(and, in recapitulated form, this chapter) by its constructionist title.
Not only does this rhetoric of design and manufacture suit the arti-
factual/architectural logic of black male representation in public white
and private black cultures, in magazines and Masonic lodges, it also
implies — so conspicuously as to almost go without saying — the anti-
essentialist position of the author that racial and gender identity as such
are socially created. In chapter 1, I argued that black men tend to be seen
photographically in white eyes, looked on as one looks on a snapshot or
some other objectified, arrested image. In chapter 2, I extended the
photographic argument to demonstrate how the production of Masonic circulation of two early portraits of African American manhood
testified, in their respective poses, to black men's historic ambition "to
approximate an image which represents a cultural ideal."[1] Correlatively,
this aim to ideality is symbolized by the realist tautology, "the circular
relations between interior states and material conditions (between psychology and sociology)," in black building and craft traditions uniquely
encouraged by Prince Hall Freemasonry.[2] What the cultural history of
Prince Hall fraternalism reveals more lucidly however about the dialectics of black masculine ideality is neither psychological nor sociological,
at root, but symbolic. In Masonry, as in the pursuit of black manhood
more broadly, "the labor of construction," as architect/philosopher
Mark Wigley has written (if in a non-Masonic context), "is never more
than the labor of representation."[3] Man-making, in other words, is

scarcely a different enterprise than image-making in either the private lodges or public lives of black men.

If the posings of Hall and Delaney, for example, are to be taken as pictorial correctives to such spectragraphic misrepresentations of black male identity as pictured in eighteenth- and nineteenth-century fugitive slave advertisements, then doubtlessly pictures constituted one more means of demonstrating black humanity and political deservedness, a companion strategy to the more familiar one of representing the proper black image scriptively in slave narratives and early black autobiography. In this chapter, I want to return to the text-based constructions of black masculine identity which, in first-person expression particularly, may owe as much to the principles of portraiture abstractly as any photograph or painting does. As African American men's first-person narratives (fictional as well as autobiographical) have consistently "alerted us to the complex sculpting of the self," to borrow a suggestive line from literary critic Richard Yarborough, they share a public rather than private function with the visual art piece.[4] Like the visual images of Hall and Delany, they reflect, "through the veiled, most likely unconscious projection into the text . . . some of [their authors'] . . . deeper fears, desires, concerns and dreams" even as he consciously attempts to shape a public persona who does not betray his "more dangerous and unruly emotions . . . lest [he] lose the audience [he was] trying to reach," black or white.[5] The authorial construction of first-person subjectivity, therefore, is finally only achieved at the expense of the exhausting effort required by the author to repress the fragmentary, dueling impulses of a divided consciousness normally kept in the reserve of the unconscious. Psychoanalytically considered, first-person narrative, including the fictional impulses in black autobiography and the autobiographical impulses of black fiction,[6] depends on more than "everything available in memory, perception, understanding, imagination, [and] desire"[7] suitable for public discourse, as the late Michael Cooke argued. It also rests upon the autobiographer's success in repressing "everything that . . . in some way or other [is] painful . . . alarming or disagreeable or shameful by the standards of the subject's personality."[8] These breaches in first-person consciousness, unearthed by the designs of psychological criticism, disclose a representational indomitability — in this essay, an essential polymorphous libidinality — that belies the pretense of black masculine ideality enacted in black men's public posings.[9] Thus, my aim in this chapter is to explore in Frederick Douglass's *Narrative of the Life of Frederick Douglass, an American Slave* and Booker T. Washington's *Up from Slavery* that vast area of repression around which the self-conscious autobiographical subject is always skirting, to trespass into the metaphorical memory-place of "those serpentine caves," as Virginia Woolf imagined it, "where one goes with a candle peering up and down, not knowing where one is stepping."[10] More to the point, this chapter is concerned with the early, developmental stage of African American male identity formation, characterized in black male autobiography by a behavioral ambivalence towards the cultural prescriptions of nineteenth- and twentieth-century racial and sexual identity, a pediatric dread corresponding, in more familiar (if still yet clinical) terms, to the polymorphous perverse. Symptomatically, this preliminary stage of black male identity is distinguished from its subsequent phase, liminal subjecthood,[11] by a vaguely Hegelian panic of ontological (if not also social) bondage and abjection,[12] a "panic of reduction,"[13] heaving the racial manchild early and headlong into the crucible matters of American race and sex.

Frederick Douglass' *Narrative* (1845) and Booker T. Washington's *Up from Slavery* (1901) are early case studies in black *boyological* development. Importantly, although both autobiographies commence with formulaic birth narratives, neither autobiographer can state precisely the date or the circumstances of his birth. The problem of racial being and nothingness is perhaps nowhere more poignantly expressed than by Washington in the epigraph to this essay: "I suspect I must have been born somewhere and at some time."[14] The bastard offspring of enslaved black mothers and obscure white fathers / masters, Douglass and Washington fashion nonoedipal dramas of slavery which reveal nuclear relations as a less significant matter to the slavocracy than the bourgeois imperatives of ownership, dominance, commodity, and (re)production. Over and above the problems posed by the strained primal configurations immanent in these autobiographical accounts, the bastard / mulatto status of Douglass and Washington would appear to figure also as a trope for the Constitutional illegitimacy of African American subjecthood, a trope that for the black writer, I suspect, had its genesis in biblical themes of Hebrew bondage and providential election.[15] Moreover, the mixed-race heroes of black men's early writing would seem to accrue biblical iconicity as allegorical figures of the American Ishmael, the extracovenantal son of the Republican Patriarch and his Black Hagar, cursed to wander the national landscape on an impossible mis-sion to find a refuge of determinacy from within the elemental indeterminacy ("born somewhere and at some time") of the slave condition.

Henry Louis Gates's "Binary Oppositions in Chapter One of *Narrative of the Life of Frederick Douglass, an American Slave Written by Himself*," in his *Figures in Black: Words, Signs, and the 'Racial' Self*, suggests a critical list of fixed binarisms (nature/culture, animal/human, barbaric/civilized, cipher/subject, black/white) governing the Manichean sign system of slavery, binarisms between which, I submit, the polymorphic drives of pubescence oscillate promiscuously, if obliviously, through a sublime middle passage of subject development. Gradually, however, the agreeably clement tides of the preliminal state swell, and the ensuing surges of a more liminal racial and gendered condition overwhelm. Suddenly the inexperienced traveler, surprised by the storm, discovers himself washed ashore, needy and disconcerted, onto the alien banks of racial and sexual self-consciousness. What follows is the troubled discovery of social meaninglessness, the slaveboy's first awareness of self-as-cipher caught inconsequentially between black and white, male and man, biology and psychology. Disclosing "the most inflexible of barriers," Gates's catalogue of binary oppositions suggests that the only real inheritance of the enslaved manchild is a vast symbolic universe of conflictual, mutually negating identifications that thwart every effort of his to be certain of when and where he was born, which racial community — black or white — is authentically his, or what the nature of manhood might be for him (given that black men and boys under slavery have lived outside of the free white contexts in which sex and gender difference were purposefully established.)[16]

If literary critics and historians have attended to issues of nativity and amalgamation in Douglass and Washington, few have pursued in either case the problems and paradoxes of sex and gender inherent in black male enslavement. Few, that is, have recognized, as critic George Cunningham has, that "within the domain of slavery, gender or culturally derived notions of man- and womanhood do not exist."[17] Cunningham's premise points plainly to what Eugene Genovese calls "the annihilating implications of chattel slavery."[18] Because the black slave belonged chiefly to a commercial order of domestic livestock, his or her sex was not the same determinant of power or protection it was in the community of slaveholders. Rather, the slave's sex would seem to have served a commodity function — the essential machinery of plantation (re)production. It follows that the slave's historical struggles for personal and political freedom are also part and parcel of his efforts to be liberated from such conditions of social cipherhood that his sex, meaningless outside of commercial contexts, signifies. This familiarly phenomenological struggle names precisely the crisis of manliness experienced by the autobiographical manchild, brought into presence by the adult narrator, in *Narrative of the Life of Frederick Douglass* and *Up from Slavery*. In both narratives, the signs of self-conflict are transparent. The mediative identifications of pubescent subjecthood surface discernibly — and often impolitely — where neither autobiographer seems to have intended it.

THE HEROIC SLAVEBOY

One confesses — or is forced to confess. . . . The most defenseless tenderness and the bloodiest of powers have a similar need of confession. Western man has become a confessing animal.

   Whence a metamorphosis in literature: we have passed from a pleasure to be recounted and heard, centering on the heroic or marvelous narration of the "trials" of bravery or sainthood, to a literature ordered according to the infinite task of extracting from the depths of oneself, in between the words, a truth which the very form of the confession holds out like a shimmering mirage. — Michel Foucault, *The History of Sexuality*

Prefiguring by nearly a century the paradigmatic spectracentric concerns of Richard Wright's *Native Son*, Frederick Douglass's *Narrative* would appear to recognize in the racial gaze on black male bodies a vaguely pornographic propensity not unlike that in Wright. In recounting the "most terrible spectacle" of his Aunt Hester's rape, Douglass reveals his own sexual vulnerability by a scopophobic worry betraying the spectragraphic surrogacy of the black woman's body for Douglass's frightful fantasies of male rape. Douglass describes Aunt Hester's rape in the most luridly suggestive terms as Captain Anthony ravages Hester, stripping her

> from neck to waist, leaving her neck, shoulders, and back entirely naked. He then told her to cross her hands, calling her at the same time a d——d b——h. After crossing her hands, he tied them with a strong rope, and led her to a stool under a large hook in the joist, put in for the purpose. He made her get upon the stool and tied her hands to the hook. *She now stood for his fair infernal purpose.*[19]

Sparing his readers any more of the unspeakable details of the event, Douglass eludes the self-implicating triangularity of the scene as voyeur, only to wind up caught by the logic of spectragraphia as the object of Anthony's sadistic desires in his own fearful imagination.[20] Douglass's silent terror, his inability to "commit to paper," as he says, a fuller disclosure of his feelings while witnessing the "horrible exhibition" of Hester's bloody violation represses the sodomitic terror. That Douglass is indeed withholding a more private, publicly unrepresentable reaction to this scene, one that contrasts the decidedly masculine self-portrait typical of the text, is incontrovertible: "I was so terrified and horror-striken at the sight, that I hid myself in a closet, and dared not venture out. . . . I expected it would be my turn next" (52). Closet symbolism aside, it is the "terrible spectacle" of his own ravished body in the place of Hester's which sends Douglass hurrying for the invisibility of a hiding place.[21]

The implication here of an erotics of slavery which, forsaking gender difference, places the enslaved biological male and the enslaved biological female equally within reach of the master's wanton hand, opposes the argument advanced by David Van Leer that the youthful Douglass did not understand "the gender specificity" of sexual violence inflicted upon slaves. While it is scarcely debatable that black women suffered far more sexual abuses in slavery, it is not to say that black men were not also victims of sexual violence, including sodomitic rape. Van Leer is wrong, then, to deny that there are sexual grounds for Douglass's panicked retreat to the closet:

[Douglass] rightly labels the scene as one of the horrors of slavery. What he does not understand is that this particular horror is not and never will be his. Not only does the boy's "turn" never come—at least not quite in this way—but the sexual undercurrents in the [Aunt Hester-Captain Anthony] passage clearly indicate the narrator's implicit understanding of the different power dynamics in male and female beatings. His failure to comment more directly on the difference marks his tacit admission that as a male he is shut out from a knowledge of this uniquely female experience.[22]

Vile though Van Lear's image of the slavocracy may be for its profligacies against black women, in his argument, slavery is given still too much credit. Van Lear's uncritical conception of rape as a heterosexual violation of women's bodies implicitly restricts the offending slaveholder's motives to an economic advantage whereby living property, under force, reproduces itself (i.e., in its offspring) at no cost, failing to adequately consider the extent to which the sexual horrors of slavery were inspired by racialist fantasies about black eros, male and female.[23] And "to the extent that the scopophilia on which the fantasy of 'racial' differentiation relies harks back to the process through which the psychic construction of sexual difference takes place," as Lee Edelman writes, "the black body, as material supplement or signifier, as that which must be possessed in order to validate the dominant subject's putative possession of the phallus" and affirm his standing as master, "must endure a symbolic inscription corresponding to that of the female body."[24] It is not unlikely, therefore, especially in light of so much of the white man's priapic preoccupations with the black male body, that the boundless prerogatives of egoistic masters were also conveniently realized on/with the enslaved bodies of black men. There is little doubt, in other words, that the sodomitic threat was as real during slavery as the heterosexual rape of women.

Admittedly, precious little of the literature representing slavery explicitly depicts men's sexual victimization. Toni Morrison's *Beloved* offers this illuminative, if unhappily brutal, exception:

> Chain-up completed, they knelt down. The dew, more likely than not, was mist by then. Heavy sometimes and if the dogs were quiet and just breathing you could hear doves. Kneeling in the mist they waited for the whim of a guard, or two, or three. Or Maybe all of them wanted it. Wanted it from one prisoner in particular or none — or all.
> "Breakfast? Want some breakfast, nigger?"
> "Yes, sir."
> "Hungry, nigger?"
> "Yes, sir."
> "Here you go."
> Occasionally a kneeling man chose a gunshot in his head as the price, maybe, of taking a bit of foreskin with him to Jesus.[25]

If the glimpsed (re)memory of a defenseless coffle of black male prisoners in Toni Morrison's *Beloved*, forced under the threat of death to fellate their white guards, is a rarity, it is not an entirely unique portrayal. Although *Beloved* is, finally, a fiction of slavery and to some, therefore, only the imagined experience of its characters, not a historical one, Morrison's portrayal of Paul D sexually assaulted on a Kentucky chain gang is not without a more historical, first-person precedent in the nineteenth-century slave narrative. That a similar violence as that depicted in Morrison, one which might molest anally just as terribly as it does orally, could indeed have threatened young Douglass, is corroborated nonfictionally by Harriet Jacobs's *Incidents in the Life of a Slave Girl* (1861).

In an often neglected passage from Jacobs's narrative, the slave heroine, now a fugitive from her master's North Carolina plantation, chances into a familiar face along the free streets of New York. Before his own flight to freedom, Jacob's fugitive friend, Luke, she recalls, belonged to a young master Jacobs describes as having become "a prey to the vices growing out of the 'patriarchal institution.'"[26] The unnamed slaveholder, having been "deprived of the use of his limbs by excess dissipation," is portrayed by Jacobs as showing all of the worst symptoms of sexual deviancy according to certain popular discourses of illness and health current in the United States from the 1830s to Freud in the twentieth century, discourses in which euphemisms like "vice," "excess," and "dissipation" connote a pathological aberration from the cultural norms of the human sexual economy.[27] According to the medical science of the period, such sudden dissipation and palsy as that manifested by Luke's master, once vigorous and virile, were the consequences of sexual perversions including masturbation and sodomy, for which the usual prognosis was progressive dementia.[28] It is no coincidence that Luke's master "took into his head the strangest freaks of despotism."[29] Purposefully, Jacobs's recollection of the reprobate slaveholder repeats the popular opinion of her day that the sodomite's sexual urges were inspired by a "strange order of ideas" in the mind.[30] In the end, the young master takes to his bed, "a mere degraded wreck of manhood," brought down in mind and body by a sexual profligacy in which Luke appears to have been constrained to participate.

The limits of public decorum would not allow Jacobs to lay bare the sexual subtext of Luke's captivity, but her memory of him having to "kneel beside the couch . . . [and] not allowed to wear anything but his shirt" would seem to tell it all.[31] Ever so polite, Jacobs nevertheless leaves little opportunity for misapprehension: "Some of these freaks," she scruples, "were of a nature too filthy to be repeated. When I fled from the house of bondage, I left poor Luke chained to the bedside of this cruel and disgusting wretch."[32] It is evident here that Jacobs's reticence intentionally suppresses details too impolite to name publicly. Her evasion recalls Douglass's earlier one ("I wish I could commit to paper the feelings with which I beheld it") only vaguely, but mimics the self-censoring of his later disparagement of Captain Anthony in *My Bondage and My Freedom* faithfully. Here Douglass loudly denounces Anthony for committing "outrages, deep, dark and nameless."[33] Critic Charles Nero has pointed to an identical display of aposiopetic pause in the Cuban slave narrative of Esteban Montejo, *The Autobiography of a Runaway Slave*, locating "physical abuse and possibly the rape of young black boys" in the elliptical space of Montejo's boyhood recollection that "if a boy was pretty and lively he was sent inside, to the master's house. And there they started softening him up . . . well, I don't know!"[34] For Douglass, Jacobs, and Montejo, then, none of whom had great trouble naming the trespass of miscegenation, few "perversions" besides sodomy would seem ineffable.

However much male-male sexual violence may be masked in Douglass or Jacobs or Montejo, all three narratives would seem to confirm that both male and female bodies under slavery were vulnerable to the sexual impositions of the master who intended to fulfill his "infernal purpose." One need no longer question *if* the compulsions of childhood sexuality exist in Douglass's *Narrative*; one only has to wonder *how much* of Douglass's sexual self is buried in the pages of his autobiography: "It was the first of a long series of such outrages, of which I was doomed to be *a witness and a participant*" (51; emphasis added). His introduction in this scene to the barbarous "hell of slavery" (51), I would argue, is also his introduction to human sexuality as its oedipal witness ("I expected it would be my turn next").

Physically withdrawn from Hester's torment, yet squarely ensconced within its psychic as well as its perspectival frames, young Douglass turns Freud's oedipal model on its head by rejecting the role of the primal child rapt by the coital labor of an oblivious mother and father. Instead, the panic-stricken slaveboy flees the scene, impotent to injure the father as the oedipal script requires. An empathic identification with Hester's indefensibility, Douglass's fear of also being raped by Anthony discloses a pubescent psychosexual libidinality situated between the more formal poles of the libidinal masculine and the libidinal feminine.[35] It is within this intermediate zone of sex and psychology, this intersected space of sexual heterogeneity between two instincts, that all boys, I submit, live.[36] Yet it is precisely this constitutional polymorphism, "this vatic bisexuality which doesn't annul [sexual] differences but stirs them up, pursues them, increases their number,"[37] that boys under patriarchy — especially slaveboys — cannot endure. Because he has learned from Hester's beating the primacy of the phallic over the feminine, Douglass's physical flight from the event repeats a more obscure, gynophobic retreat from those vaguely feminine identifications of "vatic bisexuality" distressing him toward the protective exigencies "phallic monosexuality."[38] His boyish polymorphism too perilously fraught with the cathected impulses of femaleness, the juvenile persona created by Douglass to record his early life seems hurried to differentiate himself, to counter his own "feminine" self-representation in the projected passivity of Hester, and prove the phallic perfectibility of black men. It is this phobic posture toward dynamic sexual identity generally and its feminine displays specifically, I am arguing, which provokes Douglass's sudden retaliation against Covey later on.

Although several Douglass critics have paid special attention to the slaveboy's heroic efforts to resist and overpower Covey in that crucial episode of chapter X (arguably *Narrative*'s most important scene), few have recognized the "interchangeability between power [or brute force] and [the impulses of] sexuality" in such nineteenth-century abolitionist discourse as Douglass's.[39] Consequently, the sexual undertones of Douglass's vigorous reprisal against Covey, which checks the otherwise unrestrained power of master over slave (including the "deepest, most mysterious, most fearful [power] of all: sexuality"),[40] is characteristically missed. In accord with Frantz Fanon's axiomatic belief that "[we] know how much sexuality there is in all cruelties, torture, [and] beatings,"[41] I maintain that, quite apart from the immediate danger of Covey's whip, Douglass's violent retaliation against him in chapter X of *Narrative* is fundamentally a psychosexual reaction to the whipping/rape of Hester indelibly inscribed in Douglass's memory ("I shall never forget it whilst I remember any thing" [51]). That is to say that the threat to young Douglass posed by Covey is the same threat realized by Anthony on Hester. Viewed in this way, the climactic standoff between overseer and slave which, by Douglass's own declaration, inspired in him "a sense of . . . manhood" (113) suggests a more profoundly libidinous conflict than Douglass lets on. Douglass's sudden determination to resist Covey's *coup de main* would seem to be a counterattack of psychosexual agency against the bodily trespasses of a lecherous overseer already "guilty of compelling his woman slave to commit the sin of adultery" with "a married man" whom he "used to fasten up with her every night" (105). The obsessive, associated memory of rope and lariat with so much sexual indignity in *Narrative* ("I shall never forget it") overwhelms Douglass with the potential for his own (s)exploitation ("I expected it would be my turn next") when Covey, rope in hand, attempts to subdue him by stealth.

Although Van Leer would seem an unlikely ally in this interpretation, I appeal here to his previously discussed essay, willingly risking the antagonisms its arguments pose to mine. In an ironic footnote to his principal argument concerning the "uniquely female experience" of slave rape, a footnote which seems more harmonious with this chapter's interpretive pursuit than his own, Van Leer concedes that "in the beating that opens the tenth chapter [of *Narrative*] there is some indication of a submerged homosexual threat . . . in Covey's repeated orders — and Douglass' repeated refusals — to strip."[42] Even if I disagree strongly with the text of Van Leer's essay, I do not differ with this adjunct observation. Unmistakably, the portrayal of Covey, enraged by the slave's insubordination ripping the slaveboy's clothes from his body "with the fierceness of a tiger" (102), is a graphic recapitulation of Anthony's savage assault on Hester. If, as feminist critic Jenny Franchot has argued, "Douglass's narrative construction of [Hester's punishment] privileges it as its originating moment, and thus lodges a memorial urge inside his rhetoric of indictment aimed at exposing slavery's 'foul embrace,'"[43] then the sexual dimensions of Douglass's punishment which I am positing here may be more tactical than the psychoanalytic critique I introduced from the outset might suggest. Nevertheless, I wish to pursue my original interpretive trajectory in reconsidering the contest between Douglass and Covey. To do so, it is necessary to cite a substantial portion of the episode:

> Long before daylight, I was called to go and rub, curry, and feed, the horses. I obeyed. . . . But whilst thus engaged . . . Mr. Covey entered the stable with a long rope; and just as I was half out of the loft, he caught hold of my legs, and was about tying me up. As soon as I found what he was up to, I gave a sudden spring, and as I did so, he holding to my legs, I was brought sprawling to the stable floor. Mr. Covey seemed to think he had me, and could do what he pleased; but at this moment — from whence came the spirit I don't know — I resolved to fight; and, suiting my action to the resolution,

I seized Covey hard by the throat; and as I did so, I rose. He held on to me and I to him. . . . He trembled like a leaf. This gave me assurance, and I held him uneasy, causing the blood to run where I touched him with the ends of my fingers. Mr. Covey soon called out for help. Hughes came, and while Covey held me, attempted to tie my right hand. (112)

Perhaps not accidentally, Covey's resolve to "do what he pleased" with Douglass and Hughes's struggle to "tie [Douglass's] right hand" recasts Anthony's sadistic designs on Hester's shackled body in order to execute his lascivious deeds. This, and Douglass's earlier castigation of Covey as a "snake" (103), an aspersion evoking sex and Satan, suggest something of the nature of the libidinal energy in this scene animating both protagonist and antagonist alike. Undaunted by Covey's will to corporal power, the heroic slaveboy answers Covey's ambush with a counterforce of strength sufficient to cow Covey into a physical, even "female," submission reminiscent in its vague melodrama ("He held on to me and I to him"; "He trembled like a leaf"; "I held him uneasy"; "I touched him with the ends of my fingers") of the manfully over-powered heroine in the traditional romance narrative. Inasmuch as the conventional nineteenth-century romance "also seems to be exploring the consequences of attempts to counter the increased threat of vio-lence with some sort of defiance," as Jan Radway writes, Douglass reconstructs the romantic plot that seems so much "the product of a continuing inability to imagine any situation in which a woman might acquire and use resources that . . . enable her to withstand [white] male opposition and coercion."[44] He substitutes his own strapping black self in the foregoing scene for the conventional vanquished female hero-ine.[45] Even as the more familiar plantation hierarchy of white over black, master over slave, is crucially subverted above, the paradigmatic metamorphosis begun by "I rose" also inverts the romantic dialectic of (white male) domination and (white female/ black female/ black male) subordination. It transforms Douglass from potential sexual ob-ject, prone as Hester or any romantic heroine to white male wanton-ness, into a romantically dominant subject, the transfiguring event being nothing less than a public rendering of the private triumph within the polymorphic mind of phallic will over what Van Lear would prefer to imagine as women's sexual worry: rape. Crucially, it is by a physical struggle that Douglass is, in his own words, "made a man."

Where the romantic heroine, following Radway, cannot "imagine any situation in which [she] might acquire and use resources" that help her overcome her antagonist's sexual coercion, Douglass musters a physical strength heretofore unrealized in resisting Covey. The latter's violence is counteracted by the former's as one's phallic will — Douglass's — overcomes and "feminizes" the other's — Covey's. If, in this scene, Douglass is, a slave made a man, then Covey, by the designs of a historic fiction of binary exclusivity in matters of race and sex, is a man made a slave/woman.

Crucially, then, *Narrative of the Life of Frederick Douglass* is not simply the record of a "slave [who] has become master, [a] creature . . . [a] man, [or an] object . . . [a] subject."[46] More than that, it is the narrative of a boy, oceanically pubescent, acquiring manhood by a self-conflictive renunciation of the libidinal feminine; that is, as Foucault says, by "a certain way of inverting the masculine and the feminine in oneself."[47] In overpowering Covey, Douglass wrests his manhood from the slave driver, escaping, in that selfsame maneuver, the libidinal tempest of boyish "bisexuality" (in the Cixousian sense of the word) that is made more grievous to him by his body's subjugation under "the regime of power-knowledge-pleasure" that is the peculiar institution, informing, according to its own perverse logic, the sexual subtext of the fisticuffs event.[48] Douglass's success at resisting Covey, therefore, is no small victory.

However much I am persuaded of the psychosexual significance of Douglass's self-clarifying row with Covey, I am compelled to concede a certain reductiveness to that belief. While I do not wish to step back from any of the sexual terms of this chapter's argument, I cannot avoid the truth that sexuality "is not the most intractable element in power relations."[49] Until now, my reading of Douglass's fight with Covey has tended to belie this fact, but not altogether unintentionally. As, admittedly, "relations of power are not in a position of exteriority with respect to other types of relationships (economic processes, knowledge relationships, sexual relations)," as Foucault instructs, and none of the latter can be spoken of wholly apart from the rest, to posit a central sexual subtext in *Narrative* is a critical gamble. I have risked the reductive trap here, however, in order to point out, as Foucault does, the heuristic instrumentality of sex, its abuses and — as we shall see — its allures, as a "point of support, . . . a lynchpin, for the most varied strategies"[50] of domination and rebellion immanent to the gendered ambitions of black masculine subjecthood within white Western topographies.

MYRIAD SUBTLETIES

This debt we pay to human guile;
With torn and bleeding hearts we smile,
And mouth with myriad subtleties.
— Paul Laurence Dunbar, "We Wear the Mask"

The highest art form is not that which detaches itself from the primitive use of decorative masks but that which most successfully develops that practice by dissimulating even the mechanisms of dissimulation. — Mark Wigley, "Untitled: The Housing of Gender"

If it is the potential injury of rape that provokes the panic of polymorphism in Douglass's *Narrative*, it is the criminal calumny of rape, exemplified by the quandary of sex and stereotype in Richard Wright's *Native Son* a half-century later, which seemingly inspires the drive towards a more genteel respectability of black masculine manners in Booker T. Washington's *Up from Slavery* (1901). Whereas "Douglass's central metaphor for the relationship between blacks and whites is," as David L. Dudley observes, "bloody violence, introduced and epitomized by Aaron Anthony's [pornographic] beating of Frederick's Aunt Hester"[51] (and, as I have shown above, Douglass's own highly charged brawl with Covey), Washington's account of black-white relations, on the other hand, particularly those obtaining between black male slave and white female mistress, is peace-loving and blameless. In the first chapter of the narrative, for example, Washington renders the slave "selected to sleep in the 'big house' during the absence of the [soldiering white] males" (20) a eunuchistic nonthreat to the worst fears of white manhood in the slave-holding South. Indeed, "any one attempting to harm 'young Mistress' or 'old Mistress,'" assures Washington, "would have to cross the dead body of the slave to do so" (20). It is in this loaded context of trust and trespass that "the specific trust" (20) the slave will not violate, while unspoken by Washington, accrues its particular miscegenatory meaning. Similarly, young Washington's hankering after the ginger cakes he espies his "two young mistresses and some lady visitors" (17) consuming under the plantation shade trees veils another unnameable desire, a visual trespass, an undressing of nineteenth-century white womanly virtues.

However much Washington may insist upon an image of black male innocence and sexual honor, he cannot keep from "mouth[ing] . . . myriad subtleties" of unseemly preliminal longings. No special tools of interpretation are needed, for instance, to recognize beneath the slave-boy's prodigious appetite for ginger cakes, "absolutely the most tempting and desirable things that I had ever seen" (17), a more primal desire for which ginger cake, like Eden's forbidden fruit, is merely symbolic. So alluring are the young white women's "cakes" (to exploit a pun) that "then and there" he determined that "the height of [his] ambition would be reached if [he] could get to secure and eat ginger-cakes in the way [he] saw those ladies doing" (17). The erotics of Washington's ginger cake reverie here is no less illustrative of what might be called the betrayal of the pubescent in *Up from Slavery*'s dogged effort to paint an upright picture of the black masculine than the narrator's ostensibly naive preference for nudity to the coarse dress of plantation slavery not many pages later. There, the narrator describes "the most trying ordeal" of his childhood: "the wearing of a flax shirt" (18). Made of the "cheapest and roughest" yarns, it molests the slaveboy, mind and body, like "a dozen or more chestnut burrs or a hundred small pin-points, in contact with his flesh" (18). Writes Washington: "Even to this day I can recall accurately the tortures that I underwent when putting on one of these garments. The fact that my flesh was soft and tender added to the pain. But I had no choice. I had to wear the flax shirt or none; and had it been left to me to choose, *I should have chosen to wear no covering*" (18–19; emphasis added). Washington's wish for "no covering," I submit, is part of the same erotic economy of boyish preliminality as that beneath the vague voyeurism of the earlier idyll. In his book *White over Black: American Attitudes toward the Negro, 1550–1812*, perhaps the most thoughtful documentation of the intense interracial libidinality produced by the proximity of black- and white-skinned people in America, historian Winthrop Jordan reports scenes of "Negro boys" on southern plantations "wearing only a shirt not always long enough to conceal their private parts."[52] Jordan quotes the astonishment of one eighteenth-century travel writer to such scenes' mundaneness: "I am surprised this [nudity] does not hurt the feelings of the fair Sex to see these young boys of about Fourteen and fifteen years old to Attend them. these whole nakedness Expos'd and i can Assure you It would

Surprize a person to see these d——d black boys how well they are hung [*sic*]."[53] Given the curiously "commonplace" nature of such spectacles, as Jordan characterizes them, it is hardly unreasonable to infer from Washington's shirtless yearnings exhibitionist ambitions, as the unremarked exposure of his private parts before a white (women's) audience might very well mock, if not negate, the psychophysiology of (black) masculine development. Under the self-annulling conditions of bondage, the budding slaveboy is confronted by this alarming contradiction of social being and biology. His consequent experience of self-alienation is worthy of the dehiscence of black "third-person [self-] consciousness" engendered, as Fanon asserts, by a "slow composition of [one's] self as [only] a body in the middle of a spatial and temporal world."[54] Fanon does not specify the term in which third-person consciousness is born; however, I want to put forward the threshold of physiological liminality — the panicky moment of heterogeneous sexual self-consciousness within the equally racialized and extragendered universe bequeathed him — as its first appearance.

Between the lines of chapter 1 of *Up from Slavery* lies the panic as much as the pleasure of black masculine reconcilability. Washington's determination to procure ginger cakes "if I ever got free" (17) conveys an implicit fear that he might never be free to indulge in them (or, worse, in what they symbolize). While it is possible that a slip of the pen is to account for the subtexts of fear and fantasy in these pages, I surmise that the sexual subtext, at least, is not accidental, but minstrel.

In his brief but vital study, *Modernism and the Harlem Renaissance*, Houston Baker convincingly calls attention to "the narrator's self-conscious adoption of minstrel tones" in *Up from Slavery*.[55] Strategically, Baker argues, Washington "changed the minstrel joke"[56] by wearing the minstrel mask, rhetorically speaking, with the aim of cleverly manipulating his white audience rather than clownishly entertaining them: "A liberating manipulation of masks . . . [is not] commonly ascribed to the efforts of Booker T. Washington. Yet the narrator's clear awareness of the importance of such strategies appears at the very opening of *Up from Slavery*. . . . We are two pages into the narrative when we are confronted by a "chicken-stealing darky" — as [providential] mother."[57] That a similar strategy of manipulation is behind the two scenes I have foregrounded may not only be suggested, as Baker points out, by the mathematics of "more than forty of two hundred total pages" being devoted to the art and practice of public rhetorics,[58] but it is made practically transparent later on by Washington's own rhetorical rule, explicitly stated: "I never tell an anecdote simply for the sake of telling one" (243). Six years after Paul Laurence Dunbar recast the parodic function of minstrel mask in the poem "We Wear the Mask" (still later, in the novel *The Sport of the Gods* [1901]) to disclose its ironizing function as the calculated *dis*semblence of black being, hardly the misrecognized *re*semblance of African American authenticity, Washington knew its rhetorical devices well. To be sure, his knowledge of "the guile and game of minstrelsy" is the basis of the main discursive strategy underpinning *Up from Slavery*.[59] As "a space of habitation . . . for repressed spirits of sexuality, lucid play, id satisfaction, castration anxiety, and a mirror stage of development,"[60] the minstrel mask permits Washington's autobiography to transgress the bounds of polite public discourse, to talk dirty by nineteenth-century standards, through a deceptively innocent narrative voice, a duplicity of race and sex potentially more scandalous than even that which Baker identifies as "the most scandalous instance of his deeply intentional play on minstrel form"— the image of the "chicken-thieving darky" in Washington's Atlanta Exposition Address.[61]

Despite my critical proddings toward what I have tried to convince the reader is a submerged desire for the pleasures of white women's bodies, I must concede here the possibility that the libidinal content of the boyhood chapters of *Up from Slavery* is identificatory rather than illicit. For just as the masquerade of the minstrel mask also "created an atmosphere of polymorphous license that . . . blur[red] conventional gender outlines (for men)"[62] (most clearly seen in blackface transvestism or blacked-up men "acting the wench," as it is called), the rhetorical dissemblings of *Up from Slavery* seem incapable of fully resisting identification with (white) women's bodies, however great its effort. Is it any wonder, then, that Mrs. Mary F. Mackie, a white teacher at Hampton Institute, described the autobiography of her former student in distaff terms? "'It reads like a romance,'" she declared, and further "reported that her sister was reading the chapters aloud every week to the girls of her school."[63]

Not entirely unlike Douglass's revision of the sentimental plot, Washington's still underdeveloped body, "soft and tender" under the bane of his flax shirt, recalls the susceptible feminine body of women's romance fiction. And logically so. This, in harmony with the earlier portrait of southern belle sociability, is not an extraordinary coincidence since, "the sentimentalist strategies for representing white women," as Lott underscores, "and blacks," clearly, "were often identical, each image lending the other emotional and political force."[64] One has only to consider the "romantic racialism"[65] of Harriet Beecher Stowe's *Uncle Tom's Cabin* (1853) for a model image of the "passive, sentimentalized . . . male slave"[66] that is required by Douglass and, later, by Washington in order to finally resist it by assertions of masculine counteraction.

It is not merely the recapitulation of romantic bodiliness, however, which joins Washington to the libidinal feminine. His domestic obsessions do not fail to connect (black) masculine liminality and (white) feminine proprioception. Washington's "Atlanta Exposition Address," for example, a speech duplicated in *Up from Slavery* in its entirety, relies heavily on domestic metaphors. As Claudia Tate has written, "Immediately apparent in probably the two most famous lines of Washington's 'Atlanta Exposition Address' — 'Cast down your bucket where you are' and 'In all things that are purely social, we can be as separate as the fingers, yet one as the hand in all things essential to mutual progress' — is a striking display of the modified trope of hands for veiling self-appointed agency."[67] To the extent that bucket and hand unite here to invoke women's sphere of work and culture, Washington's tropology effaces "the emancipatory discourse of [black] manhood" characteristic of Douglass's narrative even as it resists outright feminization.[68] Where Douglass counteracts the sentimentalization of black masculinity by transforming the conventional romantic plot into a masculinist melodrama, Washington employs the rhetoric of romance to foil the always already overdetermined physicality of black male rebelliousness exacerbated by Douglass and to demonstrate his own body's decidedly masculine capacity to be brought under representational (if not bodily) subjection as the sort of disciplinary man discussed in chapter 2 of this study. Further, to the degree that Washington's autobiography aims at promoting the image of the domesticated black male body, one to counter its more profligate representations in mass visual and print culture,[69] it offers a "corrective rewrite"[70] of Douglass's retaliatory brashness and representational incorrigibility, a domesticable Uncle Tom to Douglass's rebellious George Harris.[71] Rather than submit entirely to the ultimately feminizing, sentimental strategies of black male ennoblement in *Uncle Tom's Cabin*, however, *Up from Slavery* raises the bar of black masculine ideality since it asserts, at last, its masculinist preoccupations in self-regimentalism and abstract disembodiment, hopeful strategies, as I have pointed out in this book, for countering the spectragraphic conspiracy.

> Even before I had learned to read books or newspapers, I remember hearing my mother and other colored people in our part of the country speak about Frederick Douglass' wonderful life and achievements. I heard so much about Douglass when I was a boy that one of the reasons I wanted to go to school and learn to read was that I might read for myself what he had written and said. — Booker T. Washington, *My Larger Education*

Like Douglass before him who wrote two more versions of his life after *Narrative (My Bondage and My Freedom* [1855] and *Life and Times of Frederick Douglass* [1881, 1892]), Washington published his life story under two more titles, *The Story of My Life and Work* (1900) which, though written before *Up from Slavery*, had its sales restricted to the South's subscription book trade, and *My Larger Education* (1911). Following Douglass's authorial lead, Washington's three autobiographies represent nothing if not one more corroborative illustration of David Dudley's postulation that "Washington wanted to be recognized as Douglass's successor" despite the pretense of surprise and embarrassment recorded in *My Larger Education* at the urgings of so many for Washington to take up the mantle of national black leadership left in the wake of Douglass's death in February 1895.[72] Although the mass circulation of *The Story of My Life and Work* by black door-to-door salesmen in southern black districts would seem to submit Washington, like Prince Hall, to the artifactual and reproducible conditions of fin de siècle American individualism, *My Larger Education* is in fact the distinctive work among Washington's three autobiographies. In contrast to the two earlier memoirs, its debt to Douglass's autobiography is explicit, not tacit. Perhaps surprisingly, too, Washington's representational posture towards Douglass in *My Larger Education* is not corrective in the least, but imitative, reconceiving Douglass as father, not foil, to the autobiographer's self-promotion.

Just as Douglass heard it "whispered" (*Narrative*, 49) that his own father was a white man, and Washington "heard reports to the effect that [his father] was a white man who lived on one of the near-by plantations" (*Up from Slavery*, 10), Washington remembers "hearing [his] mother and other colored people . . . speak about Frederick Douglass' [*sic*] wonderful life," as if *hearing* about one's father is as close as some slaves come to the truth of the father's identity.[73] Hearing about "Frederick Douglass' wonderful life," then, and "hear[ing] so much about [him]" that the narrative of Douglass's life was "one of the first books [Washington] remember[ed] reading" (*Education*, 103) as a boy, symbolically paternalizes the elder race man, if not according to biology — "I do not even know [my biological father's] name," Washington laments (*Up from Slavery*, 10) — then perhaps according to a literary genealogy. " 'My Life and Times' . . . made a deep impression upon me," *My Larger Education* confesses, "and I read it many times" (103).[74] Washington's fondness for Douglass is transparent in *My Larger Education* and, to some extent, in *The Story of My Life and Work* as well. But the Douglass whom Washington reveres in *My Larger Education* and *The Story of My Life and Work* is not the Douglass of *Narrative*. "Uncomfortable with the militant, rebellious portrait of Frederick drawn in *Narrative*" in *My Larger Education*, "Washington prefers to concentrate on the persona of Douglass's later autobiographies," Dudley observes, "attempting, perhaps, to suggest that the Frederick of the *Narrative* is not Douglass's 'finished' or even 'true' self, but a provisional self created to survive the pressure of slavery days and then abandoned with relief when freedom arrived."[75] In *Up from Slavery*, on the other hand, perhaps owing to the deliberate designs of Walter Hines Page, then a leading publisher and Washington enthusiast, and Max Bennett Thrasher, Washington's new amanuensis, "to enhance Washington's image among the general [read: white] reading public,"[76] Washington's erstwhile homage for Douglass is supplanted by an apprentice's veneration for General Samuel C. Armstrong, "the noblest, rarest human being . . . a perfect man" (*Up from Slavery*, 59–60).

Unlike the representational spectragraphia of Douglass's violent insurgency against Covey (and his sodomitic threatening), General Armstrong exemplified the very abstract disembodiment and disciplinary individualism that had come to idealistically define the social and political preconditions of (white) American masculinity. The founder and president of the Hampton Normal and Agricultural Institute for the education and training of young African American men and women and, later, young Native Americans, Armstrong was one of the youngest generals of the Civil War — lean, athletic, handsome, and only thirty-three years old when Washington first set eyes on him. But far more enduring than his physical refinements, it would be the disembodying abstractions of his "superhuman" (*Up from Slavery*, 60) comportment and "beautiful character" (*Up from Slavery*, 78) that would survive the near complete paralysis of his body years later and compel Washington to refer to him as "the most perfect specimen of man," paralysis notwithstanding.[77] Undoubtedly, Armstrong's model of manhood owed itself, in no minor way, to his regimentalist ethic, his belief in the spiritual and intellectual merits of "self-discipline through exterior discipline."[78] Because of such ascetic convictions, and by dint of his own irrepressible military bearing, Armstrong succeeded in displaying an extraordinary accumulation of masculine self-possession for the full length of his life, even as an aging invalid deprived of the former virility of his "perfect" manhood. It was that—Armstrong's capacity to domesticate the masculine—which Washington sought to emulate: "I have observed that those who have accomplished the greatest results are those who 'keep under the body'; are those who never grow excited or lose self-control, but are always calm, self-possessed, patient and polite" (*Up from Slavery*, 182).

That Armstrong further supposed the artifactual and reproducible conditions of American individualism at the turn of the century to be natural, is revealed in the spartan regimen of Hampton's Daily Order of Exercises which resembled not so much an academic schedule as, in Harlan's words, "close order drill."[79] The familiar boot-camp regimen of "morning inspection, military drill, marching to and from classes, and system of demerits for infractions of the [school] code," maintained virtually intact for more than twenty years, conjures a disciplinary utopia of racial and masculinist uplift at once military and mechanical, achieved through the established rhythms and repetitions of the daily campus life.[80] Uniform in activity and, during drill, dress, Washington's vision of Hampton in *Up from Slavery* is unmenaced by the spectragraphical problem of overembodiment and fugitive representation (which is, in other words, the problem of the frame-up) and immanent in his picaro worries about acquiring adequate dress for a proper education ("As to clothes, when I reached Hampton I had practically nothing" [65]) and maintaining toilet ("In all my travels . . . I have always in some ways sought my daily bath" [63]). While Washington himself carried "practically nothing" to Hampton in the way of dress, the young men enrolled at Hampton during General Arm-

strong's superintendence and later were often augustly attired, protected from the "disquieting strangeness," to steal a phrase,[81] of feeling
"more naked than others" — of feeling *over*exposed, like Bigger Thomas
futilely crouched by the bed of Mary Dalton — under what would
otherwise be the familiarly onerous eye of white super-vision. For General Armstrong, we are told, regularly made a "personal inspection of
the young men in the ranks" (*Up from Slavery*, 65). No less than Washington's Tuskegee years later, then, Armstrong's Hampton was a "ma-
chine" in its own right, "making" black men *men* artifactually through
the abstracting designs of disciplinary individualism and, as with Prince
Hall and Martin R. Delaney, military posings.

Of course, as Kaja Silverman has duly noted, all posings are problematical. General Armstrong's dutiful inspection of the black and
brown men posing as cadets may well redouble the embodying effects
of the racial gaze at the very moment Armstrong wills for their abstract
disembodiment. For not only is it true that discipline, following Foucault, "increases the forces of the body (in economic terms of utility)
[while] diminish[ing] these same forces (in political terms of obedience),"[82] but Armstrong's habits of "personal inspection . . . to see
that [his students'] clothes were clean . . . [that] there [were] no
buttons off the clothing, and no grease spots" (65), point nearly micro-
scopically toward the very problem of black male bodiliness and "runaway representation" (Reid-Pharr) the general's strict body browsing
aims to subdue. While the Hampton president may well have "completely lost sight of himself," just as Washington, speaking figuratively
of the general's altruism, would worshipfully proclaim, Armstrong's
commandant supervision over so many African and Native American
boys and men would suggest in another sense that he never did lose
sight of the specter of black masculine corporeality and excess.[83] In fact,
I want to argue that what Mark Seltzer calls the white male "privilege of
relative disembodiment," which ennobled Armstrong as "a perfect
man," "*require[d]* the more deeply embodied bodies" of Hampton's
colored students "against which this privilege [could] be measured"
and felt, although it was precisely their too deeply embodied embodiment Armstrong's regimentalist pedagogy was intended to erase.[84]

Even before Washington found firm vocational footing as principal
of Tuskegee Normal and Industrial Institute, Armstrong's example was
evident in Washington's early teaching experiences. At the rural Tinkersville, West Virginia school where he had his first teaching job the

fall following his graduation from Hampton in 1875, a twenty-one-year-old Washington, the school's only teacher, impressed upon his eighty to ninety pupils — all of them males save one — the same disciplinary values he had learned at Hampton. "I require all to keep their clothes neat and clean, and their hair combed every morning," he wrote in an open letter of gratitude to his Hampton instructors published in the *Southern Workman*. "To see that this is done I have a morning inspection, as we did at Hampton."[85] Not unexpectedly did Washington add to the familiar morning inspection a daily military drill with hopes of making proper men out of a rough-and-ready tribe of unformed youths. (I suppose, too, that, with so large a class of boys, military order was as pragmatically expedient for Washington as it was ideologically preferable.) Of course, the model of military masculinism which Washington introduced to his pupils at Tinkersville would not be abandoned there. It would follow him to Tuskegee Institute in 1881. There he began employing Armstrong's methods of manly self-discipline and military standardization, as much for the reputation of his name probably — *Washington*, America's first great military leader and model man — as for the sake of his Tuskegee students. As young General Armstrong had done before him, Washington came to impress those around him with a stately bearing and, according to one biographer, "mastery over his body that few men achieved."[86] No doubt, he intended his students to succeed similarly. For "General" Washington (as one is now tempted to call him) proved no less commanding at Tuskegee than Armstrong at Hampton, nor was he any less obsessive about the symbolic domestication and regularization of the young black bodies in his charge than Armstrong. "At night, as the students marched out of chapel exercises," Louis R. Harlan has written, "he often stood at a point where each would have to pass him. 'His keen, piercing eyes were sure to detect any grease-spots that were on the students' clothes or any buttons that by chance were conspicuous by their absence from the students' clothing.'"[87] Still more obsessively, Washington hired a Commandant of Cadets to enforce an ever stricter regimen at Tuskegee. Former army officer Major Julius B. Ramsey "put the men students in uniform while on campus, drilled them into a rough state of discipline, inspected their dormitory rooms, and sought to control their behavior by a system of warnings and demerits. . . . Men students when in town were required to wear the Tuskegee school cap as an identification and encouragement to thoughtful behavior"[88]

Figure 9. Frances Benjamin Johnson, Commandant and Staff, Tuskegee Institute

(figs. 9 and 10). If Ramsey was not enough to prove Washington's insistence that Tuskegee was "not a college" exactly, as he once told the institution's students,[89] the Napoleonic principal sought to recruit to his campus Captain Charles Young, commandant at Wilberforce University and graduate of West Point. A black man, like Ramsey, Young embodied the disciplinary ideal, visually apparent, Washington envisaged for a new class of African American men, one symbolically assimilable into the American male body politic. Perhaps, though, Young was more of a man than Washington required. His terms that Washington supply real guns for the training of the Tuskegee cadets, "'very valuable things when backed by common sense and very harmless when the student has been educated to their use,'" would nevertheless undermine Washington's masculinist vision with a surplus of inescapably phallic signification menacing to Washington's eunuchistic, if still manfully rugged, ideal.[90] (At Tinkersville, Washington's boys carried sticks during drill instead of guns. When, one day, a young white mountain boy met them, "weapons" on their shoulders, rounding a nearby hill, he mistook Washington's band of boys for an advancing army and ran home to warn others of the revival of the Civil War. Fear of such a racist misrecognition as this, a dangerously public misrecognition, might well be the reason Washington captained his students "in a secluded cove in the hills" in the first place and why guns at Tuskegee were a threat to the representationalism of domesticated black mascu-

Figure 10. Frances Benjamin Johnson, Founder's Day Drill, Tuskegee Institute

linity cultivated by Washington.) Washington refused Young's terms. Young, in turn, declined the commandant's position at Tuskegee. Dignified, disciplined, and domesticated, Washington's picture of the black masculine, then, would seem as apt a case study in the cultural logistics of man-making in turn-of-the-century American culture as Henry James, say, or Rebecca Harding Davis, to name two of the primary figures in Mark Seltzer's study. For quite like the emblematic "machine-body complex" of James's *The American* (as Seltzer points out, the novel takes Americans as artifacts, things, reproduced as they are mass-produced), Washington's regimentalist preoccupations standardize black manhood through means as decidedly machinic as they are military. His veneration for the noble greatness of General Armstrong reveals how closely allied, in the mind of Washington, the military and the mechanical were. That he, too, understood the black masculine to be artifactual and reproducible is evident in his enthusiasm for General Armstrong's model. "The older I grow," he writes, "the more I am convinced that there is no education . . . that is equal to that which can be gotten from contact with great men and women. Instead of studying books so constantly, how I wish that our [black] schools and colleges might learn to study *men and things*" (*Up from Slavery*, 60; emphasis added).[91] This "miscegenation of the natural and the cultural"[92] in Washington's pedagogy of emulation, which erodes the boundaries between persons and things, animates *Up from Slavery* in a way that

106   Constructing the Black Masculine

simultaneously arrests representation in the idealized, if always uncertain objecthood of the replica, the heroically re-made man. Unmistakably, it is each one's preoccupation with the imitability of the masculine ideal, disciplined and — in Washington, at least — domesticated, that conjoins Douglass's *Narrative* and Washington's *Up from Slavery* in a pioneering partnership of black masculine beginnings in public letters. However, to more fully comprehend the exigencies of black masculine reproducibility foregrounded in this and the previous chapter of *Constructing the Black Masculine* "beyond the frequently described rough division between the male world and the female world[,] . . . it is necessary to grasp," as Bourdieu advises, the dialectics of objectification, replication, and embodiment within a more concentrated universe than the public sphere.[93] Chapter 4 seeks to locate the *habitus* (Bourdieu) or elemental structures of black masculine consciousness in the self-reflexivity of such artifactual structures as closets and cabins, huts and houses, where black male bodies wrestle between what Fanon once described as the unbearable insularity of black identity and the saving-grace achievement of self-communion.

CHAPTER FOUR

A Man's Place

Architecture, Identity, and Black Masculine Being

Architecture is the only art object we actually live in. However, we live in another construction—we do not commonly call it art—also of our own making: consciousness. — Ellen Eve Frank, *Literary Architecture*

It's been said in much less enlightened times that a woman's proper place is in the home. No body of U.S. literature ever grappled with the invidious essentialism expressed by such a proposition more tenaciously than the two full centuries of women's writing now part of our national literary and political heritage. In 1841, for instance, Catharine Beecher became arguably America's first "domestic feminist" with the publication of her *Treatise on Domestic Economy*. Although she accepted the conventional belief in the home as woman's sphere in *Treatise*, Beecher broke with the corollary belief in an ultimately masculine managerial authority over the household. In her 1869 *American Woman's Home*, coauthored with Harriet Beecher Stowe, Catharine Beecher broke more fully from the patriarchal prerogatives of domesticity, claiming instead that "women's greater capacity for self-sacrifice entitled *her* to rule the home."[1] Although she brought one important tenet of nineteenth-century domestic ideology under rigorous protofeminist scrutiny, Beecher never fully opposed those greater tenets of domestic ideology informing the (il)logic of the home as a fundamentally feminine geography. Beecher's great-niece, Charlotte Perkins Gilman, however, would go the greater distance.

Gilman, a poet, preacher, suffragist, and architectural theorist, shared Beecher's belated disdain of men's near colonial subordination of women in the home. In verse, she would write, tongue-in-cheek:

The wood-box hath no sanctity;
No glamour gilds the coal;

But the Cook-Stove is a sacred thing
To which a reverent faith we bring
And serve with heart and soul.

The Home's a temple all divine,
By the Poker and the Hod!
The Holy Stove is the alter fine,
The wife the priestess at the shrine —
Now who can be the god?[2]

Despite whatever pleasure the early Beecher might have found in the beatific imagery of women's domestic work — for she imagined women as "home ministers" and the home as a "church" — Gilman's tone is sardonic throughout.[3] For Gilman, the home is not a "temple all divine" at all but rather, as Gilman critic Polly Wynn Allen writes, "the idol whose tending diverted women from their [more] solemn duties of world service."[4] More aggressively than Beecher, Gilman rejected the platitudes of domestic ideology that sought to divide and fix the world of social and economic activity into two forever separate spheres: "man's dangerous, public realm outside [of], and woman's safe private realm inside [of], the four walls of the home."[5] Instead she imagined an architecturally radical environment "in which nature and culture coexisted in beautiful harmony. The built form of her utopian world facilitated an easy equality between men and women. It allowed men to enjoy their children's daily company as much their work. It permitted women to invest themselves more in paid work and projects of social amelioration than in the delivery of incessant household services to their families."[6] If Beecher was the nation's first domestic feminist, Gilman deserves note as her more radical heir. Certainly, other early feminists distinguished themselves in this connection as well. In fact, certain early black feminists did so brilliantly. Since no disciplinary knowledge could conceivably challenge the cultural conjunction of woman and home (or point to its white middle-class pretensions) as efficaciously as the labor history of African American women in slavery, nineteenth-century black women writers Maria W. Stewart, Elizabeth Keckley, and especially Anna Julia Cooper may well be deserving references.[7] But it is likely that the little-known Gertrude Bustill Mossell, prominent journalist, consummate race woman of the 1880s and 1890s, and cousin to Paul Robeson, was Gilman's closest, if evidently less published, counterpart.

Like her contemporary, Mossell, against the logic of the prevailing social fictions of her day, held to an "opposite point of view" in matters appertaining to women's work, contending in her brief essay of 1894 that "man as often as woman gives the keynote to the home-life" of America. "The men that usually stay in at night," she declared, "are domestic in their nature . . . [and] satisfied with being loved." This, she says, is the "open secret" of "our beloved Republic."[8] And it is precisely the romance of men's domestication — black men's, more particularly — as the "open secret" of the republic of letters that is African American men's literature, and the subtle chrysalid architecturalism of the sites of domestication, which I want to attend to in this chapter. For, as architectural theorist Mark Wigley has written in "Untitled: The Housing of Gender," sex and gender are (as race almost certainly is too) "underpinned by a spatial logic" of domestic interiority and exteriority in which the interiority of the house, quite apart from all other modern architectures, "is [conventionally] understood as a mechanism for the domestication of . . . *women*."[9] But what of *men* who linger long indoors?

Notwithstanding the particular competence and constancy of Beecher, Gilman, and Mossell to frustrate, if not altogether occlude, the all-too-ready identification of the house as uniquely woman-space, few visions of the nineteenth-century home would have challenged the spatio-binarizations of gender in the nineteenth century more vividly than Thoreau's cabinhouse at Walden Pond and Uncle Tom's small log cottage. Who can deny the symbolic resonance of Thoreau seated in demure solitude "behind my door in my little house" or Stowe's Uncle Tom ensconced in his bucolic garden shanty to raise questions about "the role of gender in the discourse of space and the role of space in the discourse of gender[?] That is to say," as Wigley aptly puts it, who can avoid questions about "the interrelationships between how the question of gender is housed and the role of gender in housing"?[10]

While the historical literature on nineteenth-century domestic (read: white) and vernacular (read: black)[11] architecture is ample enough, that which probes the ideological consequences of men's interior and "womanly" occupation of the home, urging us beyond the simplistic sexual binarisms of so-called everyday nineteenth-century life, is modest.[12] Not surprisingly, critical inquiry of black men's relation to the ineluctably racialized sexualization of the domestic sphere (to be sure, "racial difference is always complexly imbricated with sexual difference")[13] and its middle-class materiality is more modest still. This chapter, however, explores precisely that. Although it is a general truth that the domestication of men is a much-neglected subject in domesticity studies and that the number of journal pages devoted to U.S. men's gendered relationship to domestic architecture (Thoreau in his cabin, say) is regrettably meager, my purpose throughout this book has been "to place black men [more specifically] at the center as opposed to the margins" of this discourse, as Arthur Flannigan Saint-Aubin has urged.[14] It is the more particular iconicity of black Uncle Tom's gardenpatch cabin, then—a figure for the black masculinist will to abstraction behind the domesticating, despecularizing walls of houses, huts, and analogous architectures ("The whole front of [Uncle Tom's cabin] was covered by a large bignonia and a native multiflora rose, which, entwisting and interlacing, left scarce a vestige of the rough logs to be seen")[15]—that is this chapter's paragon for the domesticating exercise of the house and (its still stricter supplement) the closet on the public spectragraphical conditions of black masculine representation.

Although I have settled on the obviously romantic image of Uncle Tom's bucolic cabin as the ur-trope of architecture and identity in the following pages, *Uncle Tom's Cabin* was not the catalyst for this chapter's discursive pursuits. Perhaps surprisingly, these pages' contemplation of the space of race and gender in black masculinist production was originally inspired by the alternate iconicity of the homosexual closet as the architectural trope par excellence of contemporary identity discourse. Eve Kosofsky Sedgwick's provocative study *Epistemology of the Closet* and the broader utility I suspected lay beyond its limited European/Euro-American critical contexts, provided the formal impetus for reasoning and writing in this context. But what Sedgwick inspired and indeed inaugurated was more substantively guided by the theoretical erudition of Pierre Bourdieu whose doubly architectural and sociological thinking in *Outline of a Theory of Practice* has lent much to this undertaking to posit a working theory of black masculine identity. This chapter examines that identity as one articulated by the ways in which the mimetic architectures of black male inhabitation—closets and cabins, houses and homeplaces—project a material form of self and repeat, in their very materiality, the abstract linguistic function of the epistemological closet foregrounded by Sedgwick. Put differently, since "the social organization of the internal space of the house and the relation of this space [or its variously manifested deformations in black residential life] to external space . . . is the only means to fully grasping the structuring structures" of identity,[16] I argue, following Bourdieu, that, within African American men's cultural forms, the "internal space" of the domestic structures housing black male bodies in individualistic solitude (closets, cabins, prison cells, small rooms, houses) approximates the very "structure" of black male consciousness that theorization requires. It is an interiority at once protected from and imperiled by the superficially exterior matters of race and gender conjured in previous chapters by the phenomenology of the frame. But let us return to Sedgwick and to the trope of the closet in black men's writing for an explication. While no other book in recent memory has done more to illuminate the linguistic machinations of homosexual disguise, *Epistemology of the Closet* may hold a still greater, unrealized promise for apprehending the power of the trope of the closet in African American literature and language.[17]

OPEN SECRETS, CLOSED SPACES

While one of the first signs of the growing desire for privacy for the individual, such that "a privacy *within* the house developed beyond the privacy of the house," was the separation of the bedrooms . . . which established a masculine space, this space is not completely private. . . . The first truly private space was the man's study, a small locked room off his bedroom which no one else ever enters, an intellectual space beyond that of sexuality. Such rooms emerged in the fourteenth century and gradually became a commonplace in the fifteenth century. They were produced by transforming a piece of furniture in the bedroom — a locked writing desk — into a room, a "closet" off the bedroom. Indeed it was the first closet. — Mark Wigley, "Untitled: The Housing of Gender"

Writing the self . . . would be consistently ruled by the paradoxical proposition that the self is most itself at the moment when its defining inwardness is most secret. — D. A. Miller, "Secret Subjects, Open Secrets"

But thou, when thou prayest, enter into thy closet, and when thou hast shut the door, pray to the Father which is in secret; and thy Father which seeth in secret shall reward thee openly. — The Gospel according to St. Matthew (King James Version)

Despite the tectonic inclination to imagine the closet according to an architectural logic (for man's "experience as an activity of being —

entering and moving through interior space, seeing wall-boundaries, looking through windows, feeling stress — is governed by . . . architectural structures we perceive"),[18] the constitution of the epistemological closet theorized by Sedgwick is not foremost architectural. For Sedgwick's part, to invoke the cover of the closet is to invoke a metaphysical event rather than a built structure. The epistemological closet advanced by Sedgwick means little in the physical sense since its materiality is primarily linguistic, not architectural, a verbal sheath of silence and secrecy "built" like a protective citadel around its vulnerable subject. At bottom, the closet is a metaphor for the performance of linguistic coverture in Sedgwick. It is "a speech act of silence," she explains, "not a particular silence, but a silence that accrues particularity by fits and starts, in relation to the discourse that surrounds and differentially constitutes it."[19] Put spatially, it is an obscured interiority defined by a particular and paralyzing discursive exteriority of equivocation. That the linguistic discourse of *Epistemology* conforms so agreeably to spatialization, despite Sedgwick's ostensible indifference to the architectural meaningfulness of the trope of the closet, is owed to a phenomenology of language even Sedgwick cannot escape.

The particularistic silence of the closet gathers particularity by its contraposition to the tremulous spoken discourse "surrounding" it, as it were. Uncertainly enclosed within, a more certain space of secrecy thusly emerges with the familiar character of interiority. In Sedgwick, then, "space is itself closeted," to borrow Wigley's words, as the mimetic closet itself dissembles behind a veil of linguistic nonspace, cloaking, as Wigley points out, "the elusive architecture of the *particular closets* that are built into each [and arguably all] discourse, but [which] can only be addressed with the most oblique of gestures."[20] If indeed all "discourses are spatial mechanisms that construct [identity] before giving either [identity] or space a title," as *Epistemology of the Closet* seems so near coming out about, then the homosexualization of the trope of the closet would also seem to be merely a contingent and temporal correspondence unique to the hypersexual obsessions of our place and time since it is doubtless that the identical speech act that currently defines the closet as a queer masquerade has also already preceded its contemporaneity.[21] That is, as a verbal stratagem of identity dissemblance, the closet descends from a linguistic ancestry far broader than the whiteness of *Epistemology*'s European and Euro-American contexts or its uniquely twentieth-century display as a sign for the queer cover-up. Although one could hardly dispute the notion that "a whole cluster of the most crucial sites that form the contestation of meaning in twentieth-century Western culture are . . . marked with the historical specificity of homosocial/homosexual definition," the same crucial sites of contestation in the nineteenth century, I mean to argue, were marked first (and remain marked today) by a more visible, willful obsession with black/white definition intruding upon the Western mind.[22] Symptomatically, that speech act of taciturnity now connected with *sexual* coverture in the twentieth century, being much less exceptional to the twentieth century than imagined, acted beforehand to conceal a similarly anathematized *racial* confidence. So closely does the phenomenology of one dissemblance (sexual) repeat the other (racial) that the former one's descent from the latter one is virtually incontrovertible.[23]

In Charles Chesnutt's 1900 passing-novel *The House behind the Cedars* (which title recalls Uncle Tom's similarly obscured cabin), for example, fair-skinned Rena Walden and her still lighter brother, John Warwick, both forsake their black-skinned mother, Mis' Molly Walden, for "the free and noble [white] life" their passing affords them. Estranged from home by hundreds of unconquerable miles to South Carolina where a lucrative career in jurisprudence grants John the means and manner of white privilege, Rena and John protect the truth of their racial heritage scrupulously. Brother and sister suffer miserably, however, when their higher devotion to the principles of white Southern honor betrays a necessarily lesser dedication to a functionally "black" strategem of social survivability—passing—and obliges them to divulge to Rena's unrelenting white suitor, George Tryon, the truth of their blackness or risk a more publicly ruinous exposure later on.

Frightened that her perfect man might discover her "dark," imperfect past, the likely prospects of marriage and, ultimately, motherhood grieve Rena insufferably. To assuage her fear, John proposes to circuitously examine Tryon in the matter, gingerly broaching the truth of Rena's blackness by indirection. Rena assents and Tryon is tested. Ever the gallant, he pledges unconditional affection to Rena, though he is only half-knowing of the stigma attached to her enatic ancestry. John's tentativeness barely "touched the vital point involved; it had been at the best but a half truth" itself.[24] Rena's jubilation at Tryon's faithfulness to her is consequently short-lived:

"Oh, I am so glad!" exclaimed Rena joyfully. This report left her very happy for about three hours, or until she began to analyze carefully her brother's account of what had been said. Warwick's statement had not been specific—he had not told Tryon *the* thing. George's reply, in turn, been a mere generality. The concrete fact that oppressed her remained unrevealed, and her doubt was still unsatisfied (85; emphasis Chesnutt's).

Because the discursive territory that John is loath to tread is so clearly delineated by his painstaking circumnavigation of "*the* thing," that which he does not say resounds as emphatically as if he had candidly laid bare to Tryon the family "secret too sacred to reveal." Importantly, the rhetorical misrecognition intended by John to at once pacify and protect Rena, exactly mirrors the equivocating strategy of the homosexual closet. Chesnutt's *The House behind the Cedars* proves the epistemological point. The nonspeech of the homosexual closet is the same dissimulator of race in the black passing game. This dual heritage suggests that it has not been merely the queer *act* of the sociable body Western culture won't tolerate; neither has the occasional *fact* of that body's blackness been politely embraced.

If what we imagine as the closeted body—the body that covers itself over by some literal means, or, alternately, covers for itself by a linguistic means—may be racialized to the indifference of sexual speculations, the singularly gay character of the closet no longer holds. To point out this double function of the selfsame speech act by which racial stigmatization and illicit sex pass in the West is not to plot to purge the closet of its more familiar gay significations. Rather, it is to seek to deconstruct their ready associations. For just as the homosexual may pass for the heterosexual, by like tactics the African American who is fair enough may elude the dire consequences of color and realize a racial closet. It is the hegemony of the former phenomenon's metaphorization in architecture "as external configuration, as form and embodiment, of [queer] consciousness" I am seeking here to revise.[25]

But freeing the closet from its singularly queer moorings, even only for a moment, is not without its risks, since neither the political nor ideological fallout of such a symbological gamble can ever be predicted in advance. At stake is the particularistic conception of the closet which queer politics, especially, requires for the symbolic efficacy of its coming-out campaigns. Similarly, the effort to racialize the closet challenges the wider critical acceptance and functionability of the trope of the mask in African American history, literature, and cultural performativity.

W. E. B. Du Bois, Ralph Ellison, Constance Rourke, Lawrence Levine, Houston Baker, Henry Louis Gates, and Eric Lott have all written amply on the performativity of masking in African American cultural practice. Eric Lott's recent work on the duplicities of what bell hooks calls "radical black subjectivity" beneath the burnt-cork masks of black vaudevillians and minstrel performers proves the mask's unquestionable tropological vitality as a crucial hermeneutic for the new African Americanism which understands African American subjectivity as constitutionally diasporic, even as it is geographically so. But what is neglected in so much theorization about the mask in African American cultural studies is the dialectics of surface and supplementarity according to which such spatiality (inside/outside, beneath, behind) is produced by the mask that its play of tectonic signs is inclined towards constituting an architecture of interiority that not only produces space but is preceded by space—indeed, *enabled* by it—in the structural imagination of experience. Differently put, inasmuch as the mask is "a substitute for a spatially absent unity"[26] that refuses presence, what Wigley calls "the architecture of the mask,"[27] in subsequence and syntax inverts, but never opposes, what I have been at pains to demonstrate is the mask of architecture which passes as the closet. It may be, then, that the mask's greatest ruse is not racial or sexual or identitarian in the least, but deeply dialectical. Masks mask more than the apparent truth of who we are; they succeed best by masking their own dissembling devices. "The highest art form is not that which detaches itself from the primitive use of decorative masks," in other words, "but that which most successfully develops that practice by dissimulating even the mechanisms of dissimulation."[28] It is in this vein that the architecture of the mask has succeeded so artfully. Insofar as the mask names "*a space of habitation* . . . for repressed spirits of sexuality, lucid play, id satisfaction, castration anxiety, and a mirror stage of development," as Houston Baker put it so knowingly, it is also a closet (though contingently, since the materiality of the closet is also a mask), one as readily descriptive of the phenomenon of black male coverture as the masquerade.[29] The "space of habitation" cannot be purely psychological, however, nor even wholly metaphorical, for, as we have seen in chapter 3, a threatened corporeality may also reside there, a spatially present bodyhood in jeopardy of arrest in its very bodiliness, a bodyhood intentionally concealed by the "fits and starts" of a particular and perduring black masculinist reserve in African American men's literature.

From the earliest moments of African American men's first-person narrative in the eighteenth century—Briton Hammon and James Gronniosaw, say—to contemporary first-person narratives like Arthur Ashe's memoirs *Days of Grace* near the end of the twentieth century, closet acts have suffused the black masculinist tradition, although sex has not always been the tradition's principal concealment. Clearly the same verbal tactics of aposiopetic evasion and self-censorship inhering in the epistemological closet of queer coverture are also to account for the pervasiveness of such dialogic elisions in speech and narrative as those I wrote of in the previous chapter. The intimate disclosures of black masculine being in African American literature so preemptively frustrated affirm John Blassingame's observation that "few [black] men are able to tell the *whole* truth about themselves. Some things are either too painful to recall or to reveal to others."[30] Of course, something above pain is at stake when the souls of black folk are laid bare entirely—namely, social death. As D. A. Miller writes forcefully, "In a world where the explicit exposure of the subject would manifest how thoroughly he has been inscribed within a socially given totality, secrecy would be the spiritual exercise by which the subject is allowed to conceive of himself as a resistance" to the relentlessness of overdetermination in totalizing systems of sociality.[31]

> More precisely, secrecy would seem to be a mode whose ultimate meaning lies [not in substance of the secret so much as] in the subject's formal insistence that he is radically inaccessible to the culture that would otherwise entirely determine him. . . . [If] I cannot speak of myself without losing myself [i.e. dying a social, if not ontological, death] in the process, I can keep myself secret and—"so to speak"—change the subject[,] convinced of my indeterminability in the safety of silence.[32]

But how does one distinguish, under the cover of so much purported secrecy, the safe space of silence from the silence that signifies nothing and has no space? In part, I beg the question here since I cannot conceive of a silence that signifies nothing apart from the sonority positively differentiating it as silence. There is no silence without space. But which are the spaces that signify?

In chapter 3, I appealed to Douglass's *Narrative* of 1845 to point out the way in which the trope of the closet can be understood in black male texts as evidenced by the interiorizing strategies of circumlocution and innuendo. Although Douglass employs these strategies to circumvent the more painful details of experience, their real effect betrays him by deliberatively skirting the borders of the ineffable, the silence of which, being so strictly hedged by the limis of respectable discourse, speaks louder than words. The specific scene illustrating Douglass's protective pausings, the one meriting further mention here, is Hester's rape.

Although never expressly stated, the pornography of Anthony stripping Hester "from neck to waist," Douglass's reluctance to "commit to paper" his truer feelings about the "exhibition" (51), and his related wish to keep the unspeakable details of Anthony's crime "safely left to conjecture" (52), all imply a gross sexual misdeed where decorum precludes its explicit depiction. Almost coincidentally with the English novelist, Douglass mirrors the "gestures of secretiveness" Miller's "Secret Subjects, Open Secrets" discerns in Charles Dickens's *David Copperfield* (1850).[33] David's "diffidence of . . . narration" ("How much I suffered, it is beyond my power to tell") very nearly duplicates Douglass's ("I wish I could commit to paper the feelings with which I beheld [Anthony's assault on Hester]"). In both Dickens and in Douglass, somewhere between their traumas' allusion and elision, unspeakable secrets are silently *encrypted*, as Miller describes doubly the manner and middling of secrecy in Dickens. With Douglass, however, both the manner and metaphor of adumbration and interment are overcome, surpassed in effect, by the persistent materiality of domestic architecture.

Upon witnessing the rape event, young Douglass, his puerile sensibilities fully assaulted, seeks out personal sanctuary from the sexual torment of Anthony. Immured in an actual closet, Douglass confesses in *Narrative*: "I was so terrified and horror-stricken at the sight that I hid myself in a closet and dared not venture out. . . . I expected it would be my turn next" (52). Both in *Narrative* and in his later autobiography, *My Bondage and My Freedom*, architecture repeats the concealments of speech as the camouflage of Douglass's own sexual terror ("I expected it would be my turn next.") accedes to its always already-there spatiality "in a closet." In *My Bondage and My Freedom*, however, Douglass discovers beneath the crude utilitarian shell of that narrow refuge a more devilish usage: "My sleeping place was on the floor of [that] little, rough closet, which opened into the kitchen; and through the cracks of its unplaned boards, I could distinctly see and hear what was going on, without being seen by old master."[34] Quite unexpectedly, the withdrawn young phobic of the 1845 narrative, plausibly fearing his own rape, becomes the engaged voyeur of the 1855 *My Bondage*, his prurience soundly protected. The difference in subject positions obtaining between these two passages suggests that, like the linguistic closet, actual closets may dissimulate a range of sexual subjectivities, from same-sex victim to undercover voyeur, all simultaneously inflected by the adjunct otherness of race. What's more, the self-screening materiality of the actual closet in Douglass is capable of as many variations as the architectures of black male domesticity permit. Each of the diverse structures titularly identified in such key black masculinist writings as *Narrative of Henry Box Brown*, *Blake; or, the Huts of America*, and the previously discussed Chesnutt romance, *The House behind the Cedars*, for example, imitate the closet function. At bottom, their architectures, too, like the spatialization of the speech act of closeting, merely ornament the spatial geography — *the* thing — they outline and consequentially define.

In other words, the visible framework of all black architecture, like all architecture generally, dissimulates in that what it signifies is not a dialectics of structure or materiality only. It is, more precisely, the dialectics of an invisible space of interiority covered over by the masquerade of closet-like materiality that the exteriority of black vernacular architectures, in literary and lived experiences alike, keeps discretely guarded. Even if, in a seemingly contradictory way, the interiority of a place is bodily occupied and thus (or so it would seem) visible, the invisibility of the place defining it is nevertheless undeniable. For the inhabiting body is only one more exteriority. The invisible space of interiority — the soul of the place — is the soul of the man who occupies it. There is, then, a condition of black masculine archi-textuality in some black vernacular architectures: a quality which, when found in black men's texts, suggests we consider the representations of black vernacular architecture imitating protective closet-like functions as self-reflexive materializations of the invisible, inarticulable yearnings of black male subjecthood. Mostly it is in the architecture of houses, though, not actual closets, that the trope of the racial closet is realized in the language of African American men's literary and cultural figuration.

In his unique psychoanalysis of space and place, Gaston Bachelard, the so-called father of the French New Critics, argues that the house, which is, abstractly speaking, "the human being's first world," also maps the "topography of our intimate being."[35] It is the internalized structure of externality according to which human beings imagine, in material terms, the immateriality of the self. *The Poetics of Space* distinguishes the house as "a privileged entity for a phenomenological study of the intimate values of [the] inside space" of not just buildings but of ourselves.[36] "With the image of the house," Bachelard postulates, "we are in possession of a veritable principle of psychological integration." He argues that "not only our memories, but the things we have forgotten are 'housed.' Our soul is an abode. And by remembering 'houses' and 'rooms,' we learn to 'abide' within ourselves. Now everything becomes clear, the house images move in both directions: they are in us as much as we are in them."[37] Inasmuch, then, as issues of "home, self, and shelter have loomed paramount in the black imagination," as the late Melvin Dixon wrote in *Ride Out the Wilderness: Geography and Identity in Afro-American Literature*,[38] there is hardly a more exigent tool for apprehending the black masculine than the psychoanalytic study of space and place Bachelard calls "topoanalysis." For in black masculine life as in black masculinist literature, the home would seem to constitute a tropic preoccupation. As bell hooks has written, "many narratives of resistance struggle from slavery to the present share an obsession with the politics of space, particularly the need to construct and build houses."[39] A figure for black masculine self-possession rather than "the formal space of [adult male] departure . . . [from] the confines of the domestic, settled sphere of childhood,"[40] the house, one might say, is the very image of the structure of black masculinist consciousness as well as a principal object, materially and metaphorically speaking, of African American men's literary and cultural figuration. For quite apart from the indivisible politics and poetics of space in Douglass's *Narrative* of 1845, Booker T. Washington's *Up from Slavery*, or Chesnutt's *The House behind the Cedars*, the archi-textuality of home obtains further in not only the spatial geographies governing the slave memoirs of Henry Box Brown and Peter Randolph's *From Slave Cabin to Pulpit*, or in the "Negro shanties" that localize the hearthside lyricism of Paul Laurence Dunbar's poetry and dot the pastoral landscape of Jean Toomer's *Cane*, but also in the modernist architecture of the underground in Ralph Ellison's *Invisible Man*, in the penitentiary poetry of Bob Kaufman and

Etheridge Knight, and in the queer haunts of Melvin Dixon's *Vanishing Rooms*. African American men's literature, in other words, "is replete with speech acts and spatial images [of home] that . . . endow [its] language with the power to reinvent [the spatial] geography and identity" of black masculinist being.[41] In fact, not only African American literature but the imagination of African American cultural life generally is so "replete with [the] speech acts and spatial images" of real and symbolic homeplaces that, considered cumulatively, they constitute a unique class of "archetypal patterns" in black expressivity intimately related to the characteristic "search, discovery and achievement of [the black masculine] self."[42]

In *Art on My Mind: Visual Politics*, bell hooks represents the phenomenological power of the homeplace according to its most real, self-actualizing exercises in black men's lived experience, rendering the archi-textual pattern repeated in so many worked and written black masculinist forms semi-biographically.

> When my father's father, Daddy Jerry, a sharecropper and farmer, talked in concrete terms about his relationship to land, his longing to own and build, he spoke poetically about working with space *so that it would reveal and mirror the texture of his longings*. I never understood how Daddy Jerry "came by" a piece of land; that was the way folks talked about it then. . . . On this land Daddy Jerry built a house. I can still remember the way he and my father would sit on the porch and have deep discussions about that house; their talk evoked a poetics of space, the joy of thinking imaginatively about one's dwelling.[43]

Daddy Jerry's desire for an extrinsically conceived materiality to "reveal and reflect the texture of his [inner] longings" exemplifies the dialectical reciprocities of space and spirit that the historically sparing structures of African American living have made acute in black masculine self-searchings. Hooks's naïve "disappointment when [she] finally saw the small square brick house that [Daddy Jerry] built" contrasts sharply with "the joy of thinking imaginatively about one's dwelling." In hooks's childhood imagination, the house "seemed so utterly closed and tight."[44] But reasonably so, since Daddy Jerry's small brick house reflected something far more rudimentary than "his aesthetic sensibility," as she had come to conclude.[45] The narrowness of the structure, "utterly closed and tight," reflected the achievement of his own private and spectragraphically protected self. The joy of thinking imaginatively about one's dwelling here lies partially in the capacity of its design to enable a thinking about one's essential self. "Had I understood the interconnected politics of race, gender and class in the white-supremacist South," hooks writes, "I would have looked upon this house with the same awe as I did my favorite house," coming doubtlessly closer in that knowledge to the experience of Daddy Jerry's domestic joy.[46] And doubtlessly closer still to the truth of how Daddy Jerry, in the equivocating language of the closet, "came by" his land.

Although the trope of the homeplace may be offered to us readers or listeners of its (re)presentation as the physical ornamentation of ritual ground, the homeplace obtains more basically within the play of signs and only secondarily in space. It is, like Sedgwick's epistemological closet, a psycholinguistic formulation that merely masquerades as a spatial unit. The difference obtaining between the fundamental constitution of the homeplace (linguistic) and its incidental constitution (material) is best illustrated by the differentiation Raymond Williams has drawn between the preconscious *inner sign* and the socially operative *material sign*.

In his *Marxism and Literature*, Williams imagines the inner sign as speechless and abstract. It is transcendent. Its referent, if we can speak of such a thing, accords with the philosopher's belief in the "interiority of presence" as the material sign accords homologously with the "exteriority of representation." As such, the inner sign denotes the "space of language," to borrow an apt phrase from Susan Stewart, invisible as the unconscious, and equally silent to the point where the material sign, the architecture of inner language, coheres to differentiate the conditions of interiority and exteriority.[47] It is here, to the covert, silent space of language — to the well-fortified "interiority of presence" — where so many black masculinist subjects, otherwise "sealed into [their] own peculiarity" of spectragraphical overdetermination, retreat in order to regain subjective integrity.[48] Prior to its social communicativeness in language (i.e. speech), the homeplace already abides in his unconscious as the unvoiced, privately limned "organizations of space [he] require[s] for psychological comfort."[49] It would seem, then, that historian Mechal Sobel was justified in arguing the irony that, although the restricted size of the historical black home has always been a function of black dispossession from a materialist view, a great many blacks prior to the birth of the black middle class "*wanted* small proximate housing" because, as he says rightly, "it fit their own *inner language of building and space*."[50] The black masculinist fondness for the home, the shanty, the underground room, the crypt, and the closet, then—as opposed to the Oedipal dread of them as domesticating, even emasculating, constructions (inasmuch as our cultural logic of sex and space renders the inside place feminine)—speaks for a longing to abscond from the neurotically uncanny experience of social spectragraphia by a retreat away from the public sphere where the gaze tyrannizes into the remote interiority of that other construction of space: consciousness.

By the uncanny experience of social spectragraphia, I mean the texture of feeling Freud described as "that class of the frightening which leads back to what is known of old and long familiar."[51] Freud discovered further that the "impression of uncanniness" in the individual was commonly attributable to a certain scopic threat. Recalling the machinations of the white gaze in chapter 1, Freud wrote:

> One of the most uncanny [feelings] . . . is the dread [inspired by] the evil eye. . . . Whosoever possesses something that is at once valuable and fragile is afraid of other people's envy, in so far as he projects on them the envy he would have felt in their place. A feeling like this betrays itself by a [baneful] look even though it is not put into words. . . . What is feared is thus a secret intention of doing harm, and certain signs are taken to mean that that intention has the necessary power at its command.[52]

Although Freud seems not to have had racial representation in mind, his reflections on the uncanny explain the peculiar vulnerability of the black masculine to the denuding violence of the public "evil eye." Significantly, in the original German of Freud's essential essay "The Uncanny," "uncanny" is rendered *das Unheimliche*, literally meaning "unhomely." The uncanniness (*das Unheimliche*) of the spectragraphic condition, therefore, inheres not only in the photographical overexposure of black masculine subjects framed by a camerical look of modern intersubjectivity, but in the existential "homelessness" of photographical self-alienation. Thus, the black masculine longing for *das Heimliche*, the comfort and concealment of the home, is never merely an external affair. It is always, if in varying degrees, a liberating interiorization (closeting) as well.

Although the fervent romanticism of Jean Toomer's *Cane* has steered the greater number of comments about its themes and design outdoors into the piney, full-mooned quietude of Southern pastoralism, it is within the shanty structures that help to paint *Cane*'s dusky Gothic landscape that the artist-hero's puristic longing for black traditional simplicity, for a common place of black folk memory, is dramatized (fig. 11). In *Cane*'s third section, "Kabnis," a long semidramatic allegory, prophetically Ellisonian, the housing of psyche and sex in four discrete architectures of black domestic topography—a battered one-room shack, an adjoining closet, a littered workshop (the artisan's study), and a mysteriously inhabited underground room called "the Hole"—externalizes the hero's interior adjustments toward an unmolested wholeness of black masculinity in the materiality of vernacular architecture. Along this view, the many instances of wordplay throughout *Cane*, ones identified, for example, in the eponymy of "Karintha" (Corinth), "Carma" (karma), "Rhobert" (robot), and the very title of *Cane* itself (Cain), suggest "cabins" as a plausible architectural pun on "Kabnis."[53] As I shall show, this is a more likely play than the more contrived trick of "the title character's name read backwards . . . 'Sinbak,'" for which James Christ has argued.[54]

In sociological accord with the poetically inflected psychoanalysis of space theorized by Bachelard, Bourdieu, too, has put forward "a structural analysis of the social organization of the internal space of the house and the relation of this internal space to external space, an analysis which is not an end in itself but which . . . is the only means of fully grasping the structuring structures,"[55] the concretely conceived generative principles, of social practices and representations which, Bourdieu argues, "can be objectively 'regulated' and 'regular' without in any way being the product of obedience to rules, objectively adapting to their goals without presupposing a conscious aiming at ends or an express mastery of the operations necessary to attain them, and, being all this, collectively orchestrated without being the product of the orchestrating action of a conductor."[56] Like no other organization of space, the house (the apartment, the tenement, the barracks—wheresoever black men uncover *das Heimliche*) exteriorizes the elemental structures of black masculine consciousness according to the spatially reproducible taxonomies of race, gender, and sex "underlying all the arbitrary provisions of this culture," and their exponentiation in the architectonics of speech and silence which began this chapter.[57] That the Bourdieuvian dialectics called upon here to locate and explain the black masculine *habitus* are nonessentialist, lends yet another appeal to the sociology of

Figure 11. The cover of Norton Critical Edition of *Cane* reflecting the precarious architecture of the Southern black homeplace. Its visible conditions of isolation and disrepair externalize the otherwise invisible psychic landscape of Ralph Kabnis's self-dissolution.

space in *Outline of a Theory of Practice* for collectivizing black masculine consciousness as a system of survivalist "dispositions" through the archi-textual representativeness of *Cane*.[58]

Images of and allusions to houses, for example, abound in *Cane*. In the book's opening vignette, "Karintha," the skyward climb of pine-scented "smoke curl[ing] up and spread[ing] itself out over the valley" at dusk, contrasts the narrow framing of the black country home. "Homes in Georgia," the narrator pronounces, "are most often built on the two-room plan. In one, you cook and eat, in the other you sleep and there love goes on" (3–4). In "Becky," "a single room held down to earth . . . by a leaning chimney" crashes to the train-shaken ground upon the head of the story's scandalized heroine ("Becky was the white woman who had two sons"[9]). Houses appear in "Box Seat" and "Rhobert" with similarly devastating qualities. Although the opening lines of "Box Seat" hint hopefully at life instead of death ("Houses are shy girls whose eyes shine reticently upon the dusk body of the street . . . [and] stir the root-life of a withered people"[59]), a funereal vision gradually upstages it and prevails at story's end. As Elizabeth Schultz observed in a 1979 essay published in *Black American Literature Forum* (now *African American Review*), "Houses [in "Box Seat"] are no longer animated but [soon] become weight as dead as that of Rhobert's house in the second vignette in Part 2 of *Cane*."[59] In that vignette, "Rhobert wears a house, like a monstrous diver's helmet, on his head"; it is "a dead thing" [42]. Toomer employs the hyperbole to reflect Rhobert's overwhelming preoccupation with northern properties and the suffocating standards of bourgeois materialism. As the tragedy of "Becky" literalizes, houses in "Box Seat" and "Rhobert" tend to oppress, "crushing the life out of [their] occupants . . . . Stagnation is set against [the] fecundity [of *Cane*'s Deep-South pastoralism], isolation against communion, mechanization against sensuality, *enclosure against space*."[60] The archi-textual conditions of *Cane* do not stop there, however. The near chiaroscuro of "enclosure [set] against space" is nowhere more vivid or topoanalytically affective than in the dramedy of "Kabnis."

Imaginatively recasting his own 1921 sojourn in Sparta, Georgia, where, "in a little shack off to one side" of town, Toomer lived for two epiphanous months as the interim head of a black industrial and agricultural school,[61] "Kabnis," an allegorical drama, consists in six archi-textual scenes. Each one highlights a discretely different space along the domestic architectural landscape of fictional Sparta.

126   Constructing the Black Masculine

The architectonics of scene 1 of "Kabnis" concretize more lucidly than the rest the protagonist's conflicted journey toward interiority (i.e. toward *das Heimliche*) inasmuch as the steady dilapidations of Ralph Kabnis's shack, ensconced deep in the whispering Georgia vale, expose a speechless will to abstraction behind "whitewashed hearth and chimney," between the covers of the "warm whiteness" dressing his bed (83). Like the camouflage of fits and starts that betrays the open secret of gay identity, this scene's covers of whiteness obscure but do not abstract. In their most literal usage as bed dressing ("He slides down beneath the cover, seeking release"[83]), they do not screen him from night-riding evil or warm "the weird chill" of fear inspired by the troublesome racist refrains of "Burn, bear black children/ Till poor rivers bring/ Rest, and sweet glory/ In Camp Ground" (83). Nor can even the figurative cover of whitewash applied to hearth and chimney avoid their own sooty blackness. Moreover, nearly everywhere in Ralph Kabnis's crude quarters, cracks in the walls dividing floorboards between rough, unplaned ceiling planks, serve in Toomer's tectonic imagination as a class of near objective, archi-textual correlatives for the deeper, irrepressible fears and desires, the dangerous dreams and unruly emotions Ralph Kabnis would rather contain and keep securely "housed." The pervasive cracks in Kabnis's hut picture psychical gaps, breaches in the foundation of self-consciousness, which render objectively visible not only the threatened unity of Kabnis's personality ("I'm going bats, no doubt of that," he tells himself [87]) but the "fragmentation and disintegration" of what Kaja Silverman calls the "coherent bodily ego," the fantasy of the body perceived according to "the resistance that objects in the world have to the self."[62] In "Kabnis," the resistance of the body to "objects in the world" hardly obtains since these cracks also objectify what Mark Seltzer calls "a miscegenation of the natural and the cultural: the erosion of the boundaries that divide persons and things" by pointing precisely and ironically to the fault lines between them.[63] To the extent that "these cracks are lips the night winds use for whispering"(83), on the one hand, and that Kabnis "totters as a man would who . . . uses artificial limbs. . . . As a completely artificial man would"(85), on the other, persons and things, agents and objects, amalgamate. The cracks in Kabnis's walls, then, exteriorize psychic fracture and representational amalgamation simultaneously.

So as not to crack up, however, from the torment of fracture and the uncertainty of agency, Kabnis coaches himself with words less figurative than they outwardly appear: "Ralph, old man, pull yourself together"(87). Not altogether unexpectedly, it is *inside, within,* and *beneath* where the relief of self-reconciliation, subjects pulled together, resides: "Come now, Ralph, *go in* and make yourself go to sleep. Come now . .[*sic*] *in the door* . .[*sic*] thats right. Put the poker down. There. All right. *Slip under the sheets.* Close your eyes. Think nothing . . a long time . . [*sic*] nothing, nothing. Don't even think nothing. Blank. Not even blank. Count. No, mustnt count. Nothing . . [*sic*] blank . . [*sic*] nothing . . [*sic*] blank . . [*sic*] *space without stars in it* (87; emphasis added). Still more profoundly, Kabnis's pursuit of a refuge inside and underneath serves just as ably to embody and make extrinsic the more abstract interiorization below consciousness in sleep where there is "nothing" but "space." As Ralph Kabnis drifts off to sleep at episode's end, dramaturgy repeats plot and scene 1 fades to black.

Scene 2 cuts abruptly to "The parlor of Fred Halsey's home"(87) in its first emphatic line. While scene 3 returns to Kabnis's shack, scenes 4 and 5 forgo repeating the pretensions of Halsey's garish parlor for his littered blacksmith's shop, "an old building just off the main street of Sempter" (99). Like the cracks in the wall of Kabnis's decaying cabin that symbolically threaten to betray the illusion of a coherent bodily ego under spectragraphical conditions, an uncounted number of cracks and divots in the "age-worn, cement" walls of Halsey's workshop jeopardizes the selfsame fantasy of home-like comfortability for Halsey that Kabnis yearns. "A sort of loft above the shop proper serv[ing] as a break-water for the rain and sunshine which otherwise would have free entry to the main floor" of the place and "[a] window with as many panes broken as whole" (99) are further symbols of a more precarious interior reality, one which the image of Halsey "standing[ing] in the doorway and gaz[ing] up the street expectantly" (99) suggests is eternally threatened by the menacing exteriority of spectragraphical perils.

Below Halsey's workshop, however, "Kabnis"'s most essential architecture is situated: a dim cellar referred to as "The Hole." Appearing "huge and limitless" (105) and swimming "in a pale phosphorescence" (112), the Hole images such pure spatiality that the architectural materiality of it would seem to have been "squeezed to zero volume"[64] by book's end, and the concrete space of the Hole, transformed, beneath the surface of its own appearance, into the abstract space of the black hole of quantum physics so cleverly appropriated to African American literary theory by Houston Baker. Recently reconceiving the galactic black hole of so much concern to quantum physicists, Baker has taken that phenomenon as a metaphor for "the massive concentration of [black expressive] energy"[65] forcefully present in ritual domains of African American subcultural (if not necessarily subterranean)[66] experience. It is precisely this decisive trope "transliterated in letters of Afro-America" that metaphorically "assumes the subsurface force of the black underground" where, according to Baker, the dehiscent black self—Kabnis "cracking up," for example—uncovers "(w)holeness" and "singularity."[67] "To be *Black* and *(W)hole* is to escape incarcerating restraints of a white world," restraints which derive, as I have shown from the outset of this book, from Western ways of looking at black subjects.[68] In chapter 1, I assayed to articulate these restraints tropically, employing the twin criminological metaphors of arrest and the frame(-up) in anticipatory accord with Baker's criminological imagination ("To be *Black* and *(W)hole* is to *escape incarcerating restraints*"). "The symbolic content of Afro-American expressive culture," Baker concludes, "can thus be formulated in terms of the *black hole* conceived as a subcultural (underground, marginal, or liminal) region in which a dominant, white culture's [arrestive] representations are squeezed to zero volume, producing a new expressive order."[69] That the walls surrounding the black hole of the cellar "are of stone, wonderfully fitted" (105) is evidence of not merely the aptness of the name "the Hole"—since black holes are analogously banded by a restricting " 'event horizon,' a membrane that prevents the unaltered escape of anything which passes through"[70]—but of the construction's equivalent capacity for representing "the structures of fortified works" Lacan noted were most often "symbolized in dreams by a fortress, or a stadium."[71] Additionally, the narratological descent in scene 4 from the loft above Halsey's workshop to the workshop proper, then down at last to the cellar below, gathers so much of the accumulated verticality of the mise-en-scène into the Hole that, quite apart from all other important architectures in *Cane*, the Hole ensures what Bachelard calls "totality through depth."[72] A counterstructure to the unsteady "horizontality" of those other ground-level retreats in *Cane* externalizing the problem of racial withdrawal according to architectural images, the cellar reflects "the intimate value of verticality" which Bachelard, following Carl Jung, insists is necessary to a complete grasp of the phenomenological exercises of domestic space and place upon individual consciousness.[73] Consequently, Toomer would seem to be saying, the relentless horizontality of black masculine retreat away from the panoptical public sphere toward the private cover of home and its analogous architectures, can never yield the salvation it seeks since, as Wigley points out, "the house is itself a way of looking, a surveillance device monitoring the possessions that occupy it."[74] The real interiorizing work of black masculinity, therefore, is not in "the lockstep of linear movement within imposed definitions of reality."[75] Linearity proves a problematic progression in African American life and letters leading inevitably, if also ironically, to the black subject's unpredicted discovery of his homelessness, his chronic jeopardy. Rather, the real work of the black masculine lies in the downward excavation of identity, in a descent into the fearful, shadowy black (w)hole of self-revelation where, as "light streaks through the . . . cellar window" (Toomer, *Cane*, 117), the encrypted silence of so much black masculine secrecy achieves the voice of a new black masculinity and the pretense of old masculinist manners, symbolized in "Kabnis" by "a loose something that looks to be a gaudy ball costume" (106) the hero dons "acting a part, yet very real" (107), cast aside at book's end and hung "with an exaggerated ceremony, on its nail" (117).

Insofar as the cellar signifies the most profound sort of interiority, it pictures a man bravely facing "the buried madness, the walled-in tragedy" of black masculine life.[76] It is within the black (w)holes of language and literature, then, within the signifying concavities of black male expressivity, that we may discover a great deal about what black men both desire and fear to tell the world. For I surmise that a great many more black men may live underground in this madness than we know.

PART THREE

Looking B(l)ack

CHAPTER FIVE

"I'm Not Entirely What I Look Like"

Richard Wright, James Baldwin, and the

Hegemony of Vision; or, Jimmy's FBEye Blues

I've got to hide, he told himself. . . . He was tired of running and dodging.
Either he had to find a place to hide, or he had to surrender. A police car
swished by through the rain, its siren rising sharply. They're looking for me
all over. . . . Yes, he had to hide but where? — Richard Wright, "The Man
Who Lived Underground"

> That old FB eye
> Tied a bell to my bed stall
> Said that old FB eye
> Tied a bell to my bed stall
> Each time I love my baby, gover'ment know it all
> — Richard Wright, "FBEye Blues"

The year was 1943 when Richard Wright worked out a plan for a
monthly serial conceived, in his words, to "clarify the personality and
cultural problems of minority groups" by "using the Negro question as
an abstract and concrete frame of experience to reflect a constructive
criticism upon the culture of the nation as a whole."[1] Schematically,
"American Pages"[2] was to have offered an inexpensive, intellectual corrective to the culturally atrophying influence of popular magazines on
the American reading public. For the project's prospectus, Wright
compiled a list of one hundred or more possible issues. Features were
to include articles on African American folklore, reports on the progress of race relations, profiles of black folk who passed themselves off as
white and, conversely, whites who passed as black, as well as academic
papers simplified for a popular readership, fiction extracts, and — most
crucial for this chapter — criminal case studies. Unable to rally enough

moneyed interest in the project to finance its $16, 000 start-up costs (Marshall Fields III thought "American Pages" too much of a risk), Wright (with an impressive coterie of supporters in tow, including Horace Cayton, St. Clair Drake, and Ralph Ellison) soon aborted his "American Pages" plans. Significantly, though, several of Wright's thematic concerns survived this project's aborted hopes. Among the most enduring was a deep-seated interest in criminality, criminal discipline, and juvenile delinquency. Indulging in what was to prove a lifelong intrigue, Wright, in 1944, went on to work out yet another culturally clarifying project, one that seems to have been intent upon realizing the concrete and metaphysical "framing" of black experience metaphorically invoked in the articulated objectives of "American Pages."

As if to link the mechanical and visual function of the photographic frame to the juridical lie of the frame-up, Wright proposed to organize a photographic exhibition of young black criminal delinquents in Harlem, a curious idea that suggested a complicitous kinship between the mechanical and social processes of publicly diffusing stereotypes of black criminality. While Wright's exhibit, like his "American Pages," never materialized, the idea alone is sufficient to explain why, from a certain point of view, "Fate," Book III of his 1940 *Native Son*, might have been more aptly titled "Framed." Had Wright's objective to put up a showing of images of juvenile delinquency in 1940s Harlem been realized, it would not only have extended the logic of the photographic realism of Book III to its farthest, mimetic end, but would have undoubtedly highlighted the problem of surveillance and spectatorship as a problem just as deep, according to W. J. T. Mitchell, "as [the] various forms of reading (decipherment, decoding, interpretation, etc.)" in literary analysis.[3] I argue, in fact, that it is precisely the problem of surveillance, of the gaze of Western racialism as an untoward menace to the "coherence and ideality of the [black masculine] corporeal ego,"[4] which animates the otherwise tedious subnarrative of Book III and lends so much symbolic currency to the metaphor of enframement as the doubly signifying ur-trope of black masculine spectacularity, or what I have come to think of as the sociovisibility of black male subjects.

In the first part of this chapter, I propose to look backward from the unfulfilled criminographic ambitions of "American Pages" and the implicit panoptic critique of Wright's intended exhibition on the fictional designs of Book III of *Native Son*, in order to look forward later at the specularizing exercises of the criminographic imagination on the queer black body of James Baldwin.

In chapter 1 of *Constructing the Black Masculine*, I commented at length on Bigger Thomas's inability to articulate the absurdity of his life in Book III. I adjudged that Bigger's linguistic frustrations were the corporeally arresting consequence of a kind of picture-taking racial gaze that fixes (in two senses) or frames black male subjects within a rigid and limited grid of representational possibilities. In Book III of *Native Son*, the racial gaze congeals Bigger's seemingly anesthetized body into a Medusan rigidity that arrests representation—freezing, fixing, photographically framing him within a resolutely racist symbolic order. As a consequence, the white gaze bestializes Bigger according to anthropoidal imagery. His animalization in white eyes obtains the delineation of an "obnoxiously protrud[ing]" lower jaw, long arms "dangling . . . to his knees," and the huge "hunched" shoulders of an vicious primate (335). Even though Bigger's communist attorney, Max, assays to correctly "represent" Bigger to the court, there is no alternate repertoire of mass filmic images available to him in the sexually inflected context of Bigger's crime: "How can I . . . make the picture of what has happened to this boy show plain and powerful upon a screen of sober reason?" (446) Max hopelessly implores. Bigger's King Kong demonization is a fait accompli which Max, his revisionist intentions notwithstanding, is impotent before the state to repair. Moveover, what Book III discloses, is the more fundamental truth of the primacy of the picture over the person in the white mind. That is to say, in the white imagination, the image of the black male, or what I referred to in chapter 1 as the virtual image of him, is incriminating, not his actual person. Reduced to a visual projection of the ironical fears and fixations of white people in black hands, Bigger, our black Everyman, scares because the framed image of him is reproducible in the faces and, as I shall show shortly, the files, of black men everywhere.

If *Native Son* is the locus classicus of the faults and failures of the racial gaze in American literature, it may have its rival in American "letters" (a distinction I borrow from Michael Warner's insistence upon the formal pluralities of so-called literary expression in his *The Letters of the Republic*) in the FBI files of James Baldwin.[5] Although Baldwin's 1962 novel *Another Country*, in part a corrective rewrite of *Native Son*'s protest polemic, shares with Wright's novel a concern with the violence of the look, that effort to expose the distorting machinations of the racial gaze is but a more brief recapitulation in fiction of an extended actuality of visual violence documented in the more than seventeen hundred pages of the FBI's papers on Baldwin.[6] While Wright, too, had been secretly under the FBI's surveillance from the time he worked on the Federal Writer's Project in Chicago in 1935 until his death in 1960, never was there so intense a scrutiny of his equally itinerant life as that which vexed Baldwin. Wright's comparatively meager 181-page file reflects the enormous disparity in investigative energies spent on each man. And although it was Wright who in 1949 penned the satirical verse "FBEye Blues" (never published), it was Baldwin whose sociovisibility as a gay black male in mid-twentieth century conservative America would actualize Bigger Thomas's fictional enframement.

Perhaps not surprisingly, however, the first known mention of Baldwin in the FBI record was a 1951 reference to him in a report on Wright. An unknown source told bureau agents that Baldwin was "a young Negro writer . . . [and] a student Paris" who had "attacked the hatred themes of Wright's writings."[7] While Baldwin's very public excoriations of *Native Son* in the essays "Everybody's Protest Novel" and "Many Thousand Gone" first captured the bureau's attention, it was a 1960 report that he was a "'prominent member' of the Fair Play for Cuba Committee" that inaugurated the federal government's twenty-year surveillance of him.[8] FBI informants shadowed Baldwin and assisted the bureau in monitoring his nomadic changes of address from New York to California to Istanbul to Saint-Paul-de Vence in the south of France where he took up permanent residence in 1970, worried about the increasing violence against homosexuals in the United States. The FBI also telephoned Baldwin under numerous pretexts and, not unexpectedly, they photographed him. One compelling page of the file neatly juxtaposes a snapshot of Baldwin to one of Wright. The logic of the juxtaposition cannot be known since not so much as a caption attends the pictures. The photographic composition of the Baldwin file is nevertheless crucial to comprehending Baldwin's aggrieved sociovisibility. But more critical to uncovering the visual complicities in black male representation are the verbally manifested ekphrastic features of the file, those textual descriptions of Baldwin that do not offer us a photograph at all (dozens of memos in the file allude to photos of

Baldwin that are, in fact, absent from the dossier), but nevertheless frame him descriptively, as if to approximate in the same overdetermined, picture-taking vein as *Native Son* a pictorial representation. Here I offer two examples as complementing cases in point.

In the first instance, a 1964 *New York Post* article entitled "James Baldwin: A *New York Post* Portrait" published in six serial installments between January 13 and January 19 appears clipped from the *Post* and pasted onto twenty-four pages of the Baldwin file. Despite its first gnomish impression of him ("James Baldwin, a small, dark splinter of a man"), the profile sketches a remarkably embodied subject whose depiction not only belies the minimalism of the first glance but, like *Native Son*, reveals by virtue of its journalistic casting the public's culpability (or credulity) in the photo-graphic fetishization of black male subjects, a culpability which Baldwin's FBI papers merely formalize.[9] In page after page of the records containing the *Post* profile (Papers #100-146553-87 through #100-146553-94), Baldwin is described in some variation of "huge-eyed [if] undersized," sometimes sitting "cross-legged," rocking slowly, "pausing now and then to scratch his calf . . . [or] his elbow" or to rub his ankle. As he "stabs out his cigarette in the ashtray," we are made to notice the ashtray's place "near his knee." His knees, the report conveys, are propped up and his arms are "looping" around variously "jack-knifed" and "rubber" legs. The corporeal preoccupations in the *Post*'s six-part profile on Baldwin — inevitably now the bureau's too — belie Baldwin's "frail person" and economic build, "tiny and narrow, so thin it's hard to believe he casts a shadow." But cast a shadow he does. A shadow much more significant in the racist and homophobic imaginary than his small build could conceivably cast. For if it is indeed true that "the white male body is the relay to [social and political] legitimation," a veracity articulated by Lauren Berlant which I have made a consistent refrain of this book, and "the power to suppress that body, to cover its tracks and traces is the sign of real authority," then it is precisely the shadowy trace of blackness (to say nothing of the compounded specter of homosexuality) that misrepresents Baldwin's smallness in prosimian terms (huge eyes, "looping" arms, "rubber" legs) — terms only once removed from those which in *Native Son* describe Bigger Thomas as an ape.[10]

That the *New York Post*'s verbal picture of Baldwin is a fairly faithful reflection of the bureau's surveillance habits is supported by the text of a second document in the file reporting Baldwin's activities in Istanbul where, off and on, he spent eight years between 1961 and 1969. An extract of the report follows:

> Baldwin's method of working is strange. There are times when he writes continuously for twenty-four hours without food or drink. Under such circumstances, he does not even notice if [someone] shout[s] at him. . . . Afterwards, he lies down and sleeps. Moreover, he is in a sound state of sleep for forty-eight hours. If [anyone] is able to awaken him, how fortunate [he is].[11]

This oddly clinical report is important for the familiarly colonial way in which it imagines Baldwin as "strange," picturing him within an anthropological (if not yet anthropoidal) frame of visual reference. Moreover, it links Baldwin's "strange" behavior to writing in such a way as to mystify that labor and bring it under scopic suspicion as well. Evidently, the bureau was just as interested in Baldwin's mysterious body of writings as it was in his "strange" writing body.

When his novel *Another Country* and long essay *The Fire Next Time* were published in 1962 and 1963 respectively, the FBI intensified its surveillance of Baldwin. Whereas the bureau's motives for redoubling its efforts after *The Fire Next Time* were plainly political, the most cursory review of the papers pertaining to *Another Country* discloses that political motives were frequently confused by voyeuristic ones not unlike those of "that old FB eye" in Wright's "FBEye Blues." While it is certain, too, that Baldwin's closed 1963 meeting with then–Attorney General Robert Kennedy at the height of U.S. Civil Rights unrest was an additional catalyst for the FBI's interest in him — brazenly Baldwin suggested to Kennedy that he fire FBI Director J. Edgar Hoover — the bureau was never so obviously fixated on Baldwin's sexual tastes as when it undertook to determine whether or not *Another Country*'s homoeroticism and scenes of interracial sex transgressed federal obscenity laws.

Although the bureau's General Crimes Section concluded, curiously, that *Another Country* "contain[ed] literary merit and may be valuable to students of psychology and social behavior,"[12] this did not prevent FBI agents from keeping close watch of Baldwin's sexual habits, as if the question of *Another Country*'s pornographic potential could be solved by knowing Baldwin's sex practices ("Isn't Baldwin a well known pervert?" Hoover baited in one of his many memos). The insinuation was followed by an intense, nearly obsessive scrutiny of Baldwin's sexual behaviors, starting with the dismissive observation that "although the theme of homosexuality figured in two of his three published novels . . . it is not possible to say that he is a pervert."[13] Not much later, though, after a spate of contradictory reports, the bureau came to another more damning conclusion, one that hinged tellingly on what was not actually seen but overheard and inferred—an extrapolation, that is, of the visual from the auditory: "It has been heard that Baldwin may be a homosexual and *he appeared as if he may be one.*"[14] Conflating empirical verbal evidence and ocular speculation, the FBI surveillance of Baldwin confirmed that the white pictorial reflex could be quickened as much through eavesdropping as through eyeballing. The aural allusion in Paper #100-146553-215 suggests further the potentiality for racial specularity (as the file's missing photographs affirm) without a trapped, objectified body to provoke it. The white racialist imagination does not always require a body for its designs, only the five senses and a racial or sexual context.[15] Given what has now been proven about J. Edgar Hoover's personal obsessions with the sex lives of black men and women, with homosexuality, and, as historian David Garrow, author of *The FBI and Martin Luther King, Jr.* put it, "activities that were interracial," it is not surprising that Baldwin became a captivating site of investigation for the bureau.[16] Nor is it surprising Baldwin was considered "dangerous" in the official parlance of the bureau.

Despite the evidence of voyeuristic propensities in the FBI's relentless surveillance of a man who thought of himself, ironically enough, as "a witness" to the truth of American race matters, the bureau's tracking of Baldwin in the United States and abroad is hardly the exposé it appears it was intended to be. Nor are the FBI papers on Baldwin especially revealing of the more mundane curiosities that interest literary critics and archivists. Did Baldwin keep a journal? What periodicals did he read? Who were his turncoat friends and false lovers? Did he pray? Admittedly, there may be something of a voyeuristic urge even in such questions as these, which Baldwin, for one, might be happy these files resist. But the file remains provocative. Perhaps not for what confidences they betray about Baldwin's comings and goings—indeed, they disclose little that Baldwin did not preemptively admit to—but for what they convey about the spectacular conditions of historical black masculine identity and the chronic effort to frame the black male body, criminally and visually, for the visual pleasures of whites. The FBI's surveillance of Baldwin instantiaties what philosopher Martin Jay calls "a scopic regime" in modern Western culture, a systematic visual violation of the body that tends first to criminalize, then to eroticize black (and of late, brown) men.[17] When FBI agents trailed Baldwin to a writer's colony in upstate New York in 1945, years before the bureau's official surveillance began, to question him concerning an AWOL marine they were certain he knew, their eyeballing interrogations left him feeling "humiliated."[18] Two white male agents, "walked [Baldwin] out of [a] diner, and stood [him] against a wall":

> My color had already made me conspicuous enough in that town — this is putting it mildly indeed — and, from a distance, the townspeople stared. . . . I knew of nothing which I had done to have attracted their attention. Much later in my life, I knew very well what I had done to attract their attention, and intended, simply, to keep on keeping on. . . . I was terribly frightened, and I was desperately trying to keep one jump ahead of them — to guess what it was before they revealed it. If I could guess what it was, then I might know how to answer and know what to do. . . . They frightened me, and they humiliated me — it was like being spat upon, or pissed on, or gang-raped. (108)

Baldwin's FBI papers tell a very real story about the social and symbolic consequences of the spectacular conditions of (gay) black male subjectivity and their nearly impossible escape. Baldwin's desperation "to keep one jump ahead of them," however, to "know how to answer" and "what to do," represents nothing if not a stubborn will to defy with dancing words the criminal and sexual frame(-up), here vividly realized by the familiar enactment of a police lineup as the eyes of the whole town study him, his back pressed against a wall.

Despite evidence of this will to unmolested subjecthood, Baldwin grew ever more fearful of the bureau after the suspicious assassinations of his friends Malcolm X, Martin Luther King Jr., and Medgar Evers. Anxious that an attempt on his own life might be made, Baldwin fled the United States, "making tracks," as it were, for Istanbul, and only much later the south of France.[19] Crucial though his expatriation may be to appreciating what was either his persistent will to elude the ubiquitous dis-ease of racial specularity in America or, conversely, the magnitude of his desperation (and the two needn't be mutually exclusive drives), James Baldwin's FBI papers raise more interesting concerns about tracks of a different sort. Significantly, the FBI records of Baldwin's surveillance, like those of so many other actors in the Civil Rights and Black Power conundrums of the 1960s, are fraught with blacked-out, expurgated text. These visible deletions are meaningful not simply because of the information they conceal but because of the means by which the attempted cover-up of the bureau's suspiciously Orwellian (sometimes salaciously Orwellian) manner is achieved. It visibly marks the (un)known, often private details of Baldwin's life (his address, his friends, his lovers) with the presumed guilt of outlawry. Ironically, as Baldwin was making tracks to Eurasia, the bureau was making its own tracks on the pages of Baldwin's file, clearly blacking out text to cover its own traces after the 1966 Freedom of Information Act, thusly "marking" Baldwin in perpetuity (figs. 12 and 13).

But Baldwin's announcement of a book he was preparing to publish on the FBI, called *The Blood Counters*, would seem to be his attempt to turn the tables, marking the bureau's activities as it traced his. Although there is no evidence Baldwin ever had a finished (or early) draft—his editor at Dial Press, James Silberman, said he "lied horribly" and "had a story for everybody"[20]—the threat alone may have been a sufficient revenge. Whatever the case, it seems clear that neither the FBI nor the *New York Post* writer and Baldwin biographer Fern Marja Eckman (whose portrait of Baldwin also marks him, this time by description rather than deletion), paid very close attention to Baldwin's own potentially subversive words in that *New York Post* article: "I'm small and I have big eyes, and I come on, you know, kind of dramatic. But there's something very misleading about my manner. I'm not entirely what I look like." Perhaps what the bureau might have seen in Baldwin's big eyes and dramatic manner, if it cared to look more closely, was a resistant look, a look (in both ocular and postural terms) aiming to "reanimate and open to change" the representational potential the camera/gaze/ekphrastic text fixes and frames.[21]

To the degree that the visual pleasures of racial fetishism in *Native Son* rely on the spellbinding power of white eyes to induce the very passivity they require for their exercise ("overwhelmed by the sight of his accusers, Bigger Thomas . . . fainted dramatically this morning"), inversely, Baldwin's big eyes and dramatic manner stand to disrupt the fetishizing machinations of the racial gaze by an eyeballing disposition of his own, one that defies the hegemony of racial supervision on its own terms. Baldwin's discreetly insinuated self-portrait, mocking the

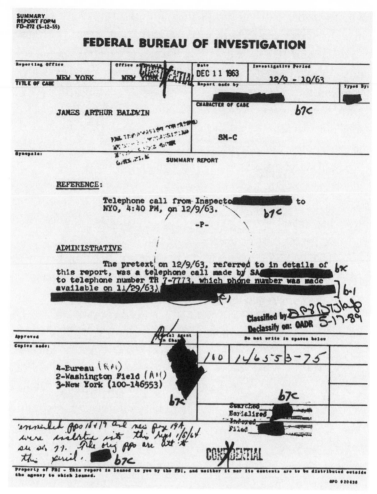

Figure 12. FBI file on James Baldwin, Dec. 11, 1963

efforts of both the *New York Post* and the FBI to verbally sketch a realistic picture of him ("there's something misleading about my manner"), may be the most illuminating material in the whole FBI record on him. For like Baldwin, black male subjects under white eyes in general are never entirely what they look like. If Wright's *Native Son* underscores the inevitable tragedy of phantasmic misrecognitions, Baldwin's theatrical mien promises a final transcendence of that tragedy. Where "the ring of steel against steel" in *Native Son* (502) symbolically seals Bigger Thomas's (mis)representational doom as an incorrigible villain, Baldwin's big eyes may well challenge Bigger's doom and affirm the truth of the private life as Roland Barthes described it: "The 'private

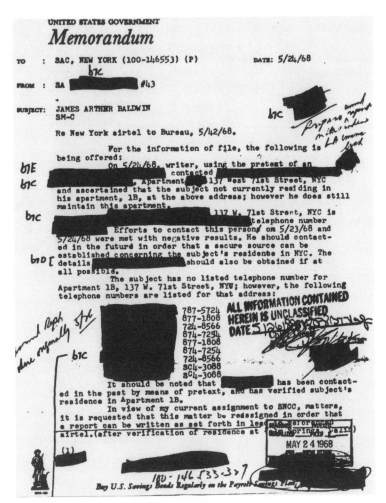

Figure 13. FBI file on James Baldwin, May 24, 1968

life' is nothing but that zone of space, of time, where [one is] not an image, an object. It is [one's] political right to be a subject which [one] must protect."[22] However invasive "the FBEye" may have been in Baldwin's private life, his big eyes and dramatic manner may well have screened him, in spite of the bureau, from the utter abjection of a more public racial and sexual visibility (figs. 14 and 15). For time made it perceptibly clear to Baldwin that the "infirmity" of "enormous eyes" "might not be [his] doom," but "might be forged into weapons" (*Devil*, 9) raised against "the devil" whose work was waged "in the eyes of the cop and the sheriff and the deputy, the landlord, the housewife, the football player: in the eyes of some junkies, the eyes of some

Figure 14. Steve Schapiro/Black Star, James Baldwin

preachers, the eyes of some governors, presidents, wardens, in the eyes of some orphans, and in the eyes of my father" (146–47). Like one's beauty, one's wretchedness dwells in the eyes of the beholder, and "he who has been treated *as* the devil recognizes the devil when they meet" (147). He who has been most menaced by him learns to resist him in the most spectacular ways. Thom Gunn captured Baldwin's subversive spectacularity lyrically in the poem "Looks." Although "Looks" is from a collection of Gunn's AIDS verse, it is difficult to imagine that the poem could not also be about Baldwin's gift for resistant looking. For the power of "Looks" resides entirely in its subject's eyes, not his illness.

> Those eyes appear to transmit energy
> And hold it back undissipated too.
> His gaze is like a star, that cannot see,
> A glow so steady he directs at you
> You try to be the first to look aside
> —Less flattered by the appearance of attention
> Than vexed by the dim stirrings thus implied
> Within a mind kept largely in suspension.
>
> Although a gaze sought out, and highly placed,
> By lovers and photographers, it is
> Too patly overwhelming for your taste.
> You step back from such mannered solemnities
> To focus on his no doubt sinewy power,
> His restless movements, and his bony cheek.
> You have seen him in the space of one half-hour
> Cross a street twenty times. You have heard him speak,
> Reading his work to the surprise of guests
> Who find that dinner was a stratagem:
> Poems in which the attracted turn to pests
>
> . . . .

Figure 15. Sedat Pakay, James Baldwin

. . . He is an actor, after all,
And it's a genuine talent he engages
In playing this one character, mean, small,
But driven like Othello by his rages

.   .   .   .

. . . as if anger could repopulate
The bony city he is trapped inside.

At times he has a lover he can hurt
By bringing home the pick-ups he despises
Because they let him pick them up. Alert
Always to looks — and they must took like prizes —
He blurs further distinction, for he knows
Nothing of strength but its apparent drift,
Tending and tending, and nothing of repose
Except within his kindled gaze, his gift.[23]

If Baldwin's "gift" is in the modernist image of his "kindled gaze," then the gift of the postmodern man of color lies in "the sinewy power" of his body. I turn now to Melvin Dixon's 1992 dance novel *Vanishing Rooms* and the choreographic work of the incomparable Bill T. Jones for a proprioceptive display of the black masculine under the hegemony of vision.

CHAPTER SIX

What Juba Knew

Dance and Desire in Melvin Dixon's *Vanishing Rooms*

To be liberated from the stigma of blackness by embracing it is to cease, forever, one's interior agreement and collaboration with the author of one's degradation. — James Baldwin, *No Name in the Street*

Of all the curious American divertissements Charles Dickens discovered during his 1842 visit to the United States, few seem to have struck him with so much satisfied amusement as a "lively young Negro" in New York City, dancing an inimitable "Negro breakdown." Dickens described the nimble young dancer in his *American Notes*: "Single shuffle, double shuffle, cut and cross-cut: snapping his fingers, rolling his eyes, turning in his knees, presenting the backs of his legs in front, spinning about on his toes and heals like nothing but the man's fingers on the tambourine; dancing with two left legs, two right legs, two wooden legs, two wire legs, two spring legs — all sorts of legs — what is this to him?"[1] The "lively hero" of Dickens's Five Points was the Master Juba himself, William Henry Lane, a free black man from Rhode Island who was, by 1845, "the greatest dancer known" in America.[2] A member of the Ethiopian Minstrels, a troupe of four white men in blackface and him, Lane was a popular minstrel performer who regularly received top billing. But "far from fitting into [the] prefitted stereotype" of the malapropian, melon-eating buffoon typically associated with blackface minstrelsy, William "Juba" Lane succeeded in presenting minstrel audiences with what only seemed as imitations of black life: Juba's "seeming counterfeit" performances, begrudged by white performers like P. T. Barnum's John Diamond, masked more authentic displays of black theatrical self-presentation than nineteenth-century audiences — or indeed twentieth-century ones — could imagine.[3] Where white minstrel imitations of black dance forms were "all stammers and jerks and gracelessness," Juba's dances were an ironic "combination of [muscular] mobility . . . flexibility of joints . . . boundings . . . slidings . . . [and] gyrations."⁴ Such "firmness of foot, such elasticity of tendon, such mutation of movement . . . such natural grace," one English critic wrote after an 1848 London performance, was never seen before in England.⁵

By the time Juba's celebrity peaked in Europe, his dancing was so accomplished that its genius often left his spectators speechless. One observer, writing for the *Illustrated London News*, wondered how Juba could "enter into [such] wonderful complications so naturally . . . and make his feet twinkle until you lose sight of them altogether in his energy?"⁶ Another witness wrote, "The manner in which he beats time with his feet, and the extraordinary command he possesses over them can only be believed by those who have been present at the exhibition."⁷ Undoubtedly the attraction of Juba's London exhibitions owed as much to a promised, percipient "aura of 'blackness' "⁸ in his act as to his "extraordinary command" of the intricacies of black dance forms. But Lane seemed to have learned to transcend the racial gaze by the time of his London performances. The "wonderful complications" of his dancing were sufficiently spellbinding to cause audiences to "lose sight" of him as spectacle, but not "without losing sight of the reality of [his raced] representation" altogether.⁹

For my purposes, however, there was no more fitting description of Juba's dancing than that published by London's *Theatrical Times*. Juba's performances were "an ideality," it proclaimed, "at once grotesque and poetical."¹⁰ The acclaim Juba received from the *Theatrical Times*, I would argue, expressed an implicit and preterit comprehension of the ways in which both "the mastery of form" and "the deformation of mastery," those strategies of black cultural performance theorized so intelligently by Houston Baker, have historically coalesced to shape black masculine subjecthood in Eurocentric contexts.¹¹

When Juba died in London in 1852, barely twenty-seven years old, he was already regarded "the most influential single performer of nineteenth-century American dance."¹² I invoke him because I believe, like Marian Hannah Winter, that Master Juba "represents an independent Black dance tradition" of masculine self-expressivity. William Henry Lane is, by my reckoning, the *pater alios* of black masculine dance history, the "initiator and determinant of the form itself," a form which lends visible expression to the difficult dialectics of black masculinity I intend to pursue here.¹³

By close consideration of Melvin Dixon's 1991 dance novel *Vanish-*

ing Rooms, I want to demonstrate that, if modern middle-class American manhood is finally an affair "between men," as Eve Sedgwick put it so famously, then black masculinity emerges as the contender identity in a bitter interracial conflict over sex and stereotype that reveals itself performatively in a dramatic improvisation on the black male body under white objectification. Inasmuch as all gender is, according to Judith Butler, "the repeated stylization of the body, a set of repeated acts within a highly rigid regulatory *frame* that congeal over time" to fashion an illusion of essence,[14] black masculinity coheres in a chronic, kinesic decolonization of the fetishized black male body under the public panopticon. Vividly illustrated in the reappropriative power of the black male dance performance, in "sweaty, sensual, fully efforted bodies" of color spectacularly asserting themselves, the black masculine's first aim is a subversion of the phantasmatic obsession.[15]

Ironically, dance is one of the few remaining disciplines that we literary-cum-cultural critics have not definitively entered upon. After film, photography, music, painting, even sport, dance is one of the last frontiers of interdisciplinarity in cultural studies. Although we seem to find few occasions for thinking or writing about dance as either an academic or popular discipline, it is, like speech and writing, a valuable sign system nevertheless, a kinetic metalanguage impervious to the signifying limitations of words. Critically regarded, dance is the visible dramatization of the invisible pursuit of "being what I am," to invoke Lacan's phrase. Because dance communicates without words, it is capable of transcending them, of telling us something more about the black masculine that the meagerness of words cannot. If it is true that black masculinity reveals itself as "a stylization of the body over space and time," as Cornel West has posited, then it is the expressive potential of black male body language that warrants an inquiry into the theory and practice of dance in black masculine contexts.[16] For from the limbo performance of the middle passage (brilliantly historicized by the eminent Guyanese writer Wilson Harris) and the calienda dances of eighteenth-century West Indian slaves to twentieth-century tap, breaking, and voguing, the history of black male performativity in dance, popular and performance, may be more crucial than we know to limning a hermeneutics of black masculinity that owes no allegiance to black macho, is not inherently heterocentric, and yet emerges from a decidedly male racial experience.[17] If dance indeed offers "recourse and access to another reality in the experience of masculinity," who then can doubt that black male dancers like Bill "Bojangles" Robinson, Arthur Mitchell, or Alvin Ailey are as critical figures as, say, Jack Johnson, Joe Louis, or Muhammad Ali in the theorization of twentieth-century black masculine identity?[18] (As Ali taught us, boxers are not that far removed from dancers. Where else but in boxing and ballet do men desire grace enough to "float like a butterfly"?) In the deepest structures of boxing and dance lies an alternate reality of black masculine subjecthood, one characterized by "new stylistic options" for identity display.[19]

In her book *Dance and the Lived Body*, Sondra Horton Fraleigh holds that to dance "is to discover [more of oneself] by uncovering, revealing and creating something not seen before . . . out of one's own bodily being."[20] To dance is to expand the repertoire of human representation, to pursue with one's body the extreme limits of self-knowledge. It is precisely this aesthetic, actualized in theme and design, that inheres in Melvin Dixon's 1991 novel *Vanishing Rooms*. Like Toni Morrison's *Jazz*, *Vanishing Rooms* is a performance piece. Its revolving narration approximates a choreographic rondo variation in four parts, never failing to keep the tallest concerns of the novel corporeal. As a "Dancing Book,"[21] *Vanishing Rooms* literalizes the figurativeness of what Henry Louis Gates Jr. called "the dance of language that is writing."[22] But dance does not only provide the design framework of this work; it is both text and subtext of the novel as well. In its representation of the black gay dancer performatively coming into being as a cohesive queer subject of color, *Vanishing Rooms* points up the symbolic power of dance as a weapon against the self-abnegating devices of everyday life and language for gay black subjects under a racial and sexual hegemony.

DECONSTRUCTING DESIRE

I think that I know something about the American masculinity which most men of my generation do not know because they have not been menaced by it in the ways that I have been. It is still true, alas, that to be an American Negro male is also to be a kind of walking phallic symbol: which means that one pays, in one's own personality, for the sexual insecurity of others. The relationship, therefore, of a white boy and a black boy is a very complex thing. — James Baldwin, "The Black Boy Looks at the White Boy"

Some boys hug each other for reassurance. — Alex Hirst, Introduction to Rotimi Fani-Kayode's *Black Male/White Male*

At the outset of *Vanishing Rooms*, Jesse and Metro, the protagonists of Dixon's novel, meet at a small Connecticut college against the backdrop of a black student protest over the college's reluctance to observe Malcolm X's birthday. Jesse is one of the students occupying the main administrative building at Wesman University in protest. Metro is a reporter for *The Wesman Herald* who shows up to cover the event. A "disadvantaged white boy from the South,"[23] Metro is all business. In a short time his "journalist's eyes" (37) find Jesse's "locked inside the building, barricaded away" (38) and looking down on him from a second-story window. Moving "from window to window, from one empty classroom to another," Jesse senses Metro moving with him on the ground. "I watched him follow me as I moved," says Jesse. "I knew we would meet somehow on the outside. . . . My hands felt empty with nothing to touch" (39). Like an exercise in body mirroring to Jesse's unchoreographed lead, their powerlessness "to touch" across the racial divide of the scene's symbolic barricades, though politically portending, intensifies the desire between them: "His stare made me feel weightless," Jesse fancies, "light angles toward him on wings suddenly fluttering from inside me and begging for air. I wanted then to get under his skin, travel at breakneck speed through his veins and right to his heart" (38). Although the barricades around Clarkson Hall are finally removed and Jesse is offered, at long last, something to touch in/on Metro's pale body, race proves a more enduring barrier between them than the police blockade.

When the demonstration ends hours later, Jesse is among those who march proudly away in symbolic militaristic victory. Armed with pad and pencil, Metro, ever the journalist, follows. Although every effort of his to get a comment from Jesse is met with steely soldier-like silence — one must keep up the nationalistic pretense — Jesse's eyes betray his indifference. Coyly, they invite Metro to his room. Without so much as a word, Metro's own eyes respond graciously, and it is not long before the pretense of the one's politics and the other's professionalism disappears. Sex ensues as Jesse revels in the warmth of Metro's thighs against his and "how close [their] faces held in making love" (10). That "making love" misnames their sex act, however, is not long hidden from view.

Despite its billings, *Vanishing Rooms* is not a love story exactly, as love stories between men go. It is, more accurately, a bitter, passionate rivalry between raced subjects in which sex is the weapon of choice.

Between Jesse and Metro, sex is nothing so much as an act of spite and envy for which the phrase "making love" is a misnomer. As Dixon himself explained in a 1991 *Christopher Street* interview: "Sexual desire can be an expression of hatred as much as it can be an expression of love. There are people who can just get off on having sex with someone *because* they hate them. The force of that hate can be as powerful as love."[24] Two rape scenes in *Vanishing Rooms,* one a gang rape of Metro and the other an attack on young Lonny Russo, exemplify the most evil of sexual hatreds. But *Vanishing Rooms* depicts the more illusive truth too that sex needn't be violent or murderous to convey enmity. Although their mutual desire for the other's body gives the affectionate impression, Jesse and Metro evince little that is loving in their reciprocal obsessions. While Metro's tragic murder in the novel is the unmistakable symbol of homophobic violence and victimization, it is also a sign of the potential destructiveness of sexual congress within impoverished relationships like Jesse's and Metro's, a peril, I hasten to add, wholly separate from the risks of unprotected sex faced by us all, daily. Theirs is a poisoned relationship sustained by each one's political and parasitic need for the other's racial bodiliness. Each one's desire for the other is, at bottom, merely iconic, the false consciousness of one desire — sexual — mistaken for another — the fundamentally political wish for patriarchal privilege — where the erotic stands in for unconsciously political desires, and the penis, an anatomical fact, is confused with the phallus, a political metaphor. What animates the sexual relationship between Jesse and Metro, to put the matter yet another way, is precisely the pursuit of *trade*.

Philip Brian Harper has theorized "the highly charged category of homosexual *trade*" elegantly. In *Private Affairs: Critical Ventures in the Culture of Social Relations*, he characterizes trade as the pursuit of nonreciprocal sex made exploitive by a nonreciprocal desire whose object of allure

> *really isn't* one's physical person per se but rather an aspect of that person abstracted from oneself and revered as a *fetish* by the pursuing party. In this case, the actual sexual consummation of the pursuit might register for all concerned as a fully reciprocal encounter, with each party deriving his pleasure and gratification from his experience of the other's body as related in a particular way to the fetish attribute.[25]

Trade is *Vanishing Room*'s cardinal conflict. Indicatively, when a rogue gang of gaybashing roughnecks chases Jesse to his apartment, hurling aspersions at him like stones, Jesse flies into Metro's arms. "He held my head and hands until I calmed down," he remembers, waxing romantic. Metro's embrace offers Jesse erotic sanctuary from the cold indignity of being imprecated as a "black nigger faggot" by his tormenters. For Jesse, Metro's body affords him a cover from the insult of racial and sexual harassment. Not surprisingly, then, Jesse's fear of the gang stalking him metamorphoses into a burning desire for Metro. "Slowly, deliberately," they couple, "believing [they] were doing something right" (15). For a moment, their sex rescues Jesse from the slanderous visibility of the "black nigger faggot." For Jesse, in this instance, the desire for Metro's body as trade is not unlike the desire *to be* Metro, "a white boy from Louisiana, [educated at] New England prep schools and college" (15).

Although Metro bitterly disputes his white-skin privilege ("Don't you think [I] have some weight to bear?"), Jesse sees differently: "You're white, Metro. At a distance you blend in with the crowd. Shit, they can see me coming, and in a riot they don't stop me to ask if I've been to college or live in the suburbs. They start beating any black head they find" (103). Jesse conveys in his reproof of Metro the resentment of a "black nigger faggot"'s double jeopardy. While Metro's queerness doesn't permit him to "blend in the crowd" as simply as Jesse imagines (Metro is murdered because of queer liabilities), the burden of blackness, a condition of visual determinism, is Jesse's alone. I emphasize the deterministic quality of Jesse's condition in order to distinguish his specularity from Metro's. This is not to deny that Metro suffers as severely under the scopic regime as Jesse. But owing to the difference race makes, each suffers the consequences of his specular condition in discretely different ways.

In his book *Homographesis*, Lee Edelman advances an inestimable theorization of homophobia as underwritten by "a powerful tropological imperative . . . to produce a visible emblem or metaphor"[26] for the homosexual person "whose sexuality must be represented as legible," visually resonant, "precisely because it 'threatens' to pass unremarked."[27] To permit that, of course, would put the so-called naturalness of heterosexuality in jeopardy. "Yet while the cultural enterprise of reading homosexuality must affirm that the homosexual is distinctively and legibly marked [i.e. made uninvisible]," according to Edelman, "it must also recognize that those markings have been, can be or can pass as, unremarked and unremarkable" in ways unavailable to racial subjects.[28] Although "'racial' discrimination, . . . like . . . [homophobia] is propped up on . . . the privileging of the scopic drive in the psychic structuring of sexual difference," homophobia and racial discrimination differ in that, unlike the racial Other, the subjecthood of the white queer is not optically predetermined.[29] Rather, homophobes read backwards onto white queer bodies, marking them—I can think of no better way to put it—a posteriori. Says troubled Lonny Russo about Metro in illustration: "I thought he was one of the guys 'cause he didn't swish. . . . This guy walked like a regular fellah. . . . He [didn't] look like a faggot" (27). Negrophobes, on the other hand, read black bodies prescriptively according to stereotypical forms and narratives that anticipate and fix the conditions of black possibility well in advance of the look.

However much Jesse may misjudge the weight borne by white queer subjects, he conveys to Metro in his rebuke ("You're white, Metro. . . . you blend in the crowd") an implicit apprehension of Lauren Berlant's point, often repeated in this book, that "the white male body is the relay to [social and political] legitimation," a body that owes its power to the ability to suppress itself by covering its racial traces.[30] He seems to know, like Berlant, that the male body of color, in contrast to the white male body, leaves its trace everywhere like ruins in the white imaginary. The persistent spectacle of dread and desire, of sin, sex, and stereotype which blackness seems to evoke reflexively in the white imagination effectively disqualifies black men for whatever authority they might otherwise have gained on the basis of shared gender. Because Jesse cannot ever hope to "suppress [his] body" or "blend in the crowd," he seeks a refuge from the unbearable spectacularity of so-called black faggotry in Metro.

Not until Metro's murder, however, does Jesse come to confront the truth of Metro's serviceability as his "underground man" (42). The tragic news that Metro is dead effects in Jesse an episode of grief so histrionic it betrays its self-interest: "Suddenly voices filled the outer hallway. Rushing footsteps. Laughter. Banging on doors somewhere. My hands shook again and my stomach tied itself in knots. Where could I hide?" (12). Jesse's worry is urgent. The (imagined?) commotion outside his apartment conjures a memory of the earlier assault. And, with Metro gone, who will protect *him*? Who, in other words, will hide the black nigger faggot from the physical and psychic violence of racism and homophobia? Eventually Jesse finds another haven in Ruella McPhee. As a black woman, Ruella, like Jesse, has her own double jeopardy to contend with. But to Jesse, she is the promise of a new hiding place, a surrogate protection whom he fitly nicknames "Rooms."

Although early on Jesse comes to believe that he has "found other spaces to touch, other windows to touch" in Ruella, ultimately the spectacle relief he is after in sex with her, as with Metro, is never realized. While Jesse and Ruella do touch, ironically they do not connect at all. For "one door [remained] locked" and only "Metro had the key" (45). If the safety Jesse requires from the taunts and torment of racial and sexual stigmatization cannot be trusted in Ruella, it is because only Metro's capacities for abstraction can secure that. Unlike Ruella, Metro is a "relay," as Berlant says, to the untraceable condition of white male corporeality. It is his touch, therefore, not hers, that sends the burning current of desire driving Jesse's libidinal energies. "I wanted *his* hands on me," he says. "Five fingers and five more. I wanted the electricity of *his* touch, *his* hands on me" (11; emphasis added). Longing for what Walt Whitman once called "the curious sympathy one feels when feeling with the hand the naked meat of the body,"[31] Jesse needs Metro's touch for the "electricity" of trade. "How many times did I tell him, 'Just touch me. Dance you fingers across my chest, my thighs. Press my flesh. Take off my clothes real slow'" (11). As Metro's "wiry" hands "do their marvelous work," exhilarating Jesse with their electric feel, they also become the medium of "relay," relieving Jesse of the weight of his color as well as his clothes. Jesse's desire is not only carnal, then, but at the very heart of the matter dialectical. The "tender . . . aching" (11) in his body yearns a deeper thing for which Metro is both prosthesis and propitiation.

It is worth the immediate notice, however, that Metro's surrogacy for Jesse is no less dire than that of Jesse for Metro. While Metro's touch allays the pain of racial insult and scopic torment, it is precisely that pain which Metro wants of Jesse. Whenever Metro beds Jesse in *Vanishing Rooms*, it is not in order to rescue him from the disgrace of "black nigger faggot." It is rather to feed the insult, and be fed in return by it. For whereas Jesse's desires are motivated by racial envy, Metro's are aroused by racial stereotype. Let me expound.

Not long after their moving from Connecticut to New York, Metro enters upon new pleasures kinkier than Jesse alone can render. At Paradise Baths, Metro hopes to seduce Jesse into them: "Don't you see? All this is part of it, what we came to New York for. The streets, the sweat, beer and cigarettes. And here? You'd walk in, anybody would walk in, hands hooked in the belt, your jeans torn just so around the crotch. You'd lean against the wood and I'd find you, smell you waiting there. I'd kneel just so and you'd talk dirty to me" (43). Suggestively, the pungent details of "sweat, beer and cigarettes," the "smell of mildew" (3), and the "stink of the warehouse" (5) convey correlatively what Metro really wants sexually: some funk.

In contrast to the slow, deliberate sex that gratifies Jesse, Metro requires the rougher, dirtier obscenities he imagines black men to embody. The raw sensualism he is after at Paradise Baths—the funkiness of black sex—he knows, aptly, less by sight than by scent. In Jesse, Metro is seeking out a "natural" blackness, a funk to confirm the half-savagery of black sex he needs to cast back at him a self-affirming shadow of his privileged and passably powerful white male self.

As Metro's compulsion grows ever more severe, and Jesse at last submits to his fantasies, the truth of the racial politics of desire driving Metro's kinky compulsions is orgasmically announced. "Take it baby. Take it all," gives way to a whiney "Give me what you are" (210) moments later. Exactly what Jesse is to him, Metro's climax cannot suppress. "Nigger" (113) slips off his tongue at the peak of pleasure so as to realize, it would seem, both the verbal and sexual irrepressibility of the ejaculation simultaneously. "What did you say?" asks Jesse, stunned. Brazenly, Metro answers, "I said, 'nigger'. . . . You wanted it low, didn't you? You wanted it dirty. . . . You wanted to ride the rough train, huh? Well, ride it, nigger." Metro's reply, of course, earns its own response. In a fury, Jesse springs wildly upon Metro, striking him. One body's defiance exercised against the power of another, Jesse expects all the while that Metro will return his rage, blow for blow. But much to his astonishment, Metro takes his licks, willingly, with dark pleasure. He "just lay there moaning and fighting the air" maniacally. "He wasn't fighting me [at all]. He wasn't even seeing me. He was pulling at himself. I stopped and watched him pulling and punching and pulling and punching again until he moaned again and stopped as abruptly as he had begun. The bed was wet, his groin was wet. His hands slippery with his own semen" (114). Metro's mad autoeroticism is a revelation to Jesse. Its self-flagellating display reveals something of the pain and pleasure involved in the ritual purgings of white identity by displacement "on the backs of blacks" (to borrow a phrase from Morrison). "I was his nigger," Jesse laments. "He called me nigger [because]. . . . I was something he couldn't stand in me or himself anymore" (128). Inasmuch as fetishism is their mutual infirmity, though, theirs is a double parasitism of sex belying race as the animating feature of their togetherness. Only through the difference accorded by race, after all, will either ever achieve the mundane out-of-body experience he is desperately seeking.

DANCE AND DECONSTRUCTION

Despite its particularities in *Vanishing Rooms*, trade between Metro and Jesse may not be far removed, finally, from the psychic reality of black and white men's contemporary lives. By realizing the homosocial/homosexual enactments of dread and desire which more broadly structure historic masculine identity, *Vanishing Rooms* proffers an imaginative critique of the unequal relations of power and desire produced by what Baldwin once called "the obscenity of color" within the broad span of male-to-male relations from combat to caring, from loathing to love. On the other hand, Dixon's emphasis on the recuperative potential of dance for the fetish-framed body is unfamiliar terrain to most of contemporary cultural criticism. In *Vanishing Rooms*, the black masculine reclaims itself, unfettered, in the dance. More specifically, it reclaims itself in a particular stylization of the gay black male body over ritualized time and space, which, following an important trope in Pierre Bourdieu's *Outline of a Theory of Practice*, I wish to call *improvisation*.

The formal distinction between choreographed performance (rehearsed dance) and improvisation (unrehearsed dance) in modern dance practice, is intentionally rejected in *Constructing the Black Masculine*. By improvisation I do not mean to invoke the unrehearsed performance specifically, but rather any motile expression, as Bourdieu would say, "play[ing] on the equivocations, innuendoes, and unspoken implications of verbal or gestural symbolism," any amount of which may be formalized in a choreography (rehearsed dance) or not.[32] More important than improvisation's physical exercise, however, are the interior deliberations over what Daniel Nagrin calls "the specific image"[33] that, in the dancer's mind, thematizes a performance and against which his improvisation asserts itself, oscillating, as Bourdieu writes in a different context, "between playfulness and seriousness, abandon and reserve, eagerness and indifference."[34] Problematically, black masculinity has for its "specific image," I argue, the picture of itself as it is misrecognized by racialists, an image that is virtual but not real. It is his virtual image, therefore, that alienates the black man from himself and for which improvisation, substituting *"strategy* for the *rule,"* seems an effectual antidote.[35]

Like Dixon's *Vanishing Rooms*, Langston Hughes's poem "Dream Variation" recognizes the resuscitative powers of the body in ritual motion. The second stanza follows:

> To fling my arms wide
> In the face of the sun
> Dance! Whirl! Whirl!
> Till the quick day is done
> Rest at pale evening . . .
> A tall, slime tree
> Night coming tenderly
> Black like me.[36]

Here, dance and desire conjoin as the romantic will to "fling my arms wide/ In the face of the sun/ Dance! Whirl! Whirl!/ Till the quick day is done" is also the will to a subject position that is, in the final analysis, as irrevocable as that "tall, slim tree," and as singular, of course, as "Black . . . me." One might imagine that the oneiric confession at the center of "Dream Variations" is a pronouncement of Hughes's hopefulness for "new stylistic options," repeating Cornel West, "for black men caught in the deadly endeavor of rejecting black machismo identity,"[37] options Hughes's dancing subject, like "Night coming tenderly," presumes to embody.

Hughes's biographer Arnold Rampersad has written that "Dream Variations," unlike other early Hughes poems, is "more contrived, though with a typically childlike, perhaps androgynous persona."[38] It is no surprise that Rampersad finds Hughes's dreamer "androgynous" since the whole choreographic repertoire, the flinging and the whirling, expands the otherwise narrow range of body improvisations currently available to black men. That a poet rather than a dancer could conceive of the greater possibilities for black masculine self-knowledge that lie in the dance (for the dancer's body-conscious mind) is not far-flung in the least. Before his death in 1989, choreographer Alvin Ailey recalled for his posthumously published autobiography *Revelations* that he and Hughes had become "good friends and often used to meet and talk, usually about music and dance—he was very fond of and knowledgeable about both."[39] Hughes had even given Ailey a few poems he hoped Ailey would put to choreography. Additionally, Hughes wrote at least one dance story. He called it "Seven People Dancing." It featured as its main character Marcel Smith, a queer Harlem epicure fond of dancing's sensual raptures. "Too fanciful to be masculine and too grotesque to be feminine," Marcel's dancing performed Rampersad's "androgynous persona" in prose.[40]

Although it is doubtful that "Seven People Dancing" or "Dream Variations" was included in the collection of works Hughes offered to Ailey, both pieces prefigure the promise of new discursive improvisations—perhaps paradigmatically androgynous ones—on what would be an otherwise dull masculinist theme.[41] In *Vanishing Rooms*, the promise of a new (black) masculinity conceived dialectically through dance is more fully realized.

The first dawning of redemption in *Vanishing Rooms*, in fact, occurs in a dance solo named after Billie Holiday's "Strange Fruit" which Jesse performs at Wesman's Spring Concert. His dance is his personal statement, he says, "of where I might go from this limited space of light and . . . movement" (102) as a (gay) black male under the public eye. Sweeping the stage "in a series of small, contracted movements in a circle," his body sweating "in the light that held [him] . . . tight . . . against the thick suggestion of night," Jesse becomes the fictional embodiment of what dance theorist Ramsay Burt refers to as dance's "restive and oppositional [resistance] to 'the body's placement within a system of power relations'" inimical to it.[42] Emblematically, Jesse's circular performance resists the boxy quadrangularity of the stage while his glistening body opposes the "thick suggestion of night" (102). Little wonder his dance bewildered so many spectators who "the next day . . . asked [him] what the dance meant" (102). Somewhat beyond verbal explanation, it enacted, in the best traditions of black dance, "an inner drama occurring on stage, . . . an activity of self-definition" in spite of its public exhibition.[43]

As with the other onlookers, Metro is also blind to the dance's depths of self-revelation. Like them, he cannot see beneath the sweaty spectacle gleaming under the spotlight the deeper constellation of tensions being dramatized in Jesse's performance. "Why did you choose that dance, Jesse? . . . why do you act like black people are the only ones oppressed?" (103). Although rankled by the arrogance of Metro's questions, Jesse won't be provoked: "Look Metro, I don't want to discuss it. It's my favorite Billie Holiday song and I wanted to dance" (103). This circumvention, a rhetorical dance-around, and Jesse's subsequent struggle to convincingly articulate for Metro his black difference, are not signs that between Jesse and Metro, both gay, their racial difference is negligible, however. Rather, Jesse's difficulty to get Metro to really see, and thus comprehend, his black particularity underscores his need to dance in the first place; for, quite apart from most other calisthentic arts, "dance functions," as one critic put it, "as a luminous symbol of *unspeakable* human truths."[44] It is "an ephemeral event whose immediate appeal *can never be captured in words.*" Jesse's eventual relent to Metro's objections in the argument that follows is thus more profoundly a capitulation to the logocentric prejudice that exalts verbal expression (the word as signifier) above body language (the gesture as signifier). As a result, Metro has little trouble convincing Jesse that their difference makes no difference at all: "We're faggots. Two faggots. That's what we are," he argues (103). Of course Jesse cannot dispute Metro. As a journalist, Metro naturally has the word on his side.

For the moment, Jesse gives up on his self-clarifying blues solo. For a while, Jesse and Metro are seen "danc[ing] together" (41). Their choreography, however, is much closer to slapstick than to a serious dance. Reconstructing their graduation-day antics, Jesse explains: "We tussled and danced in our gowns, hollering ourselves silly. I bowed to him. He pulled wide the edges of his sleeves and curtsied" (41). Later, they would leave Paradise Baths wobbling "like two dancing drunks, vying for balance" (3). But so frivolous and involuntary a production as this is far from gratifying for Jesse and, abandoning Metro on the pier near the baths to dance alone, he hurries off to the studio for practice in — of course — "improvisations" (4).

There, in class, Jesse partners with Ruella. If their duet only resembles Nagrin's, a choreography outlined and titled "A Duet" in Nagrin's *Dance and the Specific Image: Improvisation*, then the specific image before Jesse is not black and male anymore but black and female. In "A Duet," the dancers "dance looking at [their] partners and dancing about [their] partners, about his.her [*sic*] hair, clothing, personality traits, eyes — anything that gets your attention."[45] As Jesse dances "about" Ruella, it is the specific image of black womanhood with which he identifies and around which he improvises. As it is relatedly constructed in *Vanishing Rooms*, the black masculine is not so much opposed to the black feminine as it is symbiotically joined to it. This representation would seem to confirm Hortense Spillers when she writes that "the black American male embodies the only American which has had the specific occasion to learn who the female is within itself."[46] Jesse, at least, perceives this as well. He sees Ruella anew at improvisations. "She was pretty," he told himself. "And I knew right away through the dance of our black skins that if I didn't feel her full beauty, I'd never know my own" (197). Here Ruella fulfills in Jesse's self-image exactly what Metro, fighting the air, grieves.

Left alone on the pier, Metro is easy prey for the vicious mob who murders him. Although Jesse grieves bitterly for Metro, his grief is most certainly for himself as well. In a sudden reversal of circumstances, Metro's death leaves Jesse alone, as decidedly as Jesse had abandoned him by the river, to face the intolerable fact of blackness by himself. It is exactly this aloneness, though, that Jesse requires for the critical second dance of the novel, the pas de deux which liberates him at last from his fetish condition. Through Dixon's exercise of what Susan Leigh Foster calls "writing dancing," Jesse is transformed from the body-object of Metro's "rough love" (209) into a self-satisfied body-subject.[47] Jesse reclaims control over his body in a choreography that reimagines and redeems his relationship with Metro, discovering in the dance the possibility for a more authentic partnership with Metro than the racially inflected machinations of their former union allowed. In the process, Jesse overcomes the self-alienation of the surveilled body-object who "is [inevitably] made other to [himself] when [he] takes account of its appearance to others."[48] In the critical "dance for two men," Jesse's "Strange Fruit" solo is vindicated.

THE AUTOCHOREOGRAPHY OF AN EX-SNOW QUEEN

You think I'm going to please you, but I'm going to show you something we both have trouble looking at. It's in my legs and hips, my face filled with clouds passing to reveal the sun, and now clouds again, it's in my voice. Perhaps I am pretending, but this is my habitat, this place of illusion. — Bill T. Jones, *Last Night on Earth*

While *Vanishing Rooms* and Hughes's dance writings reveal some-thing vital about the symbolic effectuality of the kinetic body textu-ally, there are few articulations of the black man performatively "com-ing into being" more lucid than the genius choreographies of Bill T. Jones. Fortuitously, the correspondences between *Vanishing Rooms* and Jones's memoirs *Last Night on Earth* are striking. Reading *Last Night on Earth*, one has to fight the suspicion that it is Jones's life that *Vanishing Rooms* fictionalizes. The interracial romance, the bathhouse, and the solo dance performance of *Vanishing Rooms* all reappear in *Last Night on Earth* with uncanny similitude. However interesting these resem-blances may be, they are, in themselves, beside a much greater point. Whether or not Dixon's novel owes anything to Jones's memoirs (or Jones to Dixon's writing), the similarities permit the self-expressive limits of fiction to be transcended by the formal virtues of autochore-ography. With its combination of personal narrative, rhapsodic medita-tions, and choreographic note taking, *Last Night on Earth*, itself "a performance in text," illuminates *Vanishing Rooms*'s dance elements where literary analysis alone won't do.[49] Jones's compositional preoc-cupations following the 1988 death of his life partner Arnie Zane, clar-ify dance's subjectivizing function in *Vanishing Rooms*.

Probably no bona fide devotee of modern dance has not recognized Jones and Zane as the most visual pair in American modern dance. Few dance critics could resist discussing the stark physical contrast between Jones, "tall and black with an animal quality of movement," and Zane, "short and white with a nervous, pugnacious demeanor" (150). While there is no evidence in *Last Night* to suggest that Jones and Zane were drawn to one another, like Jesse and Metro, *because* of difference (who can rightly call these two false lovers who knew them?), it would be naïve to think that their partnership was not also sometimes vexed by racial difference, stereotype, and the seduction of fetishism. At its deep-est levels, Jones confesses, their relationship too was troubled by the demons of color and class.

In chapter seven of *Last Night*, "Amsterdam," Jones admits that the early stages of his relationship with Zane were difficult. "Our lovemak-ing and our fights took on a relentless dependency" (93). "Why does Arnie want so much?" Jones complained once to a therapist. "Why is he do business-minded? He's such a white man. He's such a Jew." "He's that way because you need him to be that way . . ." "Why do I feel used all the time?" "Because you are used. And why shouldn't you be used, since you refuse to use yourself?" (175). With his therapist's help, Jones recognized his own complicity in Zane's latent prejudice. Perhaps just as importantly, with Zane dying a slow AIDS-related death, Jones's therapist also helped him see a more genuine fear of losing Zane's bodily sanctuary/surrogacy as an incorrigible "white man" whom, Jones learns, he (Jones) "needs[s] . . . to be that way." Without Zane as collaborator and lover, Jones worried, as Jesse had, that he would lose emotional and artistic balance: "Tell me what to do, baby, I'm coming apart. You've always been the one telling me what to do" (174). Zane's rattled reply, "You'll figure it out," simple if unappeasing, was to prove prophetic. Like Jesse, Jones "figure[s] it out" in a dance.

It was only after Zane's death that Jones discovered his black masculine difference, his identity apart from the mutual dependency reflected in the all-too-familiar address "BillandArnie or ArnieandBill" (93) as friends had come to call them. In a 1992 *Transition* interview, Jones explained, "I felt very much how my world had changed when Arnie was no longer there: the work began to speak more as that of a black man. And of a gay man, too, because there was reason to."[50] As someone "who never really had to be a black artist until that other member was dead,"[51] Jones looked more purposefully to black dance once Zane was gone. What he discovered there was a consoling "tension" that not only kept him from coming apart, but challenged the smug aesthetics of white avant-gardism he and Zane had long opposed.[52] Taking full choreographic advantage of the dialectical themes of black cultural production, Jones came to realize that beyond the binary emphasis on black and white, slave and master, Africa and America common to black aesthetic practices, attention to "the mysterious intimacy between audience and performer" (164) was also vital to the processes of decolonizing the black arts. Just as crucial for Jones's career since then has been the importance of decolonizing the black male body as well.

From Jones's earliest solo performances, his critics have been consistently overwhelmed by his dark, elegant musculature. One white female critic, "*deeply* regretting the fact that he [was] gay," spoke suggestively, even wistfully, of Jones's "long limbs, the trim but defined muscles, [and] the rich mocha sheen of his skin."[53] Jones himself has never been unaware of his allure. As Henry Louis Gates Jr. wrote in 1994, "Jones . . . has an acute sense of [his] physicality." Describing himself as having the face of "a young prizefighter, with intelligent eyes, sensitive mouth, lips not too thick, nose not too flared . . . [and] an ass that is too high but firm like a racehorse,"[54] Jones's picture of himself suggests the dual nature of his performance style and compositional intent "to challenge the implicit ritualism of performance, acknowledge its boundaries and subvert them" (164). Young, intelligent, and sensitive, on the one hand, Jones's solos following Zane's death were consistently "coupled with [the kind of] wild anger and belligerence" that typifies the prizefighter or anxious stallion.[55] All along his strategy has estranged the spectator's gaze, never ingratiating it. Participating in his own fetishization in order, finally, to subvert and transcend it, Jones "does not disavow the gaze of white fascination: he works within it, plays with it," and, to recall his therapist's advice, "*uses* it."[56] And as Jones explains in *Last Night*, he has often "opted for improvisation to accomplish this" (164). In this way, "I [have been] able to deconstruct [my own] identity," Jones writes. "Deconstruction [has] yielded solos that [are] confessional, often painful, taking unpleasant emotions and exposing them spontaneously in a fashion that [is] brutal on both the audience and me" (165).

From Jones's "largely improvised solo" (165) at the American Dance Festival in 1981, the first of his self-consciously antagonizing performances, to his 1992 choreography "Last Night on Earth" and beyond, Jones has taken for his philosophy of performance what cultural theorist Michael Taussig calls "the magic of mimesis" — the notion that "in some way or another one can protect oneself from evil spirits by portraying them."[57] That is, by portraying the fetish image in his choreography, Jones gains "power over that which is portrayed,"[58] demystifying it and "out-fetishizing the fetish."[59] "Last Night on Earth," a solo composition which casts Jones as "the possibility of Eros" (238), typifies his deconstructive strategy.

Scantily clad in "a short white skirt — a tunic really" (239), obscuring gender and history with a single garment, Jones's leaps and jumps expose "a glistening sequined codpiece and [his] naked ass" (239), which flash the audience indiscreetly (Fig. 16). Then, playfully, Jones "cast[s] a coy glance at the audience, as if I were Marilyn Monroe," he explains, "in her lace bustier, teasing a bit of cleavage" (239). More duplicitous than playful, however, Jones's "glance" defies his audience with a resistant look that is not only an ocular challenge to the consolidated gaze (*le regard*) of the enchanted, but a proprioceptive self-display as well.[60] In classic vogue fashion, Jones strikes a cross-gendered, cross-racial pose

Figure 16. Beatriz Schiller, Bill T. Jones in "Last Night on Earth"

imitative of the photographic look (*l'image*) of Marilyn Monroe, whose voluptuous image is precisely that which black men, it is alleged, desire most to ravish. Whether the defiance in Jones's look (as opposed to the look of Monroe being mimicked) lies principally in the coquetry of the eyes or in his simulation of Monroe "teasing a bit of cleavage," it is clear that the dance undertakes to seduce the audience into the erotic fantasy Jones is (de)constructing on stage:

> I roll from standing to all fours, grip an imaginary partner, and thrust two times aggressively with my pelvis. I roll, repeat the rutting action, stop, stare at the audience, caught in the act, then continue with vehemence.
>
> I am dancing about fucking. Unfettered fucking. Obscene, joyous, wildly defiant, desperate fucking.

The song is over. The mood changes as I fall to the floor, allowing the audience to see me breathing heavily, clearly fatigued.

I am not a god, I am a man. (239)

While "Last Night on Earth" is a solo, the "fucking" fantasy he enacts in this choreography involves more than one persona. Jones realizes in his dance a colonial fantasy always already present in the white spectatorial gaze, which his stare is intended to disrupt. As Jones lures the audience into imaginary erotic play, they too are "caught in the act," publicly confronted by the very fetish image of black male sexuality they have privately held in their racialist minds. Jones projects their guilt before them, entrapping them within the racial fictions of their own scopic imaginations by seizing a sex partner on stage they cannot see but must eidectically imagine. Just whom each spectator "sees" Jones "fucking" so feverishly—another man or a woman, a black persona or a white one—will inevitably vary, but his or her participation in the fantasy produced by "Last Night on Earth" is invariable. Whomever it is the spectator imagines in the sex act with Jones, Jones's look suggests that he imagines he is "fucking" the spectator "with no consequence," as the colonial fantasy gets revisited on its authors with "unfettered . . . obscene . . . wildly defiant" abandon.

Perhaps only through what Gates references as "a language that is parsed by the configuration and movement of bodies" can a black man, by an aggressive improvisation on the very stereotypes that objectify and restrict his subjective possibilities (eros, for instance), ever hope to escape the unbearable psychic and social stigmas attached to him.[61] Such language, of course, needn't be that of dance only. As Jesse discovers in *Vanishing Rooms*, the expressive language of black male corporeality is "everywhere":

I watched black men everywhere for movement: in barbershops, on street corners, some reading the *New York Times*, some going in and out of expensive hotels by the front door and some by the service entrance. And I watched myself: my bend of waist while making the bed, washing dishes, stretching on the parquet floor. And I watched [my new lover] Rodney without him knowing it. . . . I saw his grace, his sureness and poise of movement. . . . I watched black Wall Street executives leaping from taxis and the man selling subway tokens near our block. I watched the kids playing handball against the supermarket wall and under the sign reading "No Ball Playing." I watched black boys dribbling imaginary basketballs while waiting to take the subway to the next playground. And some balancing real basketballs while riding in the car. (198)

Jesse's study of black men moving within and across gender, class, sexual, and physical boundaries underscores the deep structures of dance in black men's everyday lives, their particular stylizations of bodiliness, their improvisations on white American themes of subalternity. In this context, it is not difficult to see why dancing is so crucial to Jesse's representational self-recovery. Only through the deconstructive power of dance, can Jesse extricate himself from the self-abnegating "porno-house of language"[62] into which "black nigger faggot" has immolated him. His dance for two men, one black, the other white, recasts his poisoned relationship with Metro, his "underground man," in the redeeming light of a new choreography fitly performed to Duke Ellington's "A-Train." Having recognized his own difference in the lived collage of black men around him, Jesse understands by novel's end, that he, as Jones concludes, "can't even quite begin to position [himself] in the world matrix without taking into account the issue of [his] humanity as a black man."[63] Like Jones, too, Jesse comes to subjective self-knowledge, too much aware of his body's sensual and serpentine powers to be merely an object among other objects anymore.

Vanishing Rooms concludes with Jesse's pas de deux in performance. Symbolizing the culmination of his quest for black masculine subjecthood, Jesse's choreography, "the opportunity for improvisation in the rhythm, the solo, and personal statement" (199), takes him "someplace else" (200) other than the "filthy abandoned warehouse where the single word 'nigger' has already sealed [Metro's] fate" (197) and nearly his. When the performance ends, the hush of the theater erupts "into a gathering wave of hands clapping. Pools of sweat dotted the stage. The applause showered over me. . . . Then quickly, the [hall] burst into light, and the room holding us there vanished" (211). The baptismal resonances of "wave," "pools," "showered," and "light" underscore the psychic transformation the dance has inspired in Jesse.

While Dixon's portrayal of Jesse's "A-Train" choreography is colorful and spirited ("Wheels of legs spinning, leaping. Tiny runs ending in arabesque. Turn-two-three, plié-two-three. Relevé" [209]), it is brief, only a few lines long, and those who lack an appreciation for dance movement may still fail to visualize it. I suspect, however, that Bill T. Jones's

"Last Night on Earth" as well as the choreographic compositions "Absence," "Forsythia," "Achilles Loved Patroclus," "Fever Swamp" (for the Alvin Ailey Repertory Company), and his own "Pas de Deux for Two" may help us have a clearer vision of Dixon's novel and what it really means to be a black man under the public gaze in America.

A FILMIC FINALE

Bill T. Jones, of course, is only one touchstone among many for reading dance in *Vanishing Rooms*. Alongside the works of Ronald K. Brown ("Life Lesson"), Dwight Rhoden ("Black or White"), and David Rousseve ("The Whispering of Angels"), the vintage choreography of Talley Beatty merits special mention. One of the original Dunham dancers, a student of Martha Graham and one of Balanchine's first black pupils, Beatty collaborated with avant-garde filmmaker Maya Deren in 1945 to create the short film *A Study in Choreography for Camera*. In this silent experimental picture, a camera pursues Beatty chasséing through the woods. Svelte in movement and solemn in mood, no dance could be more antithetical to the racist caricature of the native African in his jungled environs. With tall, supple leaps, Beatty's dance defies the limits of the cinematic frame, conjoining such disjunctive dialectical planes as here/there, now/later, outside/inside, public/private. Connecting open woodland to the narrow architecture of studio and art gallery, he bridges the filmic geography with fluid, continuous agility, making "neighbors of distant places"[64] (fig. 17). His spins and turns beguile as his sable figure "cut[s] loose from the anchorage of a fixed center" of representational space and visual locatability.[65] While choreocritic Mary Lloyd was not necessarily incorrect to point out in *The Borzoi Book of Modern Dance* the potential "sorcellérie" Deren's camera might exercise on its black dancing subject, to fail to see Beatty as working a considerable amount of his own — shall we say — black magic is shortsighted. In *A Study of Choreography for Camera*, turning becomes transcendence and Beatty's leaps, "a sort of universal wish fulfillment to navigate the air"[66] and elude fetish-arrest under the micro-scopic lens of this (even temporally restricted) three-minute short.

Beatty's little-known collaboration with Deren is undoubtedly among the most important prefiguring works of late twentieth-century black male performance art. With the works of Juba, Jones, Brown, Rhoden, and Rousseve, it may yet have lessons to teach us about the

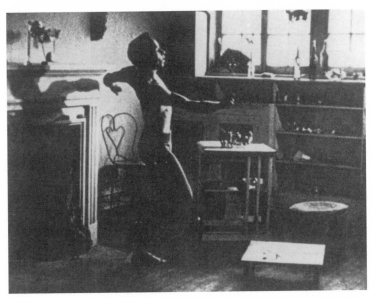

Figure 17. Maya Deren, still of Tally Beatty in *A Study in Choreography for Camera*. Here Beatty's shadow, falling away from the frame's "homely" center of gravity, renders visible an alternative reality of black masculine interiority that defies enframement and subverts the spectragraphic condition in its intimate, not othered, ghostliness.

theory and practice of black masculinist production. For, as Eric Hawkins has written, "A man dancing will have to go far beyond entertainment. A man dancing will have to stand for what a man can become."[67] This is the hope of Melvin Dixon's *Vanishing Rooms* and the promise so many dancing black men are still struggling to realize.

"What Ails You Polyphemus?"

Toward a New Ontology of Vision

in Frantz's Fanon's *Black Skin White Masks*

SON OF POSEIDON! YOU OBSCENE OCTOPUS! YOU TON OF SQUID-
SHIT, WITH YOUR EYE POURING BLACK INK! MY NAME IS NOT NO-
BODY! IT'S ODYSSEUS! AND LEARN, YOU BLOODY TYRANTS, THAT
MEN CAN STILL THINK! — Derek Walcott, *The Odyssey: A Stage Version*

"For those of us who can see, vision is, of all the modes of perception, the one which is primary and predominant, at least in the conduct
of our everyday lives." These are the words of David Michael Levin as
written in the introduction to his 1993 collection of philosophical essays, *Modernity and the Hegemony of Vision*.[1] That the recognizable truth
of everyday life articulated in modern philosophy seem always to be
couched in visual terms ("the truth is the light," "the mind's eye," "I
see" in lieu of "I understand") is a phenomenon so obvious that, until
Friedrich Nietzsche, it hardly seemed worth mentioning.

Nietzsche was the first among modern philosophers to decry
the privileged, constitutive status of ocularcentric methods of post-
Enlightenment philosophical inquiry. According to Levin, Nietzsche
attacked the monocular impulses in *The Will to Power* and *Genealogy of
Morals*, "turn[ing] the very logic of ocularcentrism against itself, alter-
ing forever the visionary ambitions of [modern] philosophy."[2] In the
twentieth century, Heidegger, Foucault, Sartre, and Derrida have all
pursued Nietzsche's lead. Each has argued, in his discrete way, that "the
thought and culture of modernity" have not only ennobled ocularcentrism but have "allowed its worst tendencies to dominate . . . in . . .
distinctively modern way[s]."[3] I want to suggest that implicit in *Black
Skin White Masks* (and in at least one instance explicit in Fanon) is still
another modernist critique of ocularcentrism, one which recognizes

the emphatically modern character of twentieth-century racial reasoning and its deep reliance in modernity on stereotype and fetishism, themselves nothing so much as fantasies of absolute difference induced by a kind of "reckless eyeballing" on the skin.

Black Skin White Masks contains not just one critique, but a powerful double critique of scopophilia in the modern age: the first is a critique of the everyday habits of seeing in racialized societies, "a matter," as Ralph Ellison wrote, "of the construction of [a set of] inner eyes . . . with which racialists look through their physical eyes upon reality" (*Invisible Man*, 3). A manner of "seeing," in other words, which subordinates the will to physically see (*voir*), as Derrida points out, to the will to meta-physically know (*savoir*), however crudely or reductively, and ultimately to the will to power (*pouvoir/puissance*).[4] The second critique of ocularcentrism extends, as Heidegger's, Foucault's, Sartre's and Derrida's do rather explicitly, from Nietzsche's complaints about philosophical monocularity. It is a critique of the hegemony of vision not only in philosophical discourse but, anticipating Foucault's panopticism, within institutions and administrations of governmentality, systems in which the dialectic hazards of the human gaze, those perpetuated by the charms of ocularcentric rationality, are worsened by formalized technologies of (super)vision. In Fanon, the designedly obscure machinations of the colonial "look of surveillance" are brought to light by a look of countersurveillance on the arresting eye of colonial power, now the object of a disruptive ocular mimicry.[5] More elaborately put,

> The principle counter-strategy [of *Black Skin White Masks*] has been to bring to the surface — into representation — that which has sustained the regimes of representation unacknowledged: to subvert the structures of "othering" in language and representation [and] image . . . and thus to turn the [ocular] mechanisms of fixed racial signification against themselves, in order to begin to constitute new subjectivities, new positions of enunciation and identification.[6]

And, not surprisingly, a new ontology of vision. Fanon follows Nietzsche, then, whose anti-ocularcentrism, Levin observes, "is itself ocularcentric." However, "this sense of the term could not be more at odds with the sense in which the thinking of (say) Plato, Descartes, and Husserl may be described as ocularcentric," he writes. "For . . . Nietzsche is effectively using an ocular metaphorics derived from the tradition to subvert the authority of ocular thinking."[7] The microphysics, one might say, of Fanon's vaguely Nietzschean subversion are most lucidly revealed in two defining scenes Bhabha has distinguished as "primal scenes . . . two myths of the origin of the marking of the subject within the racist practices and discourses of colonial culture."[8] Both scenes are animated by the coefficiency of "the pleasure of 'seeing,' which has the look as its object of desire" and "the problematic of fetishism."[9] With a view toward deconstructing the monocular menace of everyday modern life and philosophical discourse, and unmasking the perils of panopticism in the colonial setting, Fanon, I intend to demonstrate, escapes a fate like that befallen the philosopher in Derek Walcott's stage version of *The Odyssey*:

> CYCLOPS: How many've I eaten?
> ODYSSEUS: Of my crew? Just two. . . .
> Two of my crew and one philosopher.
> (*The Cyclops is picking his teeth*)
> CYCLOPS: Is this him? No more ideas. Last of his kind.[10]

My concern with the ocular in Fanon is grounded, though, in not just two, but three primal moments in *Black Skin White Masks*, moments, to invoke the irony of Bhabha's acoustic metaphor, endlessly echoed throughout the book, but especially resonant in the chapter "The Fact of Blackness." Let me focus attention on the first two of these, the two dramatic scenes of fetishism identified by Bhabha, before going on to argue for the indispensability of the third—a passionate, if still not yet primal, reverie of visual vengeance—somewhat later on. For now, I want to reflect on the ocular impulse in the earlier moments as re-capitulating what Levin calls "the assertoric gaze," that rigid, inflexible, monocular, egocentric look of objectification and, finally, conquest im-plicitly regulating difference in the confrontational opposition of self and other, subject and object.[11]

The first of the two crucial primal scenes, a small white child rushes to her mother's side, frightened by the look of the black man passing nearby. In the second scene, a hysteric boy, similarly frightened by Fanon himself, scurries to his mother's side for cover. "Mama see the Negro! I'm frightened!" is the girl's frenzied cry. "Look a nigger . . . Mama a Negro! . . . he's getting mad," is the nervous shriek of the boy. In both cases, a certain bequeathed manner of seeing provokes the children's terror. What they see in Fanon, in other words, is less a faithful picture of the Other than a "simulacrum of sensible visibility," to lift a phrase from Derrida, the trust of which reveals considerably less about the object of terror than it does about the propensity of white subjects to view black bodies as blank pages for the projection of white fears and desires.[12] Writes Fanon:

> My body was given back to me sprawled out, distorted, recolored, clad in mourning in [*sic*] that white winter day. The Negro is an animal, the Negro is bad, the Negro is mean, the Negro is ugly; look, a nigger, it's cold, the nigger is shivering, the nigger is shivering because he is cold, the little boy is trembling because he is afraid of the nigger, the nigger is shivering with cold, . . . the handsome little boy is trembling because he thinks that the Negro is quivering with rage, the little white boy throws himself into his mother's arms: Mama, the nigger's going to eat me up! . . . I sit down at the fire and I become aware of my uniform. I had not seen it. It is indeed ugly. I stop therefore, for who can tell me what beauty is?[13]

Here the assertoric gaze of the handsome boy "enframes" the troubled black body of the native in that unique Heideggerian sense that takes enframing (*das Gestell*) to signify the cultural tendency to submit to increasingly "reified . . . distorted . . . and destructively fixated" perceptions of self and others.[14] That the gazing little boy cannot perceive the "nigger" shivering, despite the logic of temperature, only quivering with black rage, confirms the monocular condition which I take to be emblematic of the difficulty racialists have of "seeing" black subjects clearly. That the native subject, his body divided from the self, suffers "sprawled out, distorted, [and] recolored" suggests how dangerously reductive, how mortally wounding, the machinations of colonial enframing can be.

Fanon's second primal scene recalls Edmund Burke's illustration of why blackness is terrible in its own nature (part IV, section XV of *A Philosophical Enquiry into the Origin of our Ideas of the Sublime and the Beautiful*).[15] Therein Burke relates the curious account of a cataracted English boy, blind very nearly since birth, who at thirteen or fourteen had his sight surgically restored. When the boy saw "a black object" for the first time, the story goes, "it gave him great uneasiness." Then, some time later, upon "accidentally seeing a Negro woman," "he was struck with great horror at the sight."[16] Burke supposes that the child's great horror is the natural operation of blackness qua darkness as a visual impression. Fanon's unmotivated revision of Burke reveals not only a kind of lingering blindness in the boy but also a willful blindness on the part of racialists like Burke to "see," as it were, the other/Other's side. Who, after all, has thought to consider what terror the so-called Negro woman must certainly have experienced, her objecthood redoubled by the look itself and the psychic backdrop of whatever "black object" first gave the little boy "uneasiness"? Certainly not Burke and few, Du Bois notwithstanding, quite like Fanon. (Of course, as film and cultural critic Lola Young has shown, the revision may disclose nothing so paradoxical as Fanon's own anoptic indifference to "the fantasies and images of black women which may inform white men's perceptions of black female sexuality."[17])

With an impulse toward the autobiographical, Fanon rewrites Burke from the point of view of the looked-on object (i.e., the thing-itself), depicting starkly what terrible risks of self-alienation lie in the irreconcilability of subject/object double-consciousness, that peculiar and painful manner, you will recall from Du Boisian thought, "of always looking at one's self through the eyes of others."[18] Hear Fanon: "On that day, completely dislocated, unable to be abroad with the other, the white man, who unmercifully imprisoned me, I took myself far off from my own presence, far indeed and make *myself* an object. What else could it be for me but an amputation, an excision, a hemorrhage that spattered my whole body with black blood?" (112). With Fanon, double-consciousness is not the "gift" it is curiously described as in Du Bois. It is a more perilous condition, the ominous potential of which is the development of a self-abnegating "third-person conscious-ness" (110), the condition of being "sealed into . . . crushing object-hood" (109) with little hope for its transcendence.

By the conclusion of *Black Skin White Masks*, however, Fanon him-self is liberated from the absolute look fixing him in the racist represen-tation of the colonial imaginary: "I try to read admiration in the eyes of others," he says, "and, if, unluckily, those eyes show me an unpleasant reflection, I find that mirror flawed. Unquestionably that other is a fool . . . I am the Hero" (212). But one does not become a hero simply by saying it. In each of the first two critical scenes which ground this epilogue's contemplations, one discerns Fanon's double critique of ocularcentrism in the reflexes of resistance invested in them. The cri-tique is accomplished in a maneuver I prefer to think of, in consonance with the theatrical project represented by Derek Walcott's stage version

of *The Odyssey*, as "acting out," a strategy for the subversion of fetishism and stereotype in which the colonized cause a scene, as not to be
trapped, framed, within one. Following immediately upon the heels of
the two primal scenes of white fright, Fanon recounts overhearing a
passerby remark, "Look how handsome that Negro is!" (114). Trembling again, the "handsome" Martiniquan is no longer shivering, however. Hot and indignant now, he is quivering with rage: "Kiss the
handsome Negro's ass, madame!" he answers. In ire, "I accomplished
two things," Fanon asserts. "I identified my enemies" and having made
this one believe he was shivering as part of his ruse, "*I made a scene*"
(114; emphasis added). Fanon's somatic free play within the linguistic
différance obtaining between signifiers "shivering" (as with cold tem-
peratures) and "quivering" (as with rage) in these juxtaposed episodes
(re)enacts, or acts out of, the fixed frames through which white eyes
look on the trembling black man. He is, as Bhabha once invited us to
consider, "working the difference"[19] (or, in this case at least, the *différance*) obtaining in the interstices between referents. He is, in a
phrase, "acting out." Of course this play of signifiers is particular to the
English translation since both "quiver" and "shiver" are rendered *trem-
bler* in the French. That the French translation does not attempt any
differentiation between causalities of Fanon's dis-ease, however, only
goes to show that the play or acting out does not depend on written or
even spoken language finally—indeed, these are part of the colonial
problem to Fanon—but on the ability of body language to so easily
escape the grasp of them both, to render, in short, ambivalence.

The idea of acting out of the fixed frames of racist representation
imposed by the monocular look of the individual or the absolute look
of institutional technologies derives its use here from Bhabha's observation that Fanon's "theatrical metaphor—the scene . . . emphasizes the
visible—the seen."[20] But, too, and perhaps more fundamentally, it is
inspired by Fanon's very real dramaturgical concerns between 1946 and
1950 just prior to his professional training in medicine and psychiatry.
In that period, between a three-year enlistment in the regular French
army during the Second World War and medical studies at the Faculté
de Médicine in Lyons, France, Fanon, who according to one early
biographer "enjoyed dramatic situations," also "began to think about
a career in drama."[21] Influenced by the existentialist productions of
Sartre, and, quite probably by the creative sensibilities of his early
mentor Aimé Césaire as well, Fanon composed three pieces for the

theater, *Parallel Hands* [*Les Mains parallèles*], *The Drowning Eye* [*L'Oeil se noie*], and *The Conspiracy* [*La Conspiration*] during the years 1948 through 1950.[22] Although none of the three plays was ever published, biographer Peter Geismar supposed that all three were "leftist existential works," "highly melodramatic," and, therefore, "not suitable for publication."[23] Geismar speculates that "Fanon grew away from them and preferred that they remained buried."[24] While he dismisses Fanon's plays as mere hand exercises for the alleviation of medical school ennui, I maintain that these obscure compositions, written in the same period that *Black Skin White Masks* was under draft,[25] are far too significant to be negligible in the bibliography of Fanon's writings and evidence a theatrical predisposition weighing upon *Black Skin White Masks*. Differently put, if one imagines Fanon's career along a vocational trajectory from soldier to aspiring dramatist to psychiatrist to the intellectual Jacobin of *Wretched of the Earth*, then *Black Skin White Masks*, published in 1952, is to be plotted just as near to the early, post–World War II Fanon — dreamy and artistically bent — as to Fanon, the clinician. *Black Skin White Masks* is a transitional text, then, neither wholly disconnected from Fanon's theatrical ambitions nor fully formed as a prescriptive document.

Fanon's repeated reference to the drama's "scenes" of encounter between native and colonist, tending as they always do to privilege the visual ("My body was given back to me sprawled out, distorted, recolored, clad in the mourning in that white winter day"), is not serendipitous. "The drama" (*le drame*) posits in the colonial context something very near to the anthropological theorist Victor Turner's conception of "social drama" or, alternatively, Clifford Geertz's notion of "the drama analogy of social life." Both performativist phrases signify a phenomenon in which "the state enacts an image of order that — a model for its beholders, in and of itself — orders society."[26] Under this influence, "the populace at large does not merely view the state's expressions as so many gaping spectators," Geertz says. Instead, the populace is "caught up bodily in them." That most of Fanon's critics have thought of *le drame* of the colonial encounter in *Black Skin White Masks* in purely psychoanalytic terms fails to "see" how vital theatrical language (and, from time to time, the theatrical genre) is to Fanon's explicit project of exposing the "'mere show,'" the psychic "masks and mummery" of everyday life under colonialism's scopic regime, which has everyone, colonizer and colonized alike, "caught up bodily" in it.[27] Of course, the problem faced by the black man in Fanon's text is that he gets not only caught up in the social drama of colonial Martinique; he gets fixed in it, and in more ways than one: "What else could it be for me but an amputation, an excision, a hemorrhage that spattered my whole body with black blood?" (112). Subjectivization is dialectical *and* phallic.

Although the reciprocal look necessary for dialectical subjectivization seems not to be an apparent feature of the two important primal scenes discussed earlier, a third moment in *Black Skin White Masks*'s critique of the hegemony of monocular vision does. I repeat the scene from the chapter "Negro and Psychopathology" below:

> The Negro . . . gives off no aura of sensuality . . . It is just that over a series of long days and long nights the image of the biological-sexual-sensual-genital-nigger has imposed himself on [the European] and [he] does not know how to get free of it. The eye is not merely a mirror, but a correcting mirror. The eye should make it possible for us to correct cultural errors. I do not say the eyes, I say the eye and there is no mystery about what that eye refers to; not to the crevice in the skull, but to that very uniform light that wells out of the reds of Van Gogh, that glides through a concerto of Tchaichowsky, that fastens itself desperately to Schiller's *Ode to Joy*, that allows itself to be conveyed by the worm-ridden bawling of Césaire. (201–202)

With this, it is clear that Fanon is not calling for the end of ocularity in *Black Skin White Masks*, but the end of monocularity, a metaphor for a single mode of colonial (super)vision maintained in the evil eye of objectification. Although he indeed speaks of "the eye" and shuns "the eyes," it is to distinguish anatomy from metaphysics. Fanon's "eye" is hardly monocular in the ordinary sense; taking in depth and color and structures of feeling, it is capable of a multiplicity of perspectives, is heterocular, and therefore compels nothing of the absolute look of monocularity, but produces a kind of visual carnival. It realizes an authentically diasporic manner of seeing, in other words, which guides the eye toward a more ethical orientation of seeing the not-self than the master/slave, subject/object, black/white, colonizer/colonized, either/or paradigm can accomplish. Just as importantly, Fanon's "eye" is, as he says, "a mirror," a "corrective mirror" specifically, endlessly refracting, reversing, and double-crossing the spectatorial space.

As I read it, *Black Skin White Masks* calls for a new ontology of sight, one which liberates slave from master and master from himself. This new ontology of sight, however, is not only about vision (*voir*); it is also an epistemology and a politics. It is about new productions of knowledge (*savoir*), new relations of power (*pouvoir/puissance*). What ails Polyphemus is precisely the monocularist's loss of the tyrant's power; in *The Odyssey*, monocular vision betrays the fiction of its own omniscience, as the cyclops Polyphemus, taking our hero too much at face value, discovers finally that monocular vision actually sees "nhbdy" at all. I prefer to think of Fanon and *Black Skin White Masks* as belonging to a similarly Odyssean tradition, one which leaves, like the scar Homer describes on Polyphemus's head, a "black wound" in the monocular vision of race and representation by which colonial power endures postcolonially.

> Concern with elimination of a vicious circle has been the only guideline for my efforts. . . . I believe that the individual should tend to take on the universality inherent in the human condition. (10)

INTRODUCTION

1　René Girard, *Deceit, Desire, and the Novel: Self and Other in Literary Structure*, trans. Yvonne Freccero (Baltimore: Johns Hopkins Univ. Press, 1976); Gayle Rubin, "The Traffic in Women: Notes toward a Political Economy of Sex" in *Toward an Anthropology of Women*, ed. Rayna R. Reiter (New York: Monthly Review Press, 1975), 157–210; Sigmund Freud, *The Standard Edition of the Complete Psychological Works of Sigmund Freud*, trans. James Strachey (London: Hogarth, 1953–74).

2　That is, inasmuch as the word "homosocial," a neologism that "describes [ostensibly nonsexual] social bonds between persons of the same sex," obtains by inescapable analogy with the "dread" of "homosexual," it is never entirely free, try as it might, from what Sedgwick calls "the orbit of [erotic] 'desire.' " Eve Kosofsky Sedgwick, *Between Men: English Literature and Male Homosocial Desire* (New York: Columbia Univ. Press, 1985), 1.

3　Hortense Spillers, "Who Cuts the Borders? Some Readings on 'America,' " in *Comparative American Identities: Race, Sex, and Nationality in the Modern Text*, ed. Spillers (New York: Routledge, 1991), 12.

4　Robyn Wiegman, *American Anatomies: Theorizing Race and Gender* (Durham, N.C.: Duke Univ. Press, 1995), 11. Emphasis Wiegman's.

5　Arthur Flannigan Saint-Aubin, "Testeria: The Dis-ease of Black Men in White Supremacist, Patriarchal Culture," *Callaloo* 17, 4 (1994): 1056.

6　Ibid.

7　This is not to say, of course, that there were not a few important works on American manhood prior to 1980. I concur with Bryce Traister, for example, that "the origins of the new American heteromasculinity studies . . . might [in fact] begin with Leslie Fiedler's *Love and Death in the American Novel*" published in 1960 (276). Traister also notes Joseph Cawelti's *Apostles of the Self-Made Man* (1965) and Joe Dubbert's *A Man's Place: Masculinity in Transition* (1979) as significant harbingers of contemporary masculinity studies scholarship. I might add to Traister's record Calvin Hernton's *Sex and Racism in America* (1965). See Bryce Traister, "Academic Viagra: The Rise of American Masculinity Studies," *American Quarterly* 52, 2 (2000): 274–304.

8　The suspicion in which many African Americanists, Africanists and postcolonialists hold the universalist pretensions of poststructuralism is not lost on this writer. I contend, however, that black and other diasporic intellectual traditions, notwithstanding the frequently alienating idiom in which poststructuralism tends to convey itself, has not gone untouched by so many theories of difference on modern black and postcolonial thinkers, especially in ethnographic and psychoanalytic reflections (see chapter 3 on race and psychoanalysis). Truth be told, certain black cultural theorists (e.g. Du Bois, Hurston, Ellison, Fanon) even anticipated certain poststructuralist ideas. Inasmuch, then, as "deconstruction, for example, seemed . . . an extension (within the dominant discourse) of the project of those already engaged in Afro-American or Black Studies — the project of theorizing about difference, absence, presences, and oppositionality," as Wahneema Lubiano has observed, it may not be unreasonable that the potential revelatory power of poststructuralism owes a secretly kept debt to the originary insights of black cultural and postcolonial studies on "diffference, absence, presences, and oppositionality." Whatever the case, I am certain, at least, of this: Only by bringing poststructuralism to bear on black subjects can the truths and lies of its universalist claims ever be finally judged. See Wahneema Lubiano, "Mapping the Interstices between Afro-American Cultural Discourse and Cultural Studies: A Prolegomenon," 19, 1 (1996): 68–77.

9   Because I am concerned with book-length critical studies principally, I will merely note the briefer but important exceptions of Kobena Mercer and Isaac Julien, "Race, Sexual Politics, and Black Masculinity: A Dossier," in *Male Order: Unwrapping Masculinity*, ed. Rowena Chapman and Jonathan Rutherford (London: Lawrence and Wishart, 1988), 97–164; bell hooks, "Reconstructing Black Masculinity" in *Black Looks: Race and Representation*, by hooks (Boston: South End Press, 1992), 87–113; bell hooks, "Representation: Feminism and Black Masculinity" in *Yearning: Race, Gender, and Cultural Politics*, by hooks (Boston: South End Press, 1990), 65–77; and Cornel West, "Black Sexuality: The Taboo Subject" in *Race Matters*, by West (New York: Beacon, 1993), 117–31.

10   To speak of the "b(l)ackside" of masculine identity in the West is, first, to speak metaphorically of the hidden (i.e. the *back*side) dimension of race which is, on the one hand, inextricable from our contemporary discourse about masculinity, yet severely neglected on the other hand. Because of the prevailing "whiteness" of scholarship on masculinity, the back- or unfamiliar side is also necessarily the *black*side; hence, the interpolation of the parenthetical *l* to the *b(l)ackside* of this discourse is de rigueur. Finally, the b(l)ackside of masculinity is meant to evoke black men's anatomical b(l)acksides because men's homosocial/homosexual relations, black and white, seem so critically governed by both/either a dread and/or desire for anality.

11   Hazel V. Carby, *Race Men* (Cambridge, Mass.: Harvard Univ. Press, 1998); Phillip Brian Harper, *Are We Not Men? Masculine Anxiety and the Problem of African-American Identity* (New York: Oxford Univ. Press, 1996); Michael Awkward, *Negotiating Difference: Race, Gender, and the Politics of Positionality*

(Chicago: Univ. of Chicago Press, 1995); Henry Louis Gates Jr., *Thirteen Ways of Looking at a Black Man* (New York: Random House, 1997); and Maggie Montesinos Sale, *The Slumbering Volcano: American Slave Ship Revolts and the Production of Rebellious Masculinity* (Durham, N.C.: Duke Univ. Press, 1997).

Also noteworthy for its specifically queer theorization of the performative inflections of black and brown masculinities in the United States is José Esteban Muñoz's terrific *Disidentifications: Queers of Color and the Performance of Politics* (Minneapolis: Univ. of Minnesota Press, 1999).

12 Marcellus Blount and George P. Cunningham, eds., *Representing Black Men* (New York: Routledge, 1996); Toni Morrison and Claudia Brodsky Lacour, eds., *Birth of a Nation'hood: Gaze, Script, and Spectacle in the O. J. Simpson Case* (New York: Random House, 1998); Devon Carbado, ed., *Black Men on Race, Gender, and Sexuality: A Critical Reader* (New York: New York Univ. Press, 1999); Don Belton, ed., *Speak My Name: Black Men on Masculinity and the American Dream* (Boston: Beacon, 1995).

13 *Journal of African American Men: A Publication of the National Council of African American Men* (New Brunswick: Transaction Publishers, 1995). The editor's note in the inaugural issue of *JAAM* (summer 1995) describes the journal as an engagement with the scholarly explorations "of the struggles and triumphs of African American men"(3). The journal invites a multidisciplinary approach through applications of theory, research, and methodology addressing both theoretical and empirical concerns relating to African American men. Special issues on sports and psychology have appeared. However, multiple academic interests are published; there are several literary analyses (such as one on Ernest Gaines's *A Lesson Before Dying*), sociological essays on economics and class structures, as well as more theoretical works on topics such as the colonized body. Although there are a great number of cultural studies on rap music and hip hop, contemporary gender roles, and filmic representation, one also finds articles on Shakespeare's *Othello* and race in Elizabethan England.

Additionally, *The Annals of the American Academy of Political and Social Science*'s 2000 special issue, *The African American Male in American Life and Thought*, edited by Jacob U. Gordon, is worth mention here as still another legitimation of the field of African American manhood across the disciplines.

14 Traister, 274.

15 Madhubuti, Haki R. and Malauna Karenga, eds., *Million Man March/Day of Absence: A Commemorative Anthology; Speeches, Commentary, Photography, Poetry, Illustrations, Documents* (Chicago: Third World Press, 1996), 140.

16 Cornel West, "Why I'm Marching in Washington," in Carbado, 26; 27.

17 Pierre Bourdieu, *Outline of a Theory of Practice*, trans. Richard Nice (Cambridge: Cambridge Univ. Press, 1977).

18 Jacques Derrida, *Memoirs of the Blind: The Self-Portrait and Other Ruins*, trans. Pascale-Anne Brault and Michael Naas (Chicago: Univ. of Chicago Press, 1993), 29.

19 On the rare occasion I use the French *le regard* in this book (and it is rare indeed), I mean to invoke the gaze as an accumulation of social, psychic, and symbolic affects through which social subjects are "screened," not simply the look. I make this differentiation here because "French has only . . . one word for vision, whereas English has two: 'look' and 'gaze.'" Kaja Silverman, *The Threshold of the Visible World* (New York: Routledge, 1996), 167.

20 Ibid., 133.

21 Kobena Mercer, *Welcome to the Jungle: New Positions in Black Cultural Studies* (New York: Routledge, 1994), 176.

22 Alex Hirst, Introduction to *Black Male/ White Male* by Rotimi Fani-Kayode (London: GMP Publishers, 1988), n.p.

23 This potential and, more generally, the pitfalls of African American allegory have been superbly considered by Jaya Kasibhatla in her unpublished paper, "The Resistance to Allegory: Richard Wright and Representation in *Native Son*." I thank Jaya for this insight. See, too, Gayatri Chakravorty Spivak, *A Critique of Postcolonial Reason: Toward a History of the Vanishing Present* (Cambridge, Mass.: Harvard Univ. Press, 1999), 198–311.

24 Susan Sontag, *On Photography* (New York: Anchor Books, 1990), 97.

25 Simon Unwin, *Analyzing Architecture* (London: Routledge, 1997), 76.

26 Homi K. Bhabha, *The Location of Culture* (London: Routledge, 1994), 75. Emphasis Bhabha's.

27 Derrida, *Memoirs*, 75.

28 Ibid., 74.

29 Charles Johnson, "A Phenomenology of the Black Body," *Michigan Quarterly Review* 32, 4 (1993): 612. Emphasis added.

30 Dana D. Nelson, *National Manhood: Capitalist Citizenship and the Imagined Fraternity of White Men* (Durham, N.C.: Duke Univ. Press, 1998), ix.

31 Loretta J. Williams, *Black Freemasonry and Middle-Class Realities* (Columbia, Mo.: Univ. of Missouri Press, 1980), 17.

32 Bourdieu, 72–73.

33 Ibid., 72.

34 Laura Mulvey, "Pandora: Topographies of the Mask and Curiosity," in *Sexuality and Space*, ed. Beatriz Colomina (New York: Princeton Architectural Press, 1992), 55.

35 Bourdieu, 76.

36 With *das Heimliche* and *das Unheimliche*, I mean to invoke the original German phrasings of Freud's essay "The 'Uncanny'" and its emphasis on the terms' former rough translation to "'homely' or 'at home'" and "unhomely" respectively. I am not unaware that modern German speakers, despite the concept of 'home' (*Heim*) being contained in the very spelling of das Heimliche and das Unheimliche, translate these twin terms as "secretive" and "uncanny."

37 Silverman, *Threshold of the Visible World*, 156.

38 Ibid.

39 Derrida, *The Truth in Painting*, trans. Geoff Bennington and Ian McLeod (Chicago: Univ. of Chicago Press, 1987), 74.

40 James Baldwin, "Everybody's Protest Novel," in *The Price of the Ticket: Collected Nonfiction, 1948–1985*, by Baldwin (New York: St. Martin's Press, 1985), 33.

41 John Edgar Wideman, *Fatheralong: A Meditation on Fathers and Sons, Race and Society* (New York: Pantheon, 1994), 71–72.

1. ON DANGERS SEEN AND UNSEEN

1   *New York Times Magazine*, 4 December 1994.

2   James Truman, introduction to *Cyclops*, by Albert Watson (Boston: Little, Brown, and Co., 1994), n.p.

3   W. J. T. Mitchell, *Picture Theory: Essays on Verbal and Visual Representation* (Chicago: Univ. of Chicago Press, 1994), 63.

4   Ibid., 49.

5   Truman, n.p.

6   Ibid.

7   Ibid.

8   Homi K. Bhabha, *The Location of Culture* (London: Routledge, 1994), 67. Emphasis and parentheses Bhabha's.

9   Ibid.

10 Kobena Mercer, "Imaging the Black Man's Sex," in *Photography/Politics Two*, ed. Jo Spence, Patrice Holland, and Simon Watney (London: Comedia, 1986), 61–69, and "Skin Head Sex Thing: Racial Difference and the Homoerotic Imaginary" *How Do I Look? Queer Film and Video*, ed. Bad Object Choices (Seattle: Bay, 1989), 169–222, reprinted as "Reading Racial Fetishism: The Photographs of Robert Mapplethorpe," in Mercer, *Welcome to the Jungle*, 171–219.

11 Ibid., 160; 164.

12 Toni Morrison, *Playing in the Dark: Whiteness and the Literary Imagination* (Cambridge, Mass.: Harvard Univ. Press, 1992), 38; 37.

13 Walter Benjamin, "The Work of Art in the Age of Mechanical Reproduction" in *Illuminations*, trans. Harry Zohn (New York: Schocken, 1969), 222.

14 Robert Hirsch, *Seizing the Light: A History of Photography* (Boston: McGraw-Hill, 2000), 9.

15 Larry J. Schaaf, *Tracings of Light: Sir John Herschel and the Camera Lucida: Drawings from the Graham Nash Collection* (San Francisco: The Friends of Photography, 1990), 7.

16 Hirsch, 7.

17 Ibid.

18 Although the stereoscope was a portable device as well, on the grounds that modern habits of looking at black men are, as I've insisted, *monocular* (for which Albert Watson's partial blindness is surely the right trope), it is fairly easy

to dismiss the stereoscope's applicability to this discourse. What modern racial vision denies in looking at black men is exactly what the stereoscope hoped to guarantee would never be lost in picture taking: depth.

19   Schaaf, 7.

20   Ibid.

21   Bernard E. Jones, ed., *Cassell's Cyclopaedia of Photography* (New York: Arno, 1973), 84.

22   John McCumber, "Derrida and the Closure of Vision," in *Modernity and the Hegemony of Vision*, ed. David Michael Levin (Berkeley: Univ. of California Press, 1993), 239.

23   Roland Barthes, *Camera Lucida: Reflections on Photography*, trans. Richard Howard (New York: Hill and Wang, 1981), 106.

24   L. A. Mannheim et al., ed., *The Focal Encyclopedia of Photography*, rev. ed. (New York: McGraw-Hill, 1969), 144.

25   Although I offer a double meaning for enframement later on in this book, I mean for the reader to hear here as many other fitting cognates as the German verb *stellen* would suggest: "*Stellen* embraces the meanings of a whole family of verbs: . . . *vorstellen* (to represent) . . . *verstellen* (to block or disguise) . . . *darstellen* (to present or exhibit), and so on. . . . All these meanings are gathered together in Heidegger's unique use of the word that is pivotal for him, *Ge-stell* (Enframing)." Editor's note in *The Question Concerning Technology and Other Essays*, by Martin Heidegger, trans. William Lovitt (New York: Harper and Row, 1977), 15.

26   Heidegger, 126.

27   Ibid., 127.

28   Ibid.

29   Derrida, *The Truth*, 9. Emphasis Derrida's.

30   Ibid., 71. Emphasis Derrida's.

31   Barthes, *Camera Lucida*, 30.

32   Petrine Archer-Straw, *Negrophilia: Avant-Garde Paris and Black Culture in the 1920s* (London: Thames and Hudson, 2000), 51.

33   Schaaf, 12. Emphasis Schaaf's.

34   Derrida, *Memoirs*, 29.

35   Ralph Ellison, *Invisible Man* (1952; reprint, New York: Vintage, 1972), 3–4. Subsequent page references will be cited parenthetically in the text.

36   I wish to point out here that much of the success of this neologism, in this chapter and elsewhere, depends upon its spelling with a medial *a* rather than the potential *o*, as the virtual conditions of black male visibility suggested by spectr*a*graphia and inherited, it would seem, from camera lucida technology are opposed to the broad metaphorical luminosity captured by a spectr*o*graph, a camera for photographing color spectrums. Spectr*o*graphia, then, might suggest in its metaphorical appeal a whole misleading array of subjective potentialities that the condition of spectr*a*graphia threatens, in its narrow racialism, to preclude.

37 Derrida, *Memoirs*, 12. Emphasis Derrida's.

38 Charles Johnson, "A Phenomenology of the Black Body," *Michigan Quarterly Review* 32, 4 (1993): 604.

39 Bernard E. Jones, 381.

40 Mitchell, 63.

41 James Baldwin, "Many Thousand Gone," in *The Price of the Ticket: Collected Nonfiction, 1948–1985*, by Baldwin (New York: St. Martin's Press, 1985), 66.

42 This is but one reason black experimental art of all forms is so urgent today: it guards the imaginativeness of black "out-thereness" (i.e. far-flung fiction) from too swift a simplification to realism (i.e. fact). It is just such a reductiveness that impoverishes white appreciability of the inventiveness of fiction in more conventional genres of black art, writing especially.

43 Lauren Berlant, "National Brands/National Bodies: *Imitation of Life*," in *Comparative American Identities: Race, Sex, and Nationality in the Modern Text*, ed. Hortense J. Spillers (New York: Routledge, 1991), 113. Emphasis added.

44 A trace is left in our psychical apparatus of the perceptions which impinge upon it. This we may describe as a *memory-trace*. . . . We shall suppose that a system in the very form of the apparatus receives the perceptual stimuli but retains no trace of them and thus has no memory, while behind it there lies a second system which transforms the momentary excitation of the first system into *permanent traces*. (emphasis added)

    Sigmund Freud, *The Interpretation of Dreams*, in *The Standard Edition of the Complete Psychological Works of Sigmund Freud*, trans. James Strachey (London: Hogarth, 1955) 5: 539.

45 Ibid. Again, I quote Freud: "It is a familiar fact that we retain permanently something more than the mere *content* of the perceptions which impinge upon the system [i.e. the trace]." Emphasis Freud's.

46 Mercer, 160.

47 Ralph Ellison, *Shadow and Act* (1953; reprint, New York: Vintage, 1964), 28.

48 Baldwin, "Many Thousand Gone," 74.

49 In the strictest sense, *ekphrasis*, the verbal representation of a visual art work, is the proper possession of classical poetics and rhetoric, not modern prose. But as W. J. T. Mitchell explains, ekphrasis may be "a more general topic (the verbal representation of visual representation)" as well. It can be, in its broadest conception, "a general 'principle'" for the composition of verbal pictures. Mitchell acknowledges the capacity of prose to reflect an ekphrasis equivalent to the poetic form. His observation that "ekphrastic prose is an equally available possibility" for the composition of verbal pictures speaks modestly to the trouble contemporary theorists of ekphrasis have hesitating between "poetry," "the verbal arts," "texts," and "writing" generally as they seek to generically locate ekphrasis. Mitchell attempts a realization of such a "possibility" by a critical appeal to "the visual-spatial features of memory" in the African Ameri-

can slave narrative. Murray Krieger achieves a similar thing by his discernments of classical ekphrasis in William Faulkner's *Light in August* and *The Bear*.

Insofar as classical ekphrasis was aimed at reproducing a work of plastic art using words for its medium, photography could not have been imagined as an ekphrastic subject. That photography is, however, equally available to ekphrasis is made evident by the anecdote beginning Mitchell's reflections on "ekphrasis and the other." In *Picture Theory*, he introduces the "problem of ekphrasis" by the boyhood remembrance of a certain duo of radio personalities who had the habit of poring over the snapshots of their summer vacation on air, giving listeners a verbal description of the local color of their favorite sites/sights. Bob and Ray invoked the visual verbally without the possibility of their listeners ever really seeing.

See Mitchell, 151–54; 184; and Murray Krieger, *Ekphrasis: The Illusion of the Natural Sign* (Baltimore: Johns Hopkins Univ. Press, 1992), 271–73. For a brief history of ekphrasis, see, too, Grant F. Scott, "The Rhetoric of Dilation: Ekphrasis and Ideology," *Word and Image* 7, 4 (1991): 301.

50 Since ekphrasis ultimately concedes its own inability to render visual forms adequately, avowing its truth as an "illusionary representation" permitted "to masquerade as a natural sign," it would seem an apt class of mimetic practice for formalizing virtual representations of the black masculine that have evolved out of the derivative vision of the camera lucida. See Krieger, xv.

51 Richard Wright, *Native Son* (1940; reprint, New York: HarperCollins, 1993), 95. All subsequent references to this novel are to this edition and page numbers will be cited parenthetically in the text.

52 Derrida, *Memoirs*, 29.

53 Sontag, 97.

54 Sigmund Freud, "Medusa's Head," in *The Standard Edition of the Complete Psychological Works of Sigmund Freud*, trans. James Strachey (London: Hogarth, 1955) 18: 273.

55 Morrison, *Playing*, 38.

56 W. E. B. Du Bois, *The Souls of Black Folk* (1903; reprint, New York: New American Library, 1969), 45.

57 Derrida, *Memoirs*, 106. Emphasis added. Apparently, Derrida is aware that gender is not "without consequence for [his] hypothesis" (5). In a footnote he observes: "Neither the biblical nor the Greek culture confers upon women an exemplary role in [the] great, paradigmatic narratives of blindness. These narratives are dominated by the filiation father/son" (5–6*n*.1). Although he cites two exceptions, Saints Lucille and Odile, it would have been better had Derrida considered the extraordinary symbolic power of that blindfolded female who, balancing the scales of justice, is the central image of U.S. juristic iconography. In a vague way, Mrs. Dalton, "in flowing white clothes [and] standing stone-still in the middle of the kitchen floor" (Wright, 68), recalls that endeared

emblem. That "she made him feel she would *judge all he did*" is still more contributive to that evocation (69; emphasis added).

58 One wonders, in this connection, if there is more to the event of their first encounter than meets the eye. When they first interact in the Dalton kitchen, Mrs. Dalton doesn't bother to ask "the new boy" his name; before long it is pretty clear that she knows already, has predetermined, he is "Bigger" (I mean to construct a double entendre here). She doesn't even have to touch him to know it. See Wright, 68–69.

59 Silverman, *Threshold of the Visible World*, 158.

60 For a succinct discussion, see Bernard W. Bell, "Richard Wright and the Triumph of Naturalism," in *The Afro-American Novel and Its Tradition* by Bell (Amherst: Univ. of Massachusetts Press, 1987), 150–67.

61 This passage did not belong to Wright's original manuscript, but it came to replace very early on a sexually explicit passage Wright had originally composed at the behest of the Book-of-the-Month-Club who would feature the novel. Because this chapter relies upon the restored text of *Native Son* where the passage under discussion does not appear (except as a note on the text), I cite the passage in this note, not parenthetically within the text. See Arnold Rampersad "Note on the Texts," in Wright, 579.

62 See previous note.

63 According to Harold Hellenbrand, the "themes of Bigger's delinquency and rebellion were so entwined with visualization that in 1944 Wright tried to organize a photographic exhibit of delinquents in Harlem. . . . Linking seeing metaphors with allusions of photography and cinema, Wright suggested the mechanical and social processes of diffusing stereotypes." See Hellenbrand, "Bigger Thomas Reconsidered: *Native Son*, Film, *King Kong*," *Journal of American Culture* 6, 1 (1983):85.

64 Laura E. Tanner, "Uncovering the Magical Disguise of Language: The Narrative Presence in Richard Wright's *Native Son*," in *Richard Wright: Critical Perspectives Past and Present*, ed. Henry Louis Gates Jr. and K. A. Appiah (New York: Amistad, 1993), 141.

65 Silverman, *Threshold of the Visible World*, 168.

66 Note the veiled phallicism and threat of homosexual rape in the image of so many "newspapermen ready with their bulbs" (388).

67 Derrida, *Truth*, 69.

68 Ed Guerrero, "The Black Man on Our Screens and the Empty Space in Representation," in *Black Male: Representations of Masculinity in Contemporary American Art*, ed. Thelma Golden (New York: Whitney Museum of American Art, 1994), 185. Emphasis Guerrero's.

69 Baldwin, "Many Thousand Gone," 74.

70 Ibid., 77.

71 Barthes, *Camera Lucida*, 15.

72 Spivak, 190. I owe this particular slant to Jaya Khasibhatla.

73 Muñoz, 4.

74 Silverman, *Threshold of the Visible World*, 203.

75 Majors and Billson, 4–5.

76 Silverman, *Threshold of the Visible World*, 202.

77 Barthes, *Camera Lucida*, 11.

78 Muñoz, 31.

79 Barthes, 10.

80 Ibid., 13.

81 Ibid., 12.

82 Silverman, *Threshold of the Visible World*, 203.

83 Ibid., 205.

84 Hirst, 3.

85 Lee Edelman, *Homographesis: Essays in Gay Literary and Cultural Theory* (New York: Routledge, 1994), 47.

86 Ibid., 57.

87 Spillers, "Who Cuts," 12. Emphasis added.

88 See Jacqueline Bobo, *Black Women as Cultural Readers* (New York: Columbia Univ. Press, 1995); Jane Gaines, "White Privilege and Looking Relations: Race and Gender in Feminist Film Theory" in *Feminist Film Theory: A Reader*, ed. Sue Thornham (New York: New York Univ. Press, 1999), 293–306; and E. Ann Kaplan, "Is the Gaze Male?" in *Feminism and Film*, ed. Kaplan (New York: Oxford Univ. Press, 2000), 119–38.

89 Richard J. Powell, *Black Art and Culture in the Twentieth Century* (New York: Thames and Hudson, 1997), 161.

90 See Judith Halberstam, *Female Masculinity* (Durham, N.C.: Duke Univ. Press, 1998).

2. "ARE WE MEN?"

1 George W. Crawford, *Prince Hall and His Followers: Being a Monograph on the Legitimacy of Negro Masonry* (New York: Crisis, 1914), 18. An incomplete list of other prominent black Freemasons before 1912 would also include Paul Cuffee, James Forten, Alexander Crummell, Edward Bouchet, W. E. B. Du Bois, and Jack Johnson.

2 Mark Seltzer, *Bodies and Machines* (New York: Routledge, 1992), 5. Note, too, that before the 1903 publication of William Grimshaw's *Official History of Freemasonry among the Colored People in North America*, no image of Hall appears to have been available. Grimshaw's is, therefore, the first.

3 Ibid., 55.

4 One of fifty foreign military lodges stationed in the American colonies. See Sidney Morse, *Freemasonry in the American Revolution* (Washington D.C.: Masonic Service Association of the United States, 1924), 16.

5   William A. Muraskin, *Middle-Class Blacks in a White Society: Prince Hall Freema-sonry in America* (Berkeley: Univ. of California Press, 1975), 32.

6   Prince Hall to William Moody of London (2 March 1784):

> Dear Brother I would inform you that this Lodge hath been founded al-most eight [*sic*] years and we have had only a Permit to Walk on St. John's Day and to Bury our Dead in manner and form. We have had no oppor-tunity to apply for a Warrant before now, though, we have been impor-tuned to send to France for one, yet we thought it best to send to the Fountain from whence we received the Light, for a Warrant; and now Dear Br. we must make you our advocate at the Grand Lodge, hoping you will be so good (in our name and Stead) to Lay this Before the Royal Grand Master and the Grand Wardens and the rest of the Grand Lodge, who we hope will not deny us nor treat us Beneath the rest of our fellow men, although Poor yet Sincere Brethren of the Craft. (Qtd. in Charles H. Wesley, *Prince Hall: Life and Legacy* [Washington, D.C.: United Supreme Council, Southern Jurisdiction, Prince Hall Affiliation, 1977], 210).

Due to several communication breakdowns and broken trusts, the official doc-ument did not arrive in the colonies until 29 April 1787. Hall's extant corre-spondences with the Mother Grand Lodge of England reveal the charter "was personally delivered to Prince Hall by James Scott, a sea captain and brother-in-law of the eminent John Hancock." Loretta J. Williams, 17.

7   Lynn Dumenil, *Freemasonry and American Culture, 1880–1930* (Princeton: Princeton Univ. Press, 1984), 9.

8   According to William Henry Grimshaw, fifty-one of the fifty-five signers of the Declaration of Independence, including Warren and Hancock, were Free-masons. It is very unlikely that any of them recognized a fraternal tie to Hall. See chapter 51 of William Grimshaw, *Official History of Freemasonry among the Colored People in North America: Tracing the Growth of Masonry from 1717 Down to the Present Day* (1903; reprint, New York: Negro Universities Press, 1969).

9   Quoted in Grimshaw, 74.

10 Sidney Kaplan and Emma Nogrady Kaplan, *The Black Presence in the Era of the American Revolution*, rev. ed. (Amherst: Univ. of Massachusetts Press, 1989), 203.

11 Seltzer, 5.

12 Loretta J. Williams, 17.

13 Sidney Kaplan, *The Black Presence in the Era of the American Revolution, 1770–1800* (Greenwich, Conn.: New York Graphic Society, 1973), 182.

14 William Robinson, "Prince Hall," in *The Heath Anthology of American Litera-ture*, vol. 1, ed. Paul Lauter (Lexington, Mass.: Heath, 1990), 685.

15 Grimshaw, 67. Whether or not Hall was a preacher has been subject to some dispute.

16 Grimshaw, 69–70.

17 Wesley, 24.

18 Booker T. Washington, *Up from Slavery* (1901; reprint, New York: Magnum, 1968), 9.

19 Charles Johnson, *Being and Race: Black Writing since 1970* (Bloomington: Indiana Univ. Press, 1988), 79.

20 Wesley, 25.

21 Washington qtd. in Wesley, 12.

22 Kaplan, 182.

23 I am compelled to qualify *photographic* here because the steel engraving might be more exactly called a proto-photograph. It was, as Hirsch called it, "something on the order of photography," generated in the 1760s "as the result of information accrued through scientific inquiries into chemistry, color and light" during this period. The engraving is produced when a photosensitive substance, usually phosphorous, is exposed to an image and captured onto a plate specially treated with the photosensitive chemicals. Hirsch observed, moreover, that "although they were organized by machines — cameras — early photographs [i.e. the engraving] resembled drawings and paintings" much more than the modern photograph. Hall's image, therefore, may be easily mistaken for a painting. Hirsch, 7; 5.

24 Wesley, 20.

25 Seltzer, 54.

26 "System of flotation" and "privilege of abstraction" are phrases taken from Seltzer, 63. See Lauren Berlant, *The Anatomy of National Fantasy: Hawthorne, Utopia, and Everyday Life* (Chicago: Univ. of Chicago Press, 1991) on abstract disembodiment and Constitutional citizenship.

27 Robert Reid-Pharr has posited the fugitive or runaway in dialectical relation to the domestic black body: where the runaway body is profligate, the domestic is respectable. My conception of the fugitive differs, I think, only insofar as I posit it in opposition to the disciplined black body. See Robert Reid-Pharr, *Conjugal Union: The Body, the House, and the Black American* (New York: Oxford Univ. Press, 1999), 15–35; 111–27.

28 Lorenzo Johnston Greene, "The New England Negro as Seen in Advertisements for Runaway Slaves," *Journal of Negro History* 29, 2 (1944): 128.

29 Billy G. Smith and Richard Wojtowicz, *Blacks Who Stole Themselves: Advertisements for Runaways in the Pennsylvania Gazette, 1728–1790* (Philadelphia, Univ. of Pennsylvania Press, 1989), 5; 13.

30 Greene, "New England Negro," 132.

31 Ibid., 135.

32 Ibid.

33 Hall also counters the runaway slave advertisements' "typical" image of the illiterate slave. Greene writes, "From the advertisements, the runaways would appear to have been overwhelmingly illiterate, for all but one of the owners said nothing concerning the ability of their slaves to read and write. Whether these

slaves were generally illiterate or whether the masters apparently believed that literacy or lack of it in their slaves would have little to do with their recovery cannot be ascertained" (Greene, "New England Negro," 139). In the context of this study, the actual literacy rate among the runaways is not as important as the perception of "overwhelming" illiteracy among them.

34 Seltzer, 155.

35 Ibid., 58.

36 Mary Ann Clawson, *Constructing Brotherhood: Class, Gender, and Fraternalism* (Princeton: Princeton Univ. Press, 1989), 81. Emphasis added. Significantly, the rite of the Third Degree is "usually considered the dramatic centerpiece of [all] Masonic ritual[s]."

37 Seltzer, 168.

38 Clawson, 13.

39 Ibid., 78.

40 For a historical overview of Prince Hall Masonic membership's numerical and regional trends, see Muraskin. For prominent Prince Hall Masons since 1723, including notable clergymen, artists, athletes, and activists, see Joseph Mason Andrew Cox, *Great Black Men of Masonry 1723–1982* (Bronx: Blue Diamond, 1982).

41 Booker T. Washington, *The Story of the Negro: The Rise of the Race from Slavery*, vol. 2 (New York: Doubleday, 1909), 60.

42 W. E. B. Du Bois and Augustus Granville Dill, eds., *The Negro American Artisan: Report of a Social Study Made by Atlanta University under the Patronage of the Trustees of the John F. Slater Fund; with Proceedings of the Seventeenth Annual Conference for the Study of the Negro Problems, Held at Atlanta University on Monday May 27th, 1912.* (1912; reprint, New York: Arno, 1968), 68.

43 Ibid., 34. The validity of the claims made by both Washington and Du Bois on the age and extensiveness of African American artisanal culture is borne out in literary representation by a wide panoply of artisanal portrayals including Frederick Douglass, the ship caulker; Nat Turner, the carpenter and wood-carver; William Craft, the fugitive cabinetmaker; and the father of Harriet Jacobs, a matchless carpenter.

44 W. E. B. Du Bois, ed., *The Negro Artisan: Report of a Social Study Made under the Direction of Atlanta University; together with the Proceedings of the Seventh Conference for the Study of Negro Problems, Held at Atlanta University, on May 27th, 1902* (Atlanta: Atlanta Univ. Press, 1902), 22.

45 *Work* is Freemasonry's own term for "the initiation of a candidate into its mysteries." Albert C. Mackey, *The Symbolism of Freemasonry: Illustrating and Explaining Its Science and Philosophy, Its Legends, Myths, and Symbols* (Chicago: Cook, 1947), 266. Paul Gilroy, *The Black Atlantic: Modernity and Double Consciousness* (Cambridge, Mass.: Harvard Univ. Press, 1993), 40.

46 James W. C. Pennington, *The Fugitive Blacksmith, or, Events in the History of James W. C. Pennington, Pastor of a Presbyterian Church, New York, Formerly a*

Slave in the State of Maryland, United States (reprint, 1849, Westport, Conn.: Negro Universities Press, 1971), 8–9.

47   Michel de Certeau, *The Practice of Everyday Life*, trans. Steven Rendall (Berkeley: Univ. of California Press, 1984), 25.

48   Ibid.

49   Ibid., vxiii.

50   Hannah Arendt, *The Human Condition* (Chicago: Univ. of Chicago Press, 1958), 93.

51   Drawing on ancient Greek distinctions, Arendt distinguishes labor, the activity of the body that slavishly "minister[s] to the necessities of life" (80) from work, the activity of productive hands that are "capable of producing a 'surplus'" (88). According to the Greeks,

> to labor meant to be enslaved by necessity, and this enslavement was inherent in the condition of human life. Because men were dominated by the necessities of life, they could win their freedom only through the domination of those whom they subjected to necessity by force. The slave's degradation was a blow of fate and a fate worse than death, because it carried with it a metamorphosis of man into something akin to a tame animal. A change in a slave's status, therefore, such as manumission by his master or a change in general political circumstance . . . automatically entailed a change in the slave's "nature." (84)

If, ideologically speaking, there is any continuity whatever between ancient Greek and modern American forms of slavery, then it is clear why Hall's efforts on behalf of enslaved and free black men to enlist and, for the freedmen, to take up the work of Freemasonry were so earnest: manumission confers upon the slave and ex-slave their humanity, while the work of the Craft, of course, makes them men.

52   Seltzer, 128.

53   Mackey, *Symbolism*, 97.

54   "The Negro is a sort of seventh son, born with a veil, and gifted with second-sight in this American world, — a world which yields him no true self-consciousness. . . . One ever feels his two-ness, — an American, a Negro; . . . two warring ideals in one dark body, whose dogged strength alone keeps it from being torn asunder." Du Bois, *Souls*, 45.

55   Albert C. Mackey, et al., *Encyclopedia of Freemasonry and Its Kindred Sciences: Comprising the Whole Range of Arts, Sciences and Literature as Connected with the Masonic Institution*, rev. ed. (1873; Chicago: Masonic History Company, 1929), 602.

56   Muraskin, 196–97.

57   Martin Robison Delany, *The Origins and Objects of Ancient Freemasonry: Its Introduction into the United States and Legitimacy among Colored Men* (Pittsburgh: Haven, 1853), 24.

58 Ibid.

59 Muraskin, 197. Emphasis added.

60 Gilroy, 19.

61 Delany, *Origins and Objects*, 37.

62 This is all the more true in light of the fact that, besides Delany, black inventors Henry Blair, the first African American inventor to receive a U.S. patent; Lewis Latimer, an associate of Thomas Edison and Alexander Graham Bell and creator of the carbon filament now used in the light bulb; and Granville T. Woods, whose inventions include the steam boiler furnace, the incubator, and railway telegraph, were also all Prince Hall Masons. See Cox.

63 Seltzer, 18.

64 Dorothy Sterling, *The Making of an Afro-American: Martin Robison Delany, 1812–1885* (Garden City, N.Y.: Doubleday, 1971), 147.

65 Garrison qtd. in Sterling, 149.

66 Sterling, 160.

67 Ibid., 219.

68 But not before he proposed a *corps d'Afrique* whose style of drill and dress would follow the Zouaves, an infantry of black African soldiers that had served the Duc D'Orleans in the Algerine war and was distinguished for its flamboyancy in drill and uniform. See Frank A. Rollin, *Life and Public Services of Martin R. Delany* (1868; reprint, New York: Kraus, 1969), 141–44.

69 Delany to E. M. Stanton, December 1863. Qtd. in Sterling, 233.

70 Michael Hatt, "'Making a Man of Him': Masculinity and the Black Body in Mid–Nineteenth-Century American Sculpture," *Oxford Art Journal* 15, 1 (1992): 24.

71 Ibid., 29.

72 Qtd. in Sterling, 246.

73 William C. Darrah, *Cartes de Visite in Nineteenth Century Photography* (Gettysburg, Pa.: Darrah, 1981), 7.

74 Ibid., 75.

75 Robert A. Mayer, "Photographing the American Presidency," *Image* 27, 3 (1984): 17.

76 Darrah, 111.

77 Slavoj Žižek, *The Fragile Absolute, or, Why Is the Christian Legacy Worth Fighting For?* (London: Verso, 2000), 23. Description of Delany in Xenia, Ohio *Sentinel*, qtd. in Sterling, 246.

78 Suzanne Schneider, "The Hottentot/Hot-to-Trot Penis: The Pornotroping of the African-American Male Body in Nineteenth Century Social and Scientific Discourse," unpublished paper, 1998. See, too, Brian Wallis's "Black Bodies, White Science: Louis Agassiz's Slave Daguerreotypes," *American Art*, summer 1995, 39–61. Note, also, that Agassiz found his slave subjects in South Carolina where Delany would begin his military service in Charleston fifteen years later.

How very different the iconography that obtained between the representative slave and the representative free man of color in mid-century South Carolina.

79 Nell Painter's *Sojourner Truth: A Life, a Symbol* includes a valuable chapter entitled "Truth in Photographs" on Truth and her photographic self-fashioning in a series of *carte de visite* portraits. My discovery of the importance of Delany's *carte* portrait is indebted to Painter's reflections on Truth. Nell Irvin Painter, *Sojourner Truth: A Life, a Symbol* (New York, Norton, 1996).

80 On Timothy Dwight and anti-Masonic sentiment, see George Johnson, "Pierre, Is That a Masonic Flag on the Moon?" *New York Times*, 24 Nov. 1996, 4E; on Louis Farrakhan, refer to Charles Paul Freund, "From Satan to Sphinx: The Masonic Mysteries of DC's Map," *Washington Post*, 5 Nov. 1995, CO3.

81 Martin Robison Delany, *Blake; or, the Huts of America: A Novel* (Boston: Beacon, 1970), 255. All subsequent page references shall be to this edition and indicated parenthetically in the text.

82 Robert S. Levine, *Martin Delany, Frederick Douglass, and the Politics of Representative Identity* (Chapel Hill: Univ. of North Carolina Press, 1997), 196.

83 Ibid., 196.

84 Mackey, *Encyclopedia*, 602.

85 Ibid.

86 Raymond Williams, *Marxism and Literature* (Oxford: Oxford Univ. Press, 1977), 40–41.

87 Mackey, *Encyclopedia*, 432.

88 Lawrence W. Levine, *Black Culture and Black Consciousness: Afro-American Folk Thought from Slavery to Freedom* (1977; reprint, New York: Oxford Univ. Press, 1978), 442.

89 Lorenzo Johnston Greene, *The Negro in Colonial New England* (New York: Atheneum, 1968), 299.

90 Linda Warfel Slaughter, *The Freedmen of the South* (1869; reprint, New York: Kraus, 1969). Qtd. in Loretta J. Williams, 30.

91 Loretta J. Williams, 44.

92 Mackey, *Encyclopedia*, 432.

93 Ibid., 433.

94 Mackey, *Symbolism*, 115.

95 Ibid., 112–13.

96 Ibid., 113.

97 For a lucid discussion of the maternal qualities of the lodge-room, see Carnes, 119–21.

98 Seltzer, 28.

3. CONSTRUCTING THE BLACK MASCULINE

1 Silverman, *Threshold of the Visible World*, 205.

2 Seltzer, 128.

3   Mark Wigley, *The Architecture of Deconstruction: Derrida's Haunt* (Cambridge, Mass.: MIT Press, 1993), 27.

4   Richard Yarborough, "The First-Person in Afro-American Fiction," in *Afro-American Literary Study in the 1990s*, ed. Houston A. Baker Jr. and Patricia Redmond (Chicago: Univ. of Chicago Press, 1989), 110.

5   Ibid., 112.

6   For a discussion of the obscured divisions between fiction and autobiography in black literary production, see Yarborough.

7   Michael Cooke, "Modern Black Autobiography in the Tradition," in *Romanticism: Vistas, Instances, Continuities*, ed. David Thorburn and Geoffrey Hartman (Ithaca: Cornell Univ. Press, 1973). Qtd. in Henry Louis Gates Jr., *Figures in Black: Words, Signs and the "Racial" Self* (New York: Oxford Univ. Press, 1987), 95.

8   Bruce Mazlish, "Autobiography and Psychoanalysis: Between Truth and Self-Deception," *Encounter* 35 (1970), 30.

9   I am not unaware of the riskiness of using the clinical language of *polymorphism*, *consciousness*, *repression*, and *libidinality* to further unfold black masculine subjecthood. I know all too well what low esteem many black scholars often hold in the systematic application of psychoanalysis to African American cultural production, dismissing psychoanalytical practices as bourgeois and conservative. To subject the so-called sable mind to the pseudoscientism of psychoanalysis, some argue, is to extend European hegemony to perilous lengths. This resistance to the psychoanalytic critique is the inevitable upshot of American conservatism's scandalous (mis)appropriations of psychoanalysis to construct so many demeaning narratives of African American mental health and intelligence. Like psychocriticism's detractors, I too am cautious of bringing the clinical language of psychoanalysis to bear on black subjectivity. Specialized terms such as *disorder*, *neurosis*, and *complex*, for example, far from generalizing the pathological condition, might well represent what Barbara Herrnstein-Smith has called simply "contingencies," which are nothing so much as elusively disguised prejudices that serve the analyst's own egoistic fantasies and "justify the exercise of [his or her] own normative authority." Herrnstein-Smith, "Contingencies of Value," *Critical Inquiry* 10, 1 (1983): 18. A clinical lexicon, therefore, can be dangerously marginalizing, effecting in its worst ethnocentric formulations cultural xenophobia wherever it is assigned outside of the context of contingencies that established it. It ought always to be regarded with healthy suspicion. But to abandon the principles of psychoanalysis altogether is to throw the baby out with the proverbial bathwater. I would submit, therefore, that responsibly and eclectically deployed psychoanalytic theory may in fact afford black literary and cultural criticism a usable — indeed, a valuable — polygraphic methodology for discerning those persistent, visceral drives which lurk just below the public black ego. Frantz Fanon's psychoana-

lytic diagnosis of the "unbearable insularity" of black identity, for instance, might only be confirmed or rejected as a condition of first-person identity in black and colonial life and literature according to the principles of the post-Freudian psychoanalysis that generated it. Similarly, the significant influence of Freudian thought on the writers of African American first-person narrative among whom are W. E. B. Du Bois, Richard Wright, and Ralph Ellison, would seem to justify the psychoanalytic pursuit here and compel a serious reconsideration of black habits of critical anti-Freudianism.

10   Virginia Woolf, *A Room of One's Own* (San Diego: Harcourt Brace Jovanovich, 1957), p. 88.

11   "Preliminal" and "liminal" are borrowed from anthropologist Arnold van Gennep. His study of "life-crisis ceremonies," *Les rites de passage* (1909), taking up among its other discursive streams "the critical problems of becoming male and female" in various societies, accords fruitfully with my own efforts in this chapter to map the same in black male contexts. Although van Gennep foregrounds the communal or tribal ceremonies (*rites*) that accompany "life-crises" (i.e., death, birth, marriage, adoption, remarriage), rather than the progressive stages of identity development I am examining, his communal *rites*, subdivided into preliminal rites (rites of separation), liminal rites (rites of transition), and postliminal rites (rites of incorporation), the totality of which symbolize the passage of a life cycle, conform very nearly to the stages of gender development I am arguing for as experienced nonceremonially in the pubescent subjects of *Narrative* and *Up from Slavery*. I deal in this chapter only with the first two stages or rites. See Arnold van Gennep, *The Rites of Passage*, trans. Monika B. Vizedom and Gabrielle L. Caffee (London: Routledge and Kegan Paul, 1977).

12   See the section called "Hegel and the Negro" in Frantz Fanon's *Black Skin White Masks* for one of the earliest attempts to properly contextualize Hegel's allegorical master/slave dialectic relative to the historical and lived experience of slavery in Europe and the New World. While Fanon correctly resists Hegel's ready applicability to the social and political contexts of slavery, he does not deny that American and European slavery depended upon psychic relations between master and slave, black and white, that could be illuminated in part by Hegel's more particularistic dialectic. See Frantz Fanon, *Black Skin White Masks*, trans. Charles Lam Markmann (New York: Grove, 1967). For a brief discussion of later readings and appropriations of Hegel in this connection, see Gilroy, 50–51.

13   Seltzer, 75.

14   Booker T. Washington, *Up from Slavery* (1901; reprint, New York: Magnum, 1968), 9. All subsequent references will be to this edition and indicated parenthetically in the text.

15   It is no accident that the King James Bible, the archetypal Western text in no small respect, was also the first (if not only) reader for many black Americans before and immediately following Emancipation. For a history of black literacy

and the Bible, refer to Janet Duitsman Cornelius, *"When I Can Read My Title Clear": Literacy, Slavery, and Religion in the Antebellum South* (Columbia: Univ. of South Carolina Press, 1991); and Renita Weems, "Reading *Her Way* through the Struggle: African American Women and the Bible," and Vincent Winbush, "The Bible and African-Americans: An Outline of an Interpretive History." Weems and Winbush are collected in Cain Hope Felder, ed., *Stony the Road We Trod: African American Biblical Interpretation* (Minneapolis: Fortress, 1991). Many scholars (Gates, for example) also credit the European picaresque for its typologization of the trope of mixed lineage inherited by black writers. See Gates, "Binary Oppositions in chapter 1 of *Narrative of the Life of Frederick Douglass, an American Slave Written By Himself*" in *Figures in Black*, 80–97.

16 Gates, *Figures in Black*, 89.

17 George Cunningham, "'Called into Existence': Gender, Desire and Voice in Douglass' *Narrative* of 1845," *Differences* 1, 3 (1989): 108.

18 Eugene D. Genovese, *The World the Slaveholders Made* (Middletown, Conn.: Wesleyan Univ. Press, 1988), xvi.

19 Frederick Douglass, *Narrative of the Life of Frederick Douglass, an American Slave* (1845; reprint, with introduction by Houston A. Baker Jr. New York: Penguin, 1987), 52. Emphasis added. All subsequent references to the *Narrative* will be to this edition and cited parenthetically in the text.

20 In *My Bondage and My Freedom*, the 1855 version of Douglass's autobiography, the slaveboy's hiding place is described as a "little, rough closet, which opened into the kitchen; and through the cracks of its unplaned boards, [Douglass] could distinctly see and hear what was going on, without being seen by old master." In all likelihood, the modern equivalent to this architecture is a simple broom closet. See Douglass, *My Bondage and My Freedom* (1855; reprint, New York: Dover, 1969), 87.

21 Clearly, queer criticism (and the work of Eve Kosofsky Sedgwick in particular) has made the closet a classic symbol of sexual coverture. The argument here, however, is not that Douglass was conscious of using the metaphor of the closet in such a way — Sedgwick is probably correct that the metaphorization of the closet as the ur-trope of homosexual concealment was imagined much later on — rather, it is that the suitability of the closet as a metaphor in Douglass owes itself, as Lacan has pointed out, to the tendency "on the mental plane" for structural metaphors like the closet to arise "spontaneously, as if issuing from the symptoms [of hysteria] themselves, to designate the mechanisms of obsessional neurosis — inversion, isolation, reduplication, cancellation and displacement." My discernments of panic, projection, and repression in Douglass's memory of Aunt Hester's rape are subsumed in Lacan's "mechanisms of obsessional neurosis." If Douglass's use of the closet shares anything with Sedgwick's theorizations in *Epistemology of the Closet*, those similarities matter less in this discussion than the closet's function as a physical refuge for the spectacle body at risk. See Eve Kosofsky Sedgwick, *Epistemology of the Closet* (Berkeley: Univ. of

California Press, 1990); and Jacques Lacan, "The Mirror Stage as Formative of the Function of the I as Revealed in Psychoanalytic Experience," in *Ecrits: A Selection*, trans. Alan Sheridan (New York: Norton, 1977), 5.

22 David Van Leer, "Reading Slavery: The Anxiety of Ethnicity in Douglass' *Narrative*," in *Frederick Douglass: New Literary and Historical Essays*, ed. Eric J. Sundquist (New York: Cambridge Univ. Press, 1990), 131.

23 While I readily admit the undeniability that black women's rape under slavery was not exclusively, or even primarily, motivated by the economic concerns of their masters—probably, their motives were compound ones—I believe Van Leer's contention that slave rape was "a uniquely female experience" misjudges the degree to which slave rape performed racial domination in the same violent way that whippings did. Even if its weapons were sexual, the slave's rape enacted a racial drama chiefly (an exercise of absolute white power over black abjection), and a sexual one only secondarily. To imagine rape under slavery as "a uniquely female experience" is to conceive of that assault as one motivated, rather than complicated, by sexual drives and erotic urges. It is to virtually deny the racial dynamic altogether. I suspect, though, that the dialectics of racial difference and domination immanent in slave rape are not completely lost on Van Leer in spite of his argument. But if he accepts the primacy of a racial dynamics at the rotted core of the slaveholder's sexual impositions on the slave body, then his insistence upon the gendered particularity of the rape experience would seem to suggest another drive, since a purely sexual one is untenable within the context of slave rape as an enactment of racial violence. Given that racial domination may be exercised on men's and women's bodies alike, and that sexual drives complicate rather than motivate sexual assaults, Van Leer unintentionally leaves us with only one other rationale for white men's assault on black women: that the slaveholder's racial sovereignty is magnified by his control over not only his slaves' bodies, male or female, but the progenitive issue of black women's bodies commercially. As the slave woman, under the force of rape, reproduces, so too does the commercial power of the slaveholder. In effect, his supremacy is redoubled. This view, however, which I take to be the only tenable justification for what is otherwise Van Leer's surprising myopia, still falls short of critical cogency vis-à-vis Douglass and renders the critic's argument lamentably ineffectual.

24 Edelman, 47.

25 Toni Morrison, *Beloved* (New York: New American Library, 1987), 107–108.

26 Harriet Jacobs, *Incidents in the Life of a Slave Girl*, in *The Classic Slave Narratives*, ed. Henry Louis Gates Jr. (New York: New American Library, 1987), 504.

27 Robert A. Nye, "Sex Difference and Male Homosexuality in French Medical Discourse," *Bulletin of the History of Medicine* 63 (1989): 41.

28 Ibid.

29 Jacobs, 504.

30 Nye, 41.

31 Jacobs, 504.

32 Ibid., 505.

33 Douglass, *Bondage*, 79.

34 Charles Nero, "Toward a Black Gay Aesthetic: Signifying in Contemporary Black Gay Literature," in *Cornerstones: An Anthology of African American Literature*, ed. Melvin Donalson (New York: St. Martin's Press, 1996), 971–89. It should be noted that the foundations of Nero's black gay aesthetic are not in the sexual abuses of black men under slavery at the hands of white men, but rather in the mutually consensual practice of homosexuality among slaves, which, if Montejo's account is a faithful picture of slavery in Cuba, "was neither unknown nor undreamt." Montejo qtd. in Nero, 975.

35 "Libidinal masculine" and "libidinal feminine" are Hélène Cixous's terms in "Laugh of the Medusa," in *Critical Theory since 1965*, ed. Hazard Adams and Leroy Searle (Tallahassee: Florida State Univ. Press, 1986), 309–20.

36 Hélène Cixous has described this space as a "location in self (réparge en soi) . . . variously manifest and insistent according to each person, male or female — of both sexes." Ibid., 314.

37 Ibid.

38 Ibid.

39 Ronald G. Walters, "The Erotic South: Civilization and Sexuality in American Abolitionism," *American Quarterly* 25, 2 (1973): 186.

40 Ibid., 180.

41 Fanon, 59.

42 Van Leer, *n*.33.

43 Jenny Franchot, "The Punishment of Ester: Frederick Douglass and the Constitution of the Feminine," in Sundquist, 150.

44 Janice A. Radway, *Reading the Romance: Women, Patriarchy, and Popular Literature* (Chapel Hill: Univ. of North Carolina Press, 1984), 72.

45 Given Douglass's active involvement in the women's suffrage movement, his familiarity with the conventions of white women's writings should come as no surprise.

46 Gates, "Binary Oppositions," 228.

47 Foucault, *History of Sexuality*, 43.

48 Ibid., 11.

49 Ibid., 103.

50 Ibid.

51 David L. Dudley, *My Father's Shadow: Intergenerational Conflict in African American Men's Autobiography* (Philadelphia: Univ. of Pennsylvania Press, 1991), 48.

52 Winthrop D. Jordan, *White over Black: American Attitudes toward the Negro, 1550–1812* (Baltimore: Penguin, 1969), 161.

53 Ibid., 159.

54 Fanon, 111.

55 Houston A. Baker Jr., *Modernism and the Harlem Renaissance* (Chicago: Univ. of Chicago Press, 1987), 30.

56 Ibid., 25.

57 Ibid., 26–27. Is there any better coincidence, in this connection, than Louis Harlan's observation that, hung outside the Negro Building of the 1895 Atlanta Cotton States and International Exposition where Washington delivered his famous Atlanta Exposition Address, was a portrait of a "handkerchief-headed 'Aunty' . . . on a large medallion." Louis R. Harlan, *Booker T. Washington: The Making of a Black Leader, 1856–1901* (New York: Oxford Univ. Press, 1972), 230.

58 Baker, *Modernism*, 31.

59 Ibid., 40.

60 Ibid., 17.

61 Ibid., 32.

62 Eric Lott, *Love and Theft: Blackface Minstrelsy and the American Working Class* (New York: Oxford Univ. Press, 1993), 27.

63 Harlan, 248.

64 Lott, 32.

65 "Romantic racialism," as Lott points out, is historian George Frederickson's term for a peculiar strain of antebellum thought which "projected an image of [African Americans] that could be construed as flattering or laudatory . . . [although it] endorsed the 'child' stereotype of the most sentimental school of proslavery paternalists and plantation romantics." Romantic racialists differed from the paternalists and plantation romancers in that they "rejected slavery . . . because it took unfair advantage," in their view, "of the Negro's [childlike] innocence," a trait that "constituted the ultimate Christian virtue." To the romantic racialists, African Americans were not inferior to Anglo-Saxons; curiously, blacks constituted "the superior race." George M. Frederickson, *The Black Image in the White Mind: The Debate on Afro-American Character and Destiny, 1817–1914* (New York: Harper and Row, 1971), 101–102.

66 Lott, 32.

67 Claudia Tate, *Domestic Allegories of Political Desire: The Black Heroine's Text at the Turn of the Century* (New York: Oxford Univ. Press, 1992), 129.

68 Ibid.

69 The opposition between the "domestic" black (male) body as a "respectable" image of black corporeality and its "profligate" alter-image, I owe to Robert Reid-Pharr's study of nineteenth-century conventions of black masculine representation in *Conjugal Union*.

70 Dudley, 44.

71 Another, better analogy could hardly be conceived here when one reads the request of Othon Guerlac, once Professor of Romance Languages at Cornell University, for permission to translate Washington's autobiography into

French: "I have no doubt that in my country where Uncle Tom's Cabin [*sic*] had such a wide success your book would meet with a very good reception." Qtd. in Harlan, 252.

72 Dudley, 39.

73 Booker T. Washington, *My Larger Education: Being Chapters from My Experience* (Garden City, N.Y.: Doubleday, Page and Co., 1911), 103. Succeeding references will be to this edition and cited parenthetically in the text.

74 As Dudley best explains, " 'My Life and Times' " is actually a confusion of the titles of Douglass's second and third autobiographies, *My Bondage and My Freedom* and *Life and Times of Frederick Douglass*. See Dudley's discussion, 41– 44.

75 Ibid., 41.

76 Harlan, 245.

77 Qtd. in Harlan, 56.

78 Ibid., 61.

79 Ibid.

80 Ibid., 63. The Daily Order of Exercises, outlined in the 1873–74 Hampton catalog and reproduced in Harlan, follows:

> AM
> 5:00 Rising Bell
> 5:45 Inspection of Men
> 6:00 Breakfast
> 6:30 Family Prayers
> 8:00 Inspection of quarters
> 8:30 Opening of school
> Roll Call and Exercises
> 8:50 to 10:20 Classes in Reading, Natural Philosophy, Arithmetic, Grammar, Geography, and Bookkeeping
> 10:20 to 10:40 Recess
> 10:40 to 12:15 Classes in Writing, Arithmetic, Grammar, History, Algebra, and Elocution
>
> PM
> 12:15 to 1:30 Dinner and intermission
> 1:30 Roll Call
> 1:40 to 2:50 Classes in Spelling, Arithmetic, Grammar, Geography, Natural Philosophy, History, Civil Government, and Moral Science
> 4:00 Cadet Drill
> 6:00 Supper
> 6:45 Evening Prayers
> 7:15 to 9:00 Evening Study Hours
> 9:30 Retiring Bell

81 Derrida, *Memoirs*, 29.

82 Michel Foucault, *Discipline and Punish: The Birth of the Prison*, trans. Alan Sheridan (New York: Vintage, 1979), 138.

83 Though Washington spoke mostly about the "boys" at Hampton, "most of the students were men and women — some as old as forty years of age" (*Up from Slavery*, 66).

84 Seltzer, 64. Emphasis added.

85 Letter, 26 March 1877, qtd. in Harlan, 83.

86 Ibid., 240.

87 Ibid., 273.

88 Ibid., 281–82.

89 Ibid., 279–80.

90 Charles Young qtd. in Harlan, 282.

91 Of course, "contact" between "great men" and boys, as we have seen earlier on in this chapter, may be a relative experience. While, for the cultural elite, it may signify the sort of productionist interface between imitable men and their perfectly replicable models (which Washington seems to have in mind), for the unlucky slaveboy like Douglass, "contact" undergoes semantic dislocation, naming instead a far less friendly association. "Contact," I mean to suggest, is not an altogether innocent pedagogy since it is also, as I believe Douglass's predicament discloses, "the basic schematic type of initiating sexual action (touching, caressing — sexuality)." Fanon, 56.

92 Seltzer, 21.

93 Bourdieu, 90.

4. A MAN'S PLACE

1 Qtd. in Dolores Hayden, *The Grand Domestic Revolution: A History of Feminist Designs for American Homes, Neighborhoods, and Cities* (Cambridge, Mass.: MIT Press, 1981), 55–56. Emphasis added.

2 Charlotte Perkins Gilman, *In This Our World*, 3d ed. Boston: Small Maynard, 1908), 160. Polly Wynn Allen's annotations in *Building Domestic Liberty: Charlotte Perkins Gilman's Architectural Feminism* (Amherst: Univ. of Massachusetts Press, 1988) remind us that a "hod" is a coal scuttle.

3 Hayden, 56.

4 Allen, 60.

5 Ibid., 16.

6 Ibid., 87–88.

7 See for example, bell hooks, *Ain't I a Woman: Black Women and Feminism* (Boston: South End Press, 1981); Jacqueline Jones, *Labor of Love, Labor of Sorrow: Black Women, Work, and the Family from Slavery to the Present* (New York: Basic Books, 1985); Deborah Gray White, *Ar'n't I a Woman?: Female Slaves in the Plantation South* (New York: Norton, 1985). Nor is there any more eloquent expression of the subversive potential in black women's work history

than Sojourner Truth's 1851 speech to the Women's Rights Convention in Akron, Ohio, "Ar'n't I a Woman?": "Look at me! Look at my arm! I have plowed, and planted, and gathered into barns, and no man could head me — and ar'n't I a woman? I could work as much and eat as much as a man (when I could get it), and bear de lash as well — and ar'n't I a woman?" Olive Gilbert, *Narrative of Sojourner Truth*, excerpted in *The Norton Anthology of African American Literature*, ed. Henry Louis Gates Jr. and Nellie Y. McKay (New York: Norton, 1997), 200.

8 Mrs. N. F. Mossell, "The Opposite Point of View," excerpted chapter from *The Work of the Afro-American Woman*, in *Words of Fire: An Anthology of African American Feminist Thought*, ed. Beverly Guy Sheftall (New York: New Press, 1995), 56–57. I am appreciative to Alice A. Deck for recently bringing Mossell to my attention. On Cooper and Mossell, see Tate.

9 Mark Wigley, "Untitled: The Housing of Gender," in *Sexuality and Space*, ed. Beatriz Colomina (New York: Princeton Architectural Press, 1992), 330; 332. Emphasis added.

10 Ibid., 329.

11 From the Latin *verna*, literally "a slave born in his master's Nothouse."

12 On nineteenth-century domestic architecture, see Wayne Andrews, *Architecture, Ambition, and Americans: A Social History of American Architecture* (New York: Free Press, 1978); David P. Handlin, *The American Home: Architecture and Society, 1815–1915* (Boston: Little, Brown, 1979); Walter Benn Michaels, "Romance and Real Estate," in *The American Renaissance Reconsidered*, ed. Michaels and Donald E. Pease (Baltimore: Johns Hopkins Univ. Press, 1985) and Peter Williams, "Constituting Class and Gender: A Social History of the Home, 1700–1901," in *Class and Space: The Making of Urban Society*, ed. Nigel Thrift and Williams (London: Routledge and Kegan Paul).

On black vernacular architecture, see Steven L. Jones, "The African-American Tradition in Vernacular Architecture," in *The Archaeology of Slavery and Plantation Life*, ed. Theresa A. Singleton (Orlando: Academic Press, 1985); Mechal Sobel, *The World They Made Together: Black and White Value in Eighteenth-Century Virginia* (Princeton: Princeton Univ. Press, 1987); Dell Upton and John Michael Vlach, eds., *Common Places: Readings in American Vernacular Architecture* (Athens: Univ. of Georgia Press, 1986); and two titles by John Michael Vlach, *By the Work of Their Hands: Studies in Afro-American Folklife* (Charlottesville: Univ. of Virginia Press, 1991); and "Not Mansions . . . but Good Enough: Slave Quarters as Bi-Cultural Expression," in *Black and White Cultural Interaction in the Antebellum South*, ed. Ted Ownby (Jackson: Univ. Press of Mississippi, 1993).

13 Silverman, *Threshold of the Visible World*, 31.

14 Saint-Aubin, 1056.

15 Harriet Beecher Stowe, *Uncle Tom's Cabin* (1852; reprint, with introduction by Russell B. Nye, New York: Washington Square, 1967), 20.

16   Bourdieu, 90.

17   Admittedly, little about *Epistemology* suggests its congruity with African American expressivity. Much to the African Americanist's regret, the literary-critical scope of *Epistemology* is decidedly white.

18   Ellen Eve Frank, *Literary Architecture: Essays toward a Tradition: Walter Pater, Gerard Manley Hopkins, Marcel Proust, Henry James* (Berkeley: Univ. of California Press, 1979), 4–5. The capacity of man to perceive at all, in other words, depends upon understanding experience "to be bounded or located in a particular space, within . . . walls, bodies, time" (6). A structural correspondence, then, is constitutive of experience, and as such predisposes man to a tectonic imagination.

19   Sedgwick, *Epistemology* 3.

20   Wigley, 389. Emphasis added.

21   Ibid.

22   Sedgwick, *Epistemology*, 72.

23   There are several passing-novels of the nineteenth century available for analysis in this connection. They include Rebecca Harding Davis, *Waiting for the Verdict* (1867); Frances E. W. Harper, *Iola Leroy* (1892); William Dean Howells, *An Imperative Duty* (1892); Mark Twain, *Pudd'nhead Wilson* (1894); Charles Chesnutt, *The House behind the Cedars* (1900); Pauline Hopkins, *Hagar's Daughter* (1902) and "The Test of Manhood" (1902); and Sutton Griggs, *The Hindered Hand* (1905).

24   Charles Chesnutt, *The House behind the Cedars* (1900; reprint, New York: Collier, 1969), 84. All subsequent references will be to this edition and will be indicated parenthetically in the text.

25   Frank, 3.

26   Wigley, 383.

27   Ibid., 370–71.

28   Ibid., 369.

29   Houston A. Baker Jr., *Modernism*, 17. Emphasis added.

30   John W. Blassingame, *The Slave Community: Plantation Life in the Antebellum South* (New York: Oxford Univ. Press, 1972), 228. Emphasis Blassingame's.

31   D. A. Miller, "Secret Subjects, Open Secrets," in *The Novel and the Police*, by Miller (Berkeley: Univ. of California Press, 1988), 207.

32   Ibid., 195.

33   Ibid., 199.

34   Douglass, *My Bondage*, 87.

35   Gaston Bachelard, *The Poetics of Space*, trans. Maria Jolas (Boston: Beacon, 1992), xxxii.

36   Ibid., 3.

37   Ibid., xxxiii.

38   Melvin Dixon, *Ride Out the Wilderness: Geography and Identity in Afro-American Literature* (Urbana: Univ. of Illinois Press, 1987), 2.

39 bell hooks, *Art on My Mind: Visual Politics* (New York: New Press, 1995), 147.

40 Mulvey, 55.

41 Dixon, *Wilderness*, 2.

42 Ibid., 5.

43 hooks, *Art*, 148. Emphasis added.

44 Ibid.

45 Ibid., 155.

46 Ibid., 148.

47 Raymond Williams, *Marxism and Literature*, 40–41. Susan Stewart, *On Longing: Narratives of the Miniature, the Gigantic, the Souvenir, the Collection* (Durham, N.C.: Duke Univ. Press, 1993), 31.

48 Fanon, 45.

49 Henry Glassie, "Eighteenth-Century Cultural Process in Delaware Valley Folk Building," in Upton and Vlach, 397. See also Glassie's *Folk Housing in Middle Virginia: Structural Analysis of Historic Artifacts* (Knoxville: Univ. of Tennessee Press, 1975) for a psycholinguistic reading of vernacular architecture as the materialization of geometrically codified thinking.

50 Sobel, 111. Emphasis added.

51 Freud, " 'Uncanny,' " 220.

52 Ibid., 240.

53 Interestingly, as the late Toomer critic Darwin T. Turner discovered, "in a manuscript typed many years after *Cane* had been published, Toomer identifies the work as 'Cain.' " Many more Toomer scholars besides Turner have taken this curiosity to "imply that Toomer originally titled *Cane* with intentional ambiguity." Darwin T. Turner, Preface to *Cane*, by Jean Toomer (1923; New York: Norton, 1988), viii. All references to the text of *Cane* will also be to this edition and indicated parenthetically in the text.

54 Jack M. Christ, "Jean Toomer's 'Bona and Paul': The Innocence and Artifice of Words," in *Jean Toomer: A Critical Evaluation*, ed. Therman B. O'Daniel (Washington, D.C.: Howard Univ. Press, 1988), 311.

55 Bourdieu, 90.

56 Ibid., 72.

57 Ibid., 89.

58 Ibid., 72.

59 Elizabeth Schultz, "Jean Toomer's 'Box Seat': The Possibility for 'Constructive Crisis,' " in O'Daniel, 299.

60 Ibid. Emphasis added.

61 Jean Toomer, "Outline of an Autobiography," in *The Wayward and the Seeking*, ed. Darwin T. Turner (Washington, D.C.: Howard Univ. Press, 1980), 123.

62 Silverman, *Threshold of the Visible World*, 20; 21. Anthony Vidler, *The Architectural Uncanny: Essays in the Modern Unhomely* (Cambridge, Mass.: MIT Press, 1992), 80.

63 Seltzer, 21.

64 Houston A. Baker Jr., *Blues, Ideology, and Afro-American Literature: A Vernacular Theory* (Chicago: Univ. of Chicago Press, 1984), 152.

65 Ibid., 145.

66 Besides Toomer's *Cane*, Ellison's *Invisible Man* and Wright's short story "The Man Who Lived Underground" each feature significant subterranean settings of black life. Victor A. Kramer has observed a parallel setting in Hart Crane's 1921 poem "Black Tambourine," a possible "source of inspiration for Jean Toomer in the composition of *Cane*, published two years later." See Kramer in O'Daniel, 121.

67 Baker, *Blues*, 151–52.

68 Ibid. Emphasis Baker's.

69 Ibid., 152.

70 Ibid., 145.

71 Jacques Lacan, "The Mirror Stage as Formative of the Function of the I as Revealed in Psychoanalytic Experience," in *Ecrits*, 5.

72 Bachelard, 23.

73 Ibid., 27.

74 Wigley, 341.

75 Robert B. Stepto, *From Behind the Veil: A Study of Afro-American Narrative*, 2d ed. (Urbana: Univ. of Illinois Press, 1991), 168.

76 Bachelard, 20.

5. "I'M NOT ENTIRELY WHAT I LOOK LIKE"

1 Richard Wright, qtd. in Michel Fabre, *The Unfinished Quest of Richard Wright*, trans. Isabel Barzun (Urbana: Univ. of Illinois Press, 1993), 258.

2 I have followed Fabre's convention of enclosing Wright's title in quotation marks.

3 Mitchell, 16.

4 Silverman, *Threshold of the Visible World*, 25.

5 See Michael Warner, *The Letters of the Republic: Publication and the Public Sphere in Eighteenth-Century America* (Cambridge, Mass.: Harvard Univ. Press, 1990).

6 The contents of the FBI papers on Baldwin that I discuss in this chapter are derived from two sources: The first is Natalie Robins's book *Alien Ink: The FBI's War on Freedom of Expression* (New York: Morrow, 1992), which devotes several pages to her research of the Baldwin papers; the second source is a copy of the seventeen-hundred-page file itself, obtained under the Freedom of Information Act. I owe Ms. Robins a great debt for permitting me access to the copied file she successfully procured. As Robins explains, however, "It is important to define what exactly a file *is*. At the point at which the documents reach anyone who has solicited them under the Freedom of Information Act, a dossier consists of separate pages of investigative reports, legal forms, interviews, memorandums, petitions, letters, articles, and news clippings that have been collected and clipped together in one [or more] folder[s] by the Federal Bu-

reau of Investigations" (17). I might add that any information in the file that the bureau deems important to the national defense or to foreign policy or that reveals the identities of informants is consistently and thoroughly expurgated. A significant portion of the Baldwin file was deleted in this manner and remains, therefore, classified.

7 Qtd. in Robins, 345.

8 Ibid., 346.

9 Here, I want to distinguish between "the photographic" and "the photo-graphic" by stressing the latter term's graphic or textual element over and above the former's mechanical or chemical operations within photography. By "the photo-graphic" I mean to evoke a writing that aspires toward picture taking, which is an activity somewhat different from picture-making ekphrasis. In the broadest sense, ekphrasis is "the verbal representation of visual representation" (Mitchell, 152). In the strictest sense, it denotes "a minor and rather obscure literary genre (poems which describe works of art)" (152). I am appealing to the broad sense of the term in order to put a name on the impulse toward verbal hypervisualization of the racial subject. One might think of "the photo-graphic" as a particular textualization of pictures subsumable under the general rubric of ekphrasis. We might take Mitchell's neologism "imagetext," "composite, synthetic [written] works . . . that combine image and text" (89n.9) as near synonym for "the photo-graphic." On ekphrasis, see Mitchell, 151–81; on imagetext, see Mitchell, 95.

10 Berlant, 113.

11 Federal Bureau of Investigation, Freedom of Information/Privacy Acts Release, File 100-146553-372 (Dec. 23, 1969).

12 File qtd. in Robins, 347.

13 Ibid., 348.

14 Ibid. Emphasis added.

15 For helping me to think through the FBI's impulse to frame Baldwin sexually by a blind devotion to image-able hearsay, I am indebted to Nicholas Boggs.

16 David J. Garrow, *The FBI and Martin Luther King, Jr.: From "Solo" to Memphis* (New York: Norton, 1981), 159.

17 Martin Jay, "Sartre, Merleau-Ponty, and the Search for a New Ontology of Sight," in *Modernity and the Hegemony of Vision*, ed. David Michael Levin (Berkeley: Univ. of California Press, 1993), 159.

18 Robins states, "The first mention of . . . James Baldwin anywhere in the FBI files occurs in 1951 — in Richard Wright's file" (345). It must be pointed out, however, that the appearance of Baldwin's name in Wright's file is only the first known mention of him, since it is likely he is also referenced in the report presumably made by the agents who accosted him in Woodstock, New York, in 1945. Since Baldwin claims he could scarcely remember the name of the deserter friend the agents were looking for, coming up only with "Teddy," it is doubtful Robins could have located, without painstakingly meticulous inves-

tigative work and inordinate time, the appropriate FBI records to confirm or dispute the originality of the 1951 Baldwin reference. See Baldwin, *The Devil Finds Work: An Essay* (New York: Dial, 1976), 107. All subsequent references are to this edition and shall be indicated parenthetically in the text.

19 Although biographer W. J. Weatherby has written that it was the FBI's surveillance that "persuade[d] [Baldwin] to make a permanent home in the south of France" (264), Baldwin's more recent biographer, David Leeming, suggests that Istanbul, not the south of France, was actually Baldwin's chosen place of retreat from the FBI during the most intense periods of surveillance. Baldwin himself said in a 1987 article for *Architectural Digest* that it was the April 4, 1968 assassination of Martin Luther King Jr. "that devastated my universe and was ultimately to lead me to this house" in Saint-Paul-de-Vence (123). See W. J. Weatherby, *James Baldwin: Artist on Fire* (New York: Dell, 1989); David Leeming, *James Baldwin: A Biography* (New York: Knopf, 1994); and Baldwin, "*Architectural Digest* Visits: James Baldwin," *Architectural Digest*, August 1987.

20 Qtd. in Robins, 349.

21 Silverman, *Threshold of the Invisible World*, 160.

22 Barthes, *Camera Lucida*, 15.

23 Thom Gunn, *The Man with Night Sweats* (London: Faber and Faber, 1992). I thank Blakey Vermeule of Northwestern University for bringing this wonderful poem to my attention.

6. WHAT JUBA KNEW

1 Charles Dickens, *American Notes*. (1842; reprint, Gloucester, Mass.: P. Smith, 1968), 110; 112.

2 Ibid., 110.

3 Lott, 113.

4 Ibid., 115.

5 Qtd. in Marian Hannah Winter, "Juba and American Minstrelsy," in *Chronicles of the American Dance*, ed. Paul David Magriel (New York: Holt, 1948), 50.

6 Qtd. in ibid.

7 Qtd. in ibid.

8 Lott, 113.

9 Ibid.

10 Qtd. in ibid.

11 See Baker, *Modernism*.

12 Winter, 39.

13 Ibid.

14 Butler, 33. Emphasis added.

15 Marta E. Savigliano, *Tango and the Political Economy of Passion* (Boulder: Westview Press, 1995), 4.

16 West, *Race Matters*, 129.

17 See Wilson Harns, "The Limbo Gateway" in *The Post-Colonial Studies Reader*,

ed. Bill Ashcroft, Gareth Griffiths, and Helen Tiffin (London: Routledge, 1995), 378–83. According to black dance historian Edward Thorpe, "one of the favorite dances which reappeared among slaves in the West Indies was the Calenda" from which the Calienda, a vigorous eighteenth-century jig "performed by males only, stripped to the waist and twirling heavy sticks in a mock fight" evolved. By contrast, the Calenda was a line dance in which "the men and women faced each other in two lines and danced to an impromptu song" intoned by the onlookers. In Calenda dancing, "the dancers made contact, slapping their thighs together, kissing and making 'lascivious' gestures." Thorpe distinguishes the Calenda from its male counterversion, the Calienda, by the supposition that, owing to its inherent homosociality, the Calienda "must have been rather different from the 'indecent' versions performed by mixed couples." Given the partial nakedness of the Calienda dancers and the phallicism of "the heavy sticks" wielded in the performance, however, the Calienda, if performatively different from the Calenda, might actually have been just as "indecent." Edward Thorpe, *Black Dance* (London: Chatto and Windus, 1989), 15.

18 Saint-Aubin, 1068.

19 West, *Race Matters*, 129.

20 Sondra Horton Fraleigh, *Dance and the Lived Body: A Descriptive Aesthetics* (Pittsburgh: Univ. of Pittsburgh Press, 1987), xxxvi.

21 The idea of the "Dancing Book" extends from Henry Louis Gates's archaeology of the Talking Book, the "ur-trope of the Anglo-African [literary] tradition." Just as the Talking Book "seems to concern itself with the possibilities of representation of the speaking black voice in writing," the "Dancing Book" as I have called it, aims to represent, in style and subject, orchestrated and improvised dance movement. We might go further, as I have suggested in the text of this chapter, to think of Toni Morrison's 1992 novel *Jazz* similarly. In a sense, *Jazz*, a novelistic approximation of the jazz sound, is the "Music Book" to Dixon's "Dancing Book." Both would seem to be postmodern derivatives of the Talking Book theorized by Gates. See Gates's *The Signifying Monkey: A Theory of Afro-American Literary Criticism* (New York: Oxford Univ. Press, 1988), xxv; 127–69.

22 Henry Louis Gates Jr., rev. of *Jazz*, by Toni Morrison, in *Toni Morrison: Critical Perspectives Past and Present*, ed. Gates and K. A. Appiah (New York: Amistad, 1993), 54.

23 Melvin Dixon, *Vanishing Rooms* (New York: Dutton, 1991), 97. All subsequent references are to this edition and will be cited parenthetically in the text.

24 Clarence Bard Cole, "Other Voices, Other Rooms: An Interview with Melvin Dixon," *Christopher Street*, May 1991, 27. Emphasis added.

25 Phillip Brian Harper, *Private Affairs: Critical Ventures in the Culture of Social Relations* (New York: New York Univ. Press, 1999), 139. Emphasis Harper's.

26 Edelman, 8.

27 Ibid., 43.

28 Ibid., 7.

29 Ibid., 46.

30 Berlant, "National Brands," 8.

31 Walt Whitman, "I Sing the Body Electric," in *The Whitman Reader*, ed. Maxwell Geismar (New York: Pocket Books, 1955), 71.

32 Bourdieu, 10.

33 See Daniel Nagrin, *Dance and the Specific Image: Improvisation* (Pittsburgh: Univ. of Pittsburgh Press, 1994).

34 Bourdieu, 10.

35 Ibid., 9. Emphasis Bourdieu's.

36 Langston Hughes, "Dream Variations," in *Collected Poems*, 40.

37 West, *Race Matters*, 129.

38 Arnold Rampersad, *The Life of Langston Hughes*, vol. 1 (New York: Oxford Univ. Press, 1986–88), 78.

39 Alvin Ailey with A. Peter Bailey, *Revelations: The Autobiography of Alvin Ailey* (Secaucus, N.J.: Carol, 1994), 88.

40 Langston Hughes, "Seven People Dancing," unpublished manuscript, n.d., Langston Hughes Papers 3485, James Weldon Johnson Collection, Beineke Library, Yale University.

41 According to Rampersad, Hughes offered Ailey his ballet libretto, "St. Louis Blues," and his long poem *Ask Your Mama* for choreographic consideration in 1955 and 1961, respectively. Whether or not the specific poems Ailey referred to in *Revelations* were related to these is not known. Ailey was also retained to provide choreographic direction to two gospel musicals by Hughes, *Black Nativity* and *Jericho Jim-Crow* (Ailey did not stay with the former production). See Rampersad, *Life*, vol. 2, 248; 343; 346–47; 371.

42 Susan Leigh Foster, "The Sygnifying Body," *Theatre Journal* 37, 1 qtd. in Ramsay Burt, *The Male Dancer: Bodies, Spectacle, Sexualities* (New York: Routledge, 1995), 46.

43 Gerald E. Myers, "African Americans and the Modern Dance Aesthetic," in *African American Genius in Modern Dance*, ed. Myers (Durham, N.C.: American Dance Festival, 1993), *n*.30.

44 Susan Leigh Foster, *Reading Dancing: Bodies and Subjects in Contemporary American Dance* (Berkeley: Univ. of California Press, 1986), xvi. Emphasis added.

45 Nagrin, 28.

46 Hortense Spillers, "Mama's Baby, Papa's Maybe: An American Grammar Book," in *Within the Circle: An Anthology of African American Literary Criticism from the Harlem Renaissance to the Present*, ed. Angelyn Mitchell (Durham, N.C.: Duke Univ. Press, 1994), 479–80.

47 Foster, xix.

48 Fraleigh, 17.

49 Bill T. Jones with Peggy Gillespie, *Last Night on Earth* (New York: Pantheon,

1995), ix. All subsequent references are to this edition and page references will be cited parenthetically in the text.

50 Eric K. Washington, "Sculpture in Flight: A Conversation with Bill T. Jones," *Transition* 62 (1993): 194.

51 Ibid., 191.

52 Ibid.

53 Qtd. in Henry Louis Gates Jr., "The Body Politic," *New Yorker*, 28 Nov. 1994, 84. Emphasis Gates's.

54 Ibid.

55 Ibid., 121.

56 Ibid. Emphasis Gates's.

57 Taussig, 13.

58 Ibid.

59 Ibid., 3. Taussig derives his theory of "the magic of mimesis" from the ritual magic practices of the Cuna Indians in and around Panama.

60 See Silverman, *Threshold of the Visible World*, 154–61.

61 Gates, "Body," 121.

62 See Calvin Thomas, *Male Matters: Masculinity, Anxiety, and the Male Body on the Line* (Urbana: Univ. of Illinois Press, 1996), 19–26; 190–94.

63 Gates, "Body," 124.

64 Dustjacket to Maya Deren, *Maya Deren: Experimental Films*, Montauk, N.Y. (Mystic Fire Video, 1986), VHS.

65 Deren quoted in Margaret Lloyd [pseud.], *The Borzoi Book of Modern Dance* (New York: Knopf, 1949), 352.

66 Ibid.

67 Erick Hawkins, *The Body Is a Clear Place, and Other Statements on Dance* (Princeton: Princeton Book Company, 1992), 56.

AFTERWORD

1 David Michael Levin, Introduction to *Modernity and the Hegemony of Vision*, ed. Levin (Berkeley: Univ. of California Press, 1993), 2.

2 Ibid., 4.

3 Ibid., 5.

4 See Derrida, *Memoirs*, 12.

5 Bhabha, *Location*, 89.

6 Stuart Hall, "The After-Life of Frantz Fanon: Why Fanon? Why Now? Why *Black Skin, White Masks*?" [*sic*] in *The Fact of Blackness*, ed. Read, 19.

7 Levin, Introduction, 4.

8 Bhabha, *Location*, 75–76.

9 Ibid., 76.

10 Derek Walcott, *The Odyssey: A Stage Version* (London: Faber and Faber, 1993), 69–70.

11 David Michael Levin, *The Opening of Vision: Nihilism and the Postmodern Situation* (New York: Routledge, 1988), 440.

12 Derrida, *Memoirs*, 29.

13 Frantz Fanon, *Black Skin White Masks*, trans. Charles Lam Markmann, 1952 (New York: Grove Press, 1967), 113–4. All subsequent citations will be to this edition and indicated parenthetically in the text of this chapter.

14 Levin, Introduction, 5.

15 Although the proper title of part IV, section XV is "*Darkness* is terrible in its own nature" (my emphasis), "the ideas of darkness and blackness are much the same," according to Burke. "They differ only in this, that blackness is a more confined idea." Edmund Burke, *A Philosophical Enquiry into the Origin of Our Ideas of the Sublime and Beautiful*, ed. Adam Phillips (1757; Oxford: Oxford Univ. Press, 1990), 131.

16 Ibid.

17 Lola Young, "Missing Persons: Fantasising Black Women in *Black Skin, White Masks*" [*sic*] in *The Fact of Blackness*, ed. Read, 93.

18 Du Bois, *Souls*, 45.

19 This phrase of Bhabha's has lingered with me since I first heard it in Bhabha's 1996 keynote address to the "Locations, Cultures, Topographies: Diaspora in Cultural Criticism" conference at Yale University.

20 Bhabha, *Location*, 76.

21 Peter Geismar, *Fanon*. (New York: Grove, 1971), 35; 43.

22 See B. Marie B. Perinbam's bibliography in her *Holy Violence: The Revolutionary Thought of Frantz Fanon: An Intellectual Biography* (Washington, D.C.: Three Continents, 1982), 153–76. Fanon's plays are also mentioned by Geismar and by Pierre Bouvier, *Fanon* (Paris: Éditions Universitaires, 1971), but one is hard-pressed to locate any further references to these compositions anywhere.

23 Geismar, 49.

24 Ibid.

25 In the making for more than seven years, according to Bouvier (31). According to Geismar, *Black Skin White Masks* "developed out of a series of separate essays and speeches" (14) that Fanon set about to cohere into a unified work between 1948 and 1951.

26 Clifford Geertz, "Blurred Genres: The Refiguration of Social Thought," in *Critical Theory since 1965*, ed. Adams and Searle, 520.

27 Ibid., 518.

Ailey, Alvin, with A. Peter Bailey. *Revelations: The Autobiography of Alvin Ailey.* Secaucus, N.J.: Carol, 1994.

Alexander, Elizabeth. "'Can you be BLACK and look at this?': Reading the Rodney King Video(s)." In *Black Male: Representations of Masculinity in Contemporary American Art,* ed. Thelma Golden, 91–110. New York: Whitney Museum of American Art, 1994.

Allen, Polly Wynn. *Building Domestic Liberty: Charlotte Perkins Gilman's Architectural Feminism.* Amherst: Univ. of Massachusetts Press, 1988.

Andrews, Wayne. *Architecture, Ambition, and Americans: A Social History of American Architecture.* New York: Free Press, 1978.

Archer-Straw, Petrine. *Negrophilia: Avant-Garde Paris and Black Culture in the 1920s.* London: Thames and Hudson, 2000.

Arendt, Hannah. *The Human Condition.* Chicago: Univ. of Chicago Press, 1958.

Awkward, Michael. *Negotiating Difference: Race, Gender, and the Politics of Positionality.* Chicago: Univ. of Chicago Press, 1995.

Bachelard, Gaston. *The Poetics of Space.* Trans. Maria Jolas. Boston: Beacon, 1994.

Baker, Houston A., Jr. *Blues, Ideology, and Afro-American Literature: A Vernacular Theory.* Chicago: Univ. of Chicago Press, 1984.

———. *Modernism and the Harlem Renaissance.* Chicago: Univ. of Chicago Press, 1987.

Baldwin, James. "*Architectural Digest* Visits: James Baldwin." *Architectural Digest,* August 1987, 122–25.

———. *The Devil Finds Work: An Essay.* New York: Dial, 1976.

———. "Everybody's Protest Novel." In *The Price of the Ticket: Collected Nonfiction, 1948–1985,* by Baldwin, 27–39. New York: St. Martin's Press, 1985.

———. "Here Be Dragons." In *The Price of the Ticket: Collected Nonfiction, 1948–1985,* by Baldwin, 677–90. New York: St. Martin's Press, 1985.

———. "Many Thousand Gone." In *The Price of the Ticket: Collected Nonfiction, 1948–1985,* by Baldwin, 65–78. New York: St. Martin's Press, 1985.

Barthes, Roland. *Camera Lucida: Reflections on Photography.* Trans. Richard Howard. New York: Hill and Wang, 1981.

———. *S/Z.* Trans. Richard Miller. New York: Hill and Wang, 1974.

Bell, Bernard W. *The Afro-American Novel and Its Tradition.* Amherst: Univ. of Massachusetts Press, 1987.

Belton, Don, ed. *Speak My Name: Black Men on Masculinity and the American Dream*. Boston: Beacon, 1995.

Benjamin, Walter. *Illuminations*. Trans. Harry Zohn. New York: Schocken, 1969.

Benn Michaels, Walter. "Romance and Real Estate." In *The American Renaissance Reconsidered*, ed. Michaels and Donald E. Pease, 156–82. Baltimore: Johns Hopkins Univ. Press, 1985.

Berlant, Lauren. *The Anatomy of National Fantasy: Hawthorne, Utopia, and Everyday Life*. Chicago: Univ. of Chicago Press, 1991.

———. "National Brands/National Bodies: *Imitation of Life*." In *Comparative American Identities: Race, Sex, and Nationality in the Modern Text*, ed. Hortense J. Spillers, 110–40. New York: Routledge, 1991.

"The Black Man is Terrible Trouble. Whose Fault Is That?" *New York Times Magazine*, 4 Dec. 1994.

Bhabha, Homi K. Keynote address. Locations, Cultures, Topographies: Diaspora in Cultural Criticism Conference, Yale University, New Haven. April 1996.

———. *The Location of Culture*. London: Routledge, 1994.

Blassingame, John W. *The Slave Community: Plantation Life in the Antebellum South*. New York: Oxford Univ. Press, 1972.

Blount, Marcellus, and George P. Cunningham, eds. *Representing Black Men*. New York: Routledge, 1996.

Bourdieu, Pierre. *Outline of a Theory of Practice*. Trans. Richard Nice. Cambridge: Cambridge Univ. Press, 1977.

Bouvier, Pierre. *Fanon*. Paris: Éditions Universitaires, 1971.

Burke, Edmund. *A Philosophical Enquiry into the Origin of Our Ideas of the Sublime and Beautiful*. 1757. Ed. Adam Phillips. Oxford: Oxford Univ. Press, 1990.

Burt, Ramsay. *The Male Dancer: Bodies, Spectacle, Sexualities*. New York: Routledge, 1995.

Butler, Judith. *Gender Trouble: Feminism and the Subversion of Identity*. New York: Routledge, 1990.

Carbado, Devon, ed. *Black Men on Race, Gender, and Sexuality: A Critical Reader*. New York: New York Univ. Press, 1999.

Carby, Hazel V. *Race Men*. Cambridge, Mass.: Harvard Univ. Press, 1998.

Carnes, Mark C. *Secret Ritual and Manhood in Victorian America*. New Haven: Yale Univ. Press, 1989.

Chesnutt, Charles. *The House behind the Cedars*. 1900. Reprint, New York: Collier, 1969.

Christ, Jack M. "Jean Toomer's 'Bona and Paul': The Innocence and Artifice of Words." In *Jean Toomer: A Critical Evaluation*, ed. Therman B. O'Daniel, 311–17. Washington, D. C.: Howard Univ. Press, 1988.

Cixous, Hélène. "Laugh of the Medusa." In *Critical Theory since 1965*, ed. Hazard Adams and Leroy Searle, 309–20. Tallahassee: Florida State Univ. Press, 1986.

Clawson, Mary Ann. *Constructing Brotherhood: Class, Gender, and Fraternalism*. Princeton: Princeton Univ. Press, 1989.

Cole, Clarence Bard. "Other Voices, Other Rooms: An Interview with Melvin Dixon." *Christopher Street*, May 1991, 24–7.

Cooke, Michael. "Modern Black Autobiography in the Tradition." In *Romanticism: Vistas, Instances, Continuities*, ed. David Thorburn and Geoffrey Hartman, 255–80. Ithaca: Cornell Univ. Press, 1973.

Cornelius, Janet Duitsman. *"When I Can Read My Title Clear": Literacy, Slavery, and Religion in the Antebellum South*. Columbia: Univ. of South Carolina Press, 1991.

Cox, Joseph Mason Andrew. *Great Black Men of Masonry 1723–1982*. Bronx: Blue Diamond, 1982.

Crary, Jonathan. *Techniques of the Observer: On Vision and Modernity in the Nineteenth Century*. Cambridge, Mass.: MIT Press, 1990.

Crawford, George W. *Prince Hall and His Followers: Being a Monograph on the Legitimacy of Negro Masonry*. New York: Crisis, 1914.

Culler, Jonathan. *On Deconstruction: Theory and Criticism after Structuralism*. Ithaca: Cornell Univ. Press, 1982.

Cunningham, George. "'Called into Existence': Gender, Desire and Voice in *Douglass' Narrative of 1845*." *Differences* 1, 3 (1989): 108–36.

Darrah, William C. *Cartes de Visite in Nineteenth Century Photography*. Gettysburg, Pa.: Darrah, 1981.

Davis, Harry E. *A History of Freemasonry among Negroes in America*. Cleveland[?]: United Supreme Council, Ancient and Accepted Scottish Rite of Freemasonry, Northern Jurisdiction, USA (Prince Hall Affiliation), 1946.

Davis, Rebecca Harding. *Waiting for the Verdict*. 1867. Upper Saddle River, N.J.: Gregg Press, 1968.

de Certeau, Michel. *The Practice of Everyday Life*. Trans. Steven Rendall. Berkeley: Univ. of California Press, 1984.

Delany, Martin Robison. *Blake; or, the Huts of America: A Novel*. 1859. Reprint, with an introduction by Floyd J. Miller. Boston: Beacon, 1970.

———. *The Origins and Objects of Ancient Freemasonry: Its Introduction into the United States and Legitimacy among Colored Men*. Pittsburgh: Haven, 1853.

———. *Principia of Ethnology: The Origin of Races and Color, With an Archaeological Compendium of Ethiopian and Egyptian Civilization from Years of Careful Examination and Inquiry*. Philadelphia: Harper, 1880.

Deren, Maya. *Maya Deren: Experimental Films*. Montauk, N.Y.: Mystic Fire Video, 1986. VHS.

Derrida, Jacques. *Memoirs of the Blind: The Self-Portrait and Other Ruins*. Trans. Pascale-Anne Brault and Michael Naas. Chicago: Univ. of Chicago Press, 1993.

———. *The Truth in Painting*. Trans. Geoff Bennington and Ian McLeod. Chicago: Univ. of Chicago Press, 1987.

Dickens, Charles. *American Notes*. 1842. Reprint, with an introduction by Christopher Lasch. Gloucester, Mass.: P. Smith, 1968.

Dixon, Melvin. *Ride Out the Wilderness: Geography and Identity in Afro-American Literature*. Urbana: Univ. of Illinois Press, 1987.

———. *Vanishing Rooms*. New York: Dutton, 1991.

Douglass, Frederick. *My Bondage and My Freedom*. 1855. Reprint, with a new introduction by Philip S. Foner. New York: Dover, 1969.

———. *Narrative of the Life of Frederick Douglass, an American Slave*. 1845. Reprint, with introduction by Houston A. Baker Jr. New York: Penguin, 1987.

Du Bois, W. E. B. *The Souls of Black Folk*. 1903. Reprint, with introductions by Nathan Hare and Alvin F. Poussaint. New York: New American Library, 1982.

Du Bois, W. E. B., and Augustus Granville Dill, eds. *The Negro American Artisan: Report of a Social Study Made by Atlanta University under the Patronage of the Trustees of the John F. Slater Fund; with Proceedings of the Seventeenth Annual Conference for the Study of the Negro Problems, Held at Atlanta University on Monday, May 27th, 1902*. 1902. Reprint, New York: Arno, 1968.

Dudley, David L. *My Father's Shadow: Intergenerational Conflict in African American Men's Autobiography*. Philadelphia: Univ. of Pennsylvania Press, 1991.

Dumenil, Lynn. *Freemasonry and American Culture, 1880–1930*. Princeton: Princeton Univ. Press, 1984.

Edelman, Lee. *Homographesis: Essays in Gay Literary and Cultural Theory*. New York: Routledge, 1994.

Ellison, Ralph. *Invisible Man*. 1952. Reprint, New York: Vintage, 1972.

———. *Shadow and Act*. 1953. Reprint, New York: Vintage, 1964.

Fabre, Michel. *The Unfinished Quest of Richard Wright*. Trans. Isabel Barzun. Urbana: Univ. of Illinois Press, 1993.

Fanon, Frantz. *Black Skin White Masks*. Trans. Charles Lam Markmann. New York: Grove, 1967.

Fernandez, James W. *Persuasions and Performances: The Play of Tropes in Culture*. Bloomington: Indiana Univ. Press, 1986.

Foster, Susan Leigh. *Reading Dancing: Bodies and Subjects in Contemporary American Dance*. Berkeley: Univ. of California Press, 1986.

Foucault, Michel. *Discipline and Punish: The Birth of the Prison*. Trans. Alan Sheridan. New York: Vintage, 1979.

———. *The History of Sexuality*. Trans. Robert Hurley. New York: Pantheon, 1978.

Fraleigh, Sondra Horton. *Dance and the Lived Body: A Descriptive Aesthetics*. Pittsburgh: Univ. of Pittsburgh Press, 1987.

Frank, Ellen Eve. *Literary Architecture: Essays toward a Tradition: Walter Pater, Gerard Manley Hopkins, Marcel Proust, Henry James*. Berkeley: Univ. of California Press, 1979.

Franchot, Jenny. "The Punishment of Ester: Frederick Douglass and the Constitution of the Feminine." In *Frederick Douglass: New Literary and Historical Essays*, ed. Eric J. Sundquist, 141–65. New York: Cambridge Univ. Press, 1990.

Fredrickson, George M. *The Black Image in the White Mind: The Debate on Afro-American Character and Destiny, 1817–1914*. New York: Harper and Row, 1971.

Freud, Sigmund. *The Interpretation of Dreams*. In *The Standard Edition of the Complete Psychological Works of Sigmund Freud*, vols. 4–5, trans. James Strachey. London: Hogarth, 1955.

——. "Medusa's Head." In *The Standard Edition of the Complete Psychological Works of Sigmund Freud*, vol. 18, trans. James Strachey, 273–74. London: Hogarth, 1955.

——. "The 'Uncanny.'" In *The Standard Edition of the Complete Psychological Works of Sigmund Freud*, vol. 17, trans. James Strachey, 217–52. London: Hogarth, 1955.

Freund, Charles Paul. "From Satan to Sphinx: The Masonic Mysteries of DC's Map." *Washington Post*, 5 Nov. 1995, CO3.

Garrow, David J. *The FBI and Martin Luther King, Jr.: From 'Solo' to Memphis*. New York: Norton, 1981.

Gates, Henry Louis, Jr. "The Body Politic." *New Yorker*, 28 Nov. 1994.

——. *Figures in Black: Words, Signs, and the "Racial" Self*. New York: Oxford Univ. Press, 1987.

——. Review of *Jazz*, by Toni Morrison. In *Toni Morrison: Critical Perspectives Past and Present*, ed. Gates and K. A. Appiah, 52–55. New York: Amistad, 1993.

——. *The Signifying Monkey: A Theory of Afro-American Literary Criticism*. New York: Oxford Univ. Press, 1988.

——. *Thirteen Ways of Looking at a Black Man*. New York: Random House, 1997.

Geertz, Clifford. "Blurred Genres: The Refiguration of Social Thought." In *Critical Theory since 1965*, ed. Hazard Adams and Leroy Searle, 514–23. Tallahassee: Florida State Univ. Press, 1986.

Geismar, Peter. *Fanon*. New York: Grove, 1971.

Genovese, Eugene D. *The World the Slaveholders Made: Two Essays in Interpretation*. Middletown, Conn.: Wesleyan Univ. Press, 1988.

Gilbert, Olive. *Narrative of Sojourner Truth*. 1850. In *The Norton Anthology of African American Literature*, ed. Henry Louis Gates Jr. and Nellie Y. McKay, 199–201, New York:Norton, 1997.

Gilman, Charlotte Perkins. *In This Our World*. 3d ed. Boston: Small Maynard, 1908.

Gilroy, Paul. *The Black Atlantic: Modernity and Double Consciousness*. Cambridge, Mass.: Harvard Univ. Press, 1993.

Girard, René. *Deceit, Desire, and the Novel: Self and Other in Literary Structure*. Trans. Yvonne Freccero. Baltimore: Johns Hopkins Univ. Press, 1976.

Glassie, Henry. "Eighteenth-Century Cultural Process in Delaware Valley Folk Building." In *Common Places: Reading in American Vernacular Architecture*, ed. Dell Upton and John Michael Vlach, 394–425. Athens: Univ. of Georgia Press, 1986.

——. *Folk Housing in Middle Virginia: Structural Analysis of Historic Artifacts*. Knoxville: Univ. of Tennessee Press, 1975.

Golden, Thelma, ed. *Black Male: Representations of Masculinity in Contemporary American Art*. New York: Whitney Museum of American Art, 1994.

Gooding-Williams, Robert, ed. *Reading Rodney King/Reading Urban Uprising*. New York: Routledge, 1993.

Gordon, Jacob U., ed. *The African American Male in American Life and Thought*. Thousand Oaks, Calif.: Sage, 2000.

Greenberg, David F. *The Construction of Homosexuality*. Chicago: Univ. of Chicago Press, 1988.

Greene, Lorenzo Johnston. *The Negro in Colonial New England*. New York: Atheneum, 1968.

———. "The New England Negro as Seen in Advertisements for Runaway Slaves." *Journal of Negro History* 29, 2 (1944): 125–46.

Griggs, Sutton E. *The Hindered Hand; or, The Reign of the Repressionist*. 1905. Reprint, Miami, Fla.: Mnemosyne, 1969.

Grimshaw, William Henry. *Official History of Freemasonry among the Colored People in North America: Tracing the Growth of Masonry from 1717 Down to the Present Day*. New York: Negro Universities Press, 1969.

Guerrero, Ed. "The Black Man on Our Screens and the Empty Space in Representation." In *Black Male: Representations of Masculinity in Contemporary American Art*, ed. Thelma Golden, 181–89. New York: Whitney Museum of American Art, 1994.

Gunn, Thom. *The Man with Night Sweats*. London: Faber and Faber, 1992.

Halberstam, Judith. *Female Masculinity*. Durham, N.C.: Duke Univ. Press, 1998.

Hall, Stuart. "The After-Life of Frantz Fanon: Why Fanon? Why Now? Why *Black Skin, White Masks*?" [*sic*] in *The Fact of Blackness: Frantz Fanon and Visual Representation*, ed. Alan Read, 12–37. London: Institute of Contemporary Arts, 1996.

Handlin, David P. *The American Home: Architecture and Society, 1815–1915*. Boston: Little, Brown, 1979.

Harlan, Louis R. *Booker T. Washington: The Making of a Black Leader, 1856–1901*. New York: Oxford Univ. Press, 1972.

Harper, Phillip Brian. *Are We Not Men? Masculine Anxiety and the Problem of African-American Identity*. New York: Oxford Univ. Press, 1996.

———. *Private Affairs: Critical Ventures in the Culture of Social Relations*. New York: New York Univ. Press, 1999.

Harris, Wilson. "The Limbo Gateway." In *The Post-Colonial Studies Reader*, ed. Bill Ashcroft, Gareth Griffiths, and Helen Tiffin, 378–83. London: Routledge, 1995.

Hatt, Michael. " 'Making a Man of Him': Masculinity and the Black Body in Mid–Nineteenth-Century American Sculpture." *Oxford Art Journal*, 15, 1 (1992): 21–35.

Hawkins, Erick. *The Body Is a Clear Place, and Other Statements on Dance*. Princeton: Princeton Book Company, 1992.

Hayden, Dolores. *The Grand Domestic Revolution: A History of Feminist Designs for American Homes, Neighborhoods, and Cities*. Cambridge, Mass.: MIT Press, 1981.

Hearn, Jeff. *The Gender of Oppression: Men, Masculinity and the Critique of Marxism.* Brighton: Wheatsheaf, 1987.

Heidegger, Martin. *The Question Concerning Technology, and Other Essays.* Trans. William Lovitt. New York: Harper and Row, 1977.

Hellenbrand, Harold. "Bigger Thomas Reconsidered: *Native Son,* Film, *King Kong.*" *Journal of American Culture* 6, 1 (1983): 84–95.

Herrnstein-Smith, Barbara. "Contingencies of Value." *Critical Inquiry* 10, 1 (1983): 1–35.

Hirsch, Robert. *Seizing the Light: A History of Photography.* Boston: McGraw-Hill, 2000.

Hirst, Alex. Introduction to *Black Male/White Male,* by Rotimi Fani-Kayode. London: GMP Publishers, 1988.

Hoch, Paul. *White Hero Black Beast: Racism, Sexism and the Mask of Masculinity.* London: Pluto Press, 1979.

hooks, bell. *Ain't I a Woman: Black Women and Feminism.* Boston: South End Press, 1981.

———. *Art on My Mind: Visual Politics.* New York: New Press, 1995.

———. *Black Looks: Race and Representation.* Boston: South End Press, 1992.

———. *Yearning: Race, Gender, and Cultural Politics.* Boston: South End Press, 1990.

Hopkins, Pauline. *Hagar's Daughter.* 1901–1902. In *The Magazine Novels of Pauline Hopkins.* New York: Oxford Univ. Press, 1988.

Howells, William Dean. *An Imperative Duty: A Novel.* New York: Harper, 1892.

Hughes, Langston. *The Collected Poems of Langston Hughes.* Ed. Arnold Rampersad and David Roessel. New York: Vintage, 1995.

———. "Seven People Dancing." Unpublished manuscript, n.d. Langsten Hughes Papers 3485. In James Weldon Johnson Collection Beineke Library, Yale University.

Jacobs, Harriet. *Incidents in the Life of a Slave Girl.* In *The Classic Slave Narratives,* ed. Henry Louis Gates Jr. New York: New American Library, 1987.

Jay, Martin. "Sartre, Merleau-Ponty, and the Search for a New Ontology of Sight." In *Modernity and the Hegemony of Vision,* ed. David Michael Levin, 143–85. Berkeley: Univ. of California Press, 1993.

Johnson, Charles. *Being and Race: Black Writing since 1970.* Bloomington: Indiana Univ. Press, 1988.

———. "A Phenomenology of the Black Body." *Michigan Quarterly Review* 32, 4 (1993): 598–614.

Johnson, George. "Pierre, Is That a Masonic Flag on the Moon?" *New York Times,* 24 Nov. 1996, 4E.

Jones, Bernard E., ed. *Cassell's Cyclopaedia of Photography.* New York: Arno, 1973.

Jones, Bill T., with Peggy Gillespie. *Last Night on Earth.* New York: Pantheon, 1995.

Jones, Jacqueline. *Labor of Love, Labor of Sorrow: Black Women, Work, and the Family from Slavery to the Present.* New York: Basic Books, 1985.

Jones, Steven L. "The African-American Tradition in Vernacular Architecture." In *The Archaeology of Slavery and Plantation Life*, ed. Theresa A. Singleton, 195–213. Orlando: Academic Press, 1985.

Jordan, Winthrop D. *White over Black: American Attitudes toward the Negro, 1550–1812*. Baltimore: Penguin, 1969.

Journal of African American Men: A Publication of The National Council of African American Men. New Brunswick: Transaction Publishers, 1995–.

Kaplan, Sidney. *The Black Presence in the Era of the American Revolution, 1770–1880*. Greenwich, Conn.: New York Graphic Society, 1973.

Kaplan, Sidney and Emma Nogrady Kaplan. *The Black Presence in the Era of the American Revolution*. Rev. ed. Amherst: Univ. of Massachusetts Press, 1989.

Krieger, Murray. *Ekphrasis: The Illusion of the Natural Sign*. Baltimore: Johns Hopkins Univ. Press, 1992.

Lacan, Jacques. *Écrits: A Selection*. Trans. Alan Sheridan. New York: Norton, 1977.

——. *The Four Fundamental Concepts of Psycho-Analysis*. Trans. Alan Sheridan. New York: Norton, 1978.

Leeming, David. *James Baldwin: A Biography*. New York: Knopf, 1994.

Leverenz, David. *Manhood and the American Renaissance*. Ithaca: Cornell Univ. Press, 1989.

Levin, David Michael, ed. *Modernity and the Hegemony of Vision*. Berkeley: Univ. of California Press, 1993.

——. *The Opening of Vision: Nihilism and the Postmodern Situation*. New York: Routledge, 1988.

Levine, Lawrence W. *Black Culture and Black Consciousness: Afro-American Folk Thought from Slavery to Freedom*. 1977. Reprint, New York: Oxford Univ. Press, 1978.

Levine, Robert S. *Martin Delany, Frederick Douglass, and the Politics of Representative Identity*. Chapel Hill: Univ. of North Carolina Press, 1997.

Lloyd, Margaret [pseud.]. *The Borzoi Book of Modern Dance*. New York: Knopf, 1949.

Lott, Eric. *Love and Theft: Blackface Minstrelsy and the American Working Class*. New York: Oxford Univ. Press, 1993.

Lubiano, Wahneema H. "Mapping the Interstices between Afro-American Cultural Discourse and the Culture Studies: A Prolegomenon." *Callaloo* 19, 1 (1996): 68–77.

Mackey, Albert G. *Encyclopedia of Freemasonry and Its Kindred Sciences: Comprising the Whole Range of Arts, Sciences and Literature as Connected with the Masonic Institution*. 1873. 2 vols. Rev. ed. Chicago: Masonic History Company, 1929.

——. *The Symbolism of Freemasonry: Illustrating and Explaining Its Science and Philosophy, Its Legends, Myths, and Symbols*. Chicago: Cook, 1947.

Madhubuti, Haki R. *Black Men: Obsolete, Single, Dangerous? Afrikan American Families in Transition: Essays in Discovery, Solution, and Hope*. Chicago: Third World Press, 1990.

Madhubuti, Haki R. and Malauna Karenga, eds. *Million Man March/Day of Absence: A Commemorative Anthology; Speeches, Commentary, Photography, Poetry, Illustrations, Documents*. Chicago: Third World Press, 1996.

Majors, Richard, and Janet Mancini Billson. *Cool Pose: The Dilemmas of Black Manhood in America*. New York: Lexington Books, 1992.

Mannheim, L. A., et al., eds. *The Focal Encyclopedia of Photography*. Rev. ed. New York: McGraw-Hill, 1969.

Mayer, Robert A. "Photographing the American Presidency." 27, 3 (1984): 1–36.

Mazlish, Bruce. "Autobiography and Psychoanalysis: Between Truth and Self-Deception." *Encounter* 35 (1970): 28–37.

McCumber, John. "Derrida and the Closure of Vision." In *Modernity and the Hegemony of Vision*, ed. David Michael Levin, 234–51. Berkeley: Univ. of California Press, 1993.

Mercer, Kobena. *Welcome to the Jungle: New Positions in Black Cultural Studies*. New York: Routledge, 1994.

Mercer, Kobena, and Isaac Julien, "Race, Sexual Politics, and Black Masculinity: A Dossier." *Male Order: Unwrapping Masculinity*, ed. Rowena Chapman and Jonathan Rutherford, 97–164. London: Lawrence and Wishart, 1988.

Middleton, Peter. *The Inward Gaze: Masculinity and Subjectivity in Modern Culture*. London: Routledge, 1992.

Miller, D. A. *The Novel and the Police*. Berkeley: Univ. of California Press, 1988.

Mitchell, W. J. T. *Picture Theory: Essays on Verbal and Visual Representation*. Chicago: Univ. of Chicago Press, 1994.

Morrison, Toni. *Beloved*. New York: Plume, 1987.

———. *Playing in the Dark: Whiteness and the Literary Imagination*. Cambridge, Mass.: Harvard Univ. Press, 1992.

Morrison, Toni, and Claudia Brodsky Lacour, eds. *Birth of a Nation'hood: Gaze, Script, and Spectacle in the O. J. Simpson Case*. New York: Random House, 1998.

Morse, Sidney. *Freemasonry in the American Revolution*. Washington, D.C.: Masonic Service Association of the United States, 1924.

Mossell, Gertrude Bustill. "A Lofty Study." In *Words of Fire: An Anthology of African American Feminist Thought*, ed. Beverly Guy-Sheftall, 60–61. New York: New Press, 1995.

———. "The Opposite Point of View." In *Words of Fire: An Anthology of African American Feminist Thought*, ed. Beverly Guy-Sheftall, 56–59. New York: New Press, 1995.

Mulvey, Laura. "Pandora: Topographies of the Mask and Curiosity." In *Sexuality and Space*, ed. Beatriz Colomina, 53–71. New York: Princeton Architectural Press, 1992.

Muñoz, José Esteban. *Disidentifications: Queers of Color and the Performance of Politics*. Minneapolis: Univ. of Minnesota Press, 1999.

Muraskin, William A. *Middle-Class Blacks in a White Society: Prince Hall Freemasonry in America*. Berkeley: Univ. of California Press, 1975.

Myers, Gerald E. "African Americans and the Modern Dance Aesthetic." In *African American Genius in Modern Dance*, ed. Myers, 30–33. Durham, N.C.: American Dance Festival, 1993.

Nagrin, Daniel. *Dance and the Specific Image: Improvisation*. Pittsburgh: Univ. of Pittsburgh Press, 1994.

Nelson, Dana D. *National Manhood: Capitalist Citizenship and the Imagined Fraternity of White Men*. Durham, N.C.: Duke Univ. Press, 1998.

Nero, Charles. "Toward a Black Gay Aesthetic: Signifying in Contemporary Black Gay Literature." In *Cornerstones: An Anthology of African American Literature*, ed. Melvin Donalson, 971–89. New York: St. Martin's Press, 1996.

Nye, Robert A. "Sex Difference and Male Homosexuality in French Medical Discourse." *Bulletin of the History of Medicine* 63 (1989): 32–51.

O'Daniel, Therman. *Jean Toomer: A Critical Evaluation*. Washington, D. C..: Howard University Press, 1988.

Painter, Nell Irvin. *Sojourner Truth: A life, a Symbol*. New York: Norton, 1996.

Pennington, James W. C. *The Fugitive Blacksmith; or, Events in the History of James W. C. Pennington, Pastor of a Presbyterian Church, New York, Formerly a Slave in the State of Maryland, United States*. 1849. Reprint, Westport, Conn.: Negro Universities Press, 1971.

Perinbam, B. Marie. *Holy Violence: The Revolutionary Thought of Frantz Fanon: An Intellectual Biography*. Washington, D.C.: Three Continents, 1982.

Powell, Richard J. *Black Art and Culture in the Twentieth Century*. New York: Thames and Hudson, 1997.

Radway, Janice A. *Reading the Romance: Women, Patriarchy, and Popular Literature*. Chapel Hill: Univ. of North Carolina Press, 1984.

Rampersad, Arnold. *The Life of Langston Hughes*. 2 vols. New York: Oxford Univ. Press, 1986–88.

———. Notes to *Native Son*, by Richard Wright. New York: HarperCollins, 1993.

Rampersad, Arnold, and David Roessel, eds. *The Collected Poems of Langston Hughes*. New York: Vintage, 1995.

Reid-Pharr, Robert *Conjugal Union: The Body, the House, and the Black American*. New York: Oxford Univ. Press, 1999.

———. "Violent Ambiguity: Martin Delany, Bourgeois Sadomasochism, and the Production of Black National Masculinity." In *Representing Black Men*, ed. Marcellus Blount and George P. Cunningham, 73–94. New York: Routledge, 1996.

Robins, Natalie. *Alien Ink: The FBI's War on Freedom of Expression*. New York: Morrow, 1992.

Robinson, William. "Prince Hall." In *The Heath Anthology of American Literature*, vol. 1, ed. Paul Lauter, 685–86. Lexington, Mass.: Heath, 1990.

Rollin, Frank A. *Life and Public Services of Martin R. Delany*. 1868. Reprint, New York: Kraus, 1969.

Rotundo, E. Anthony. *American Manhood: Transformations in Masculinity from the Revolution to the Modern Era*. New York: Basic Books, 1993.

Rubin, Gayle. "The Traffic in Women: Notes toward a Political Economy of Sex."
In *Toward an Anthropology of Women*, ed. Rayna R. Reiter, 157–210. New York:
Monthly Review Press, 1975.

Rutherford, Jonathan. *Men's Silences: Predicaments in Masculinity*. London: Routledge, 1992.

Saint-Aubin, Arthur Flannigan. "Testeria: The Dis-ease of Black Men in White
Supremacist, Patriarchal Culture." *Callaloo* 17, 4 (1994): 1054–73.

Sale, Maggie Montesinos. *The Slumbering Volcano: American Slave Ship Revolts
and the Production of Rebellious Masculinity*. Durham, N.C.: Duke Univ. Press,
1997.

Savigliano, Marta E. *Tango and the Political Economy of Passion*. Boulder: Westview
Press, 1995.

Schaaf, Larry J. *Tracings of Light: Sir John Herschel and the Camera Lucida: Drawings
from the Graham Nash Collection*. San Francisco: The Friends of Photography,
1990.

Schultz, Elizabeth. "Jean Toomer's 'Box Seat': The Possibility for 'Constructive Crisis.'" In *Jean Toomer: A Critical Evaluation*, ed. Therman B. O'Daniel, 297–310.
Washington, D.C.: Howard Univ. Press, 1988.

Scott, Grant F. "The Rhetoric of Dilation: Ekphrasis and Ideology." *Word and
Image* 7, 4 (1991): 301–310.

Sedgwick, Eve Kosofsky. *Between Men: English Literature and Male Homosocial
Desire*. New York: Columbia Univ. Press, 1985.

———. *Epistemology of the Closet*. Berkeley: Univ. of California Press, 1990.

Seidler, Victor J. *Rediscovering Masculinity: Reason, Language and Sexuality*. London: Routledge, 1989.

Seltzer, Mark. *Bodies and Machines*. New York: Routledge, 1992.

Silverman, Kaja. *Male Subjectivity at the Margins*. New York: Routledge, 1992.

———. *The Threshold of the Visible World*. New York: Routledge, 1996.

Slaughter, Linda Warfel. *The Freedmen of the South*. 1869. Reprint, New York:
Kraus, 1969.

Smith, Billy G., and Richard Wojtowicz. *Blacks Who Stole Themselves: Advertisements
for Runaways in the Pennsylvania Gazette, 1728–1790*. Philadelphia: Univ. of Pennsylvania Press, 1989.

Smith, Valerie. "Gender and Afro-Americanist Literary Theory and Criticism." In
Speaking of Gender, ed. Elaine Showalter, 56–70. New York: Routledge, 1989.

Sobel, Mechal. *The World They Made Together: Black and White Values in Eighteenth-
Century Virginia*. Princeton: Princeton Univ. Press, 1987.

Sontag, Susan. *On Photography*. New York: Anchor Books, 1990.

Spillers, Hortense. "Mama's Baby, Papa's Maybe: An American Grammar Book."
In *Within the Circle: An Anthology of African American Literary Criticism from the
Harlem Renaissance to the Present*, ed. Angelyn Mitchell, 554–81. Durham, N.C.:
Duke Univ. Press, 1994.

———. "Who Cuts the Borders? Some Readings on 'America.'" In *Comparative*

American Identities: Race, Sex, and Nationality in the Modern Text, ed. Spillers, 1–22. New York: Routledge, 1991.

Spivak, Gayatri Chakravorty. *A Critique of Postcolonial Reason: Toward a History of the Vanishing Present*. Cambridge, Mass.: Harvard Univ. Press, 1999.

Staples, Robert. *Black Masculinity: The Black Male's Role in American Society*. San Francisco: Black Scholar Press, 1982.

Stepto, Robert B. *From Behind the Veil: A Study of Afro-American Narrative*. 2d ed. Urbana: Univ. of Illinois Press, 1991.

Sterling, Dorothy. *The Making of an Afro-American: Martin Robison Delany, 1812–1885*. Garden City, N.Y.: Doubleday, 1971.

Stewart, Susan. *In Longing: Narratives of the Miniature, the Gigantic, the Souvenir, the Collection*. Durham, N.C.: Duke Univ. Press, 1993.

Stowe, Harriet Beecher. *Uncle Tom's Cabin*. 1852. Reprint, with introduction by Russel B. Nye, New York: Washington Square, 1967.

Tanner, Laura E. "Uncovering the Magical Disguise of Language: The Narrative Presence in Richard Wright's *Native Son*." In *Richard Wright: Critical Perspectives Past and Present*, ed. Henry Louis Gates Jr. and K. A. Appiah, 132–48. New York: Amistad, 1993.

Tate, Claudia. *Domestic Allegories of Political Desire: The Black Heroine's Text at the Turn of the Century*. New York: Oxford Univ. Press, 1992.

Taussig, Michael. *Mimesis and Alterity: A Particular History of the Senses*. New York: Routledge, 1993.

Thomas, Calvin. *Male Matters: Masculinity, Anxiety, and the Male Body on the Line*. Urbana: Univ. of Illinois Press, 1996.

Thorpe, Edward. *Black Dance*. London: Chatto and Windus, 1989.

Toomer, Jean. *Cane*. 1923. Ed. Darwin T. Turner. New York: Norton, 1988.

——. "Outline of an Autobiography" in *The Wayward and the Seeking*, ed. Darwin T. Turner, 123. Washington, D. C.: Howard Univ. Press, 1988.

Traister, Bryce. "Academic Viagra: The Rise of American Masculinity Studies." *American Quarterly* 52, 2 (2000): 274–304.

Truman, James. Introduction to *Cyclops*, by Albert Watson. Boston: Little, Brown, and Co., 1994.

Twain, Mark. *The Tragedy of Pudd'nhead Wilson; and, the Comedy, Those Extraordinary Twins*. 1894. Reprint, with foreword by Shelly Fisher Fishkin, introduction by Shirley Anne Williams, afterword by David Lionel Smith, New York: Oxford Univ. Press, 1996.

Ullman, Victor. *Martin R. Delany: The Beginnings of Black Nationalism*. Boston: Beacon, 1971.

Unwin, Simon. *Analysing Architecture*. London: Routledge, 1997.

Upton, Dell, and John Michael Vlach, eds. *Common Places: Readings in American Vernacular Architecture*. Athens: Univ. of Georgia Press, 1986.

van Gennep, Arnold. *The Rites of Passage*. Trans. Monika B. Vizedom and Gabrielle L. Caffee. London: Routledge and Kegan Paul, 1977.

Van Leer, David. "Reading Slavery: The Anxiety of Ethnicity in Douglass' *Narrative*." In *Frederick Douglass: New Literary and Historical Essays*, ed. Eric J. Sundquist, 118–40. New York: Cambridge Univ. Press, 1990.

Vidler, Anthony. *The Architectural Uncanny: Essays in the Modern Unhomely*. Cambridge, Mass.: MIT Press, 1992.

Vlach, John Michael. *By the Work of Their Hands: Studies in Afro-American Folklife*. Charlottesville: Univ. of Virginia Press, 1991.

——. "Not Mansions . . . but Good Enough: Slave Quarters as Bi-Cultural Expression." In *Black and White Cultural Interaction in the Antebellum South*, ed. Ted Ownby, 89–114. Jackson: Univ. Press of Mississippi, 1993.

Walcott, Derek. *The Odyssey: A Stage Version*. London: Faber and Faber, 1993.

Wallace, Michele. *Black Macho and the Myth of the Superwoman*. New York: Dial, 1979.

Wallis, Brian. "Black Bodies, White Science: Louis Agassiz's Slave Daguerreotypes." *American Art* (summer 1995): 39–61.

Walters, Ronald G. "The Erotic South: Civilization and Sexuality in American Abolitionism." *American Quarterly* 25, 2 (1973): 177–201.

Warner, Michael. *The Letters of the Republic: Publication and the Public Sphere in Eighteenth-Century America*. Cambridge, Mass.: Harvard Univ. Press, 1990.

Washington, Booker T. *My Larger Education: Being Chapters from My Experience*. Garden City, N.Y.: Doubleday, Page and Co., 1911.

——. *The Story of My Life and Work*. Reprint, with an introduction by J. L. M. Curry, New York: Negro Universities Press, 1969.

——. *The Story of the Negro: The Rise of the Race from Slavery*, vol. 2. New York: Doubleday, Page, 1909.

——. *Up from Slavery*. 1901. Reprint, New York: Magnum, 1968.

Washington, Eric K. "Sculpture in Flight: A Conversation with Bill T. Jones." *Transition* 62 (1993): 188–202.

Watson, Albert. *Cyclops*. Boston: Little, Brown, 1994.

Weatherby, W. J. *James Baldwin: Artist on Fire*. New York: Dell, 1989.

Weems, Renita. "Reading *Her* Way through the Struggle: African American Women and the Bible." In *Stony the Road We Trod: African American Biblical Interpretation*, ed. Cain Hope Felder, 57–77. Minneapolis: Fortress, 1991.

Wesley, Charles H. *Prince Hall: Life and Legacy*. Washington, D.C.: United Supreme Council, Southern Jurisdiction, Prince Hall Affiliation, 1977.

West, Cornel. *Race Matters*. New York: Beacon, 1993.

——. "Why I'm Marching in Washington." In *Black Men on Race, Gender, and Sexuality: A Critical Reader*, ed. Devon Carbado, 26–27. New York: New York Univ. Press, 1999.

White, Deborah Gray. *Ar'n't I a Woman?: Female Slaves in the Plantation South*. New York: Norton, 1985.

Whitman, Walt. "I Sing the Body Electric." In *The Whitman Reader*, ed. Maxwell Geismar, 63–72. New York: Pocket Books, 1955.

Wideman, John Edgar. *Fatheralong: A Meditation on Fathers and Sons, Race and Society*. New York: Pantheon, 1994.

Wiegman, Robyn. *American Anatomies: Theorizing Race and Gender*. Durham, N.C.: Duke Univ. Press, 1995.

Wigley, Mark. *The Architecture of Deconstruction: Derrida's Haunt*. Cambridge, Mass.: MIT Press, 1993.

——. "Untitled: The Housing of Gender." In *Sexuality and Space*, ed. Beatriz Colomina, 327–89. New York: Princeton Architectural Press, 1992.

Williams, Loretta J. *Black Freemasonry and Middle-Class Realities*. Columbia, Mo.: Univ. of Missouri Press, 1980.

Williams, Peter. "Constituting Class and Gender: A Social History of the Home, 1700–1901." In *Class and Space: The Making of Urban Society*, ed. Nigel Thrift and Williams, 154–204. London: Routledge and Kegan Paul, 1987.

Williams, Raymond. *Marxism and Literature*. Oxford: Oxford Univ. Press, 1977.

Winbush, Vincent. "The Bible and African-Americans: An Outline of an Interpretive History." In *Stony the Road We Trod: African American Biblical Interpretation*, ed. Cain Hope Felder, 81–97. Minneapolis: Fortress, 1991.

Winter, Marian Hannah. "Juba and American Minstrelsy." In *Chronicles of the American Dance*, ed. Paul David Magriel, 39–63. New York: Holt, 1948.

Woolf, Virginia. *A Room of One's Own*. 1929. Reprint, New York: Harcourt Brace Jovanovich, 1957.

Wright, Richard. *Native Son*. 1940. Reprint, New York: HarperCollins, 1993.

Yarborough, Richard. "The First-Person in Afro-American Fiction." In *Afro-American Literary Study in the 1990s*, ed. Houston A. Baker Jr. and Patricia Redmond, 105–34. Chicago: Univ. of Chicago Press, 1989.

Young, Lola. "Missing Persons: Fantasising Black Women in *Black Skin, White Masks*." [*sic*] In *The Fact of Blackness: Frantz Fanon and Visual Representation*, ed. Alan Read, 86–101. London: Institute of Contemporary Arts, 1996.

Žižek, Slavoj. *The Fragile Absolute; or Why Is the Christian Legacy Worth Fighting For?* London: Verso, 2000.

INDEX

Enframement (*cont.*)
and, 30; translated from German, 184
n.25; Watson and, 28; as ur-trope of
black masculine visibility, 8, 28. *See
also* Frame(-up); Gaze; Spectragraphia; Traces
Enframing, 6, 29, 173
Epistemology of the Closet (Sedgwick),
111–14, 197 n.21, 204 n.17
Exceptionalism, 54, 75

Fani-Kayode, Rotimi: *Black Male/White
Male,* 48, 150
Fanon, Frantz, 91, 97; anti-ocularcen-
trism and, 171–72; *Black Skin White
Masks,* 14, 170–78, 212 n.25; The
Conspiracy, 176; *The Drowning Eye,*
176; dramaturgical concerns and,
175–76; enframement and, 14–15; on
Hegel, 196 n.12; *Parallel Hands,* 176;
and third-person consciousness, 97,
174; *The Wretched of the Earth,* 176
Farrakhan, Louis, 76
"FBEye Blues" (Wright), 136, 138
Federal Bureau of Investigation (FBI):
James Baldwin and, 135–43, 206 n.6,
207–8 nn.18–19; Richard Wright
and, 136. *See also* Freedom of Information Act (1966)
Female masculinity, 49
Feminism, 3; black, 3, 5
Fetishism, 20; James Baldwin's FBI papers and, 137; Homi Bhabha and,
24–25; and black bodies, 29; in *Black
Skin White Masks,* 172; Bill T. Jones
and, 162, 164–66; modernism and,
29; photography and, 20–21; racial
gaze and, 30; in *Vanishing Rooms,*
157; Watson and, 20, 22–25, 48
Film: in *Native Son,* 40, 41
First-person narrative. *See* Narrative,
first-person
Foucault, Michel, 2, 94, 103, 171

Fox Talbot, Henry, 27–28
Fraleigh, Sondra Horton: *Dance and the
Lived Body,* 150
Frame, 8–9, 29, 32, 47, 112, 149, 175.
See also *Debordement*; Frame(-up)
Frame(-up), 8; James Baldwin and,
140; in *Black Skin White Masks,* 14–
15; in *Native Son,* 41–44. *See also* Enframement; Gaze; Spectragraphia;
Traces
Fraternalism. *See* Freemasonry
Freedom of Information Act (1966),
141, 206 n.6. *See also* Federal Bureau
of Investigations (FBI)
Freemasonry: artisan figure in, 63–65,
69; black, 10, 11, 53–56, 58–69, 75–
82, 188 n.1; birth of, 54–56; important posts in, 78, 80; paranoia concerning, 75–76; promotion of artifactual process, 62, 66; realist tautology
and, 66; rite of Third Degree, 63, 191
n.36; symbolism of lodge-room in,
67, 76–78, 80; white, 55, 65, 67–68;
women and, 80; "work" of, 191 n.45.
See also Lodge-room, Masonic
Freud, Sigmund, 39, 90; on castration
complex, 37; *das Heimliche* and, 12,
123, 124, 182 n.36; *das Unheimliche*
and, 12, 123, 182 n.36; *Interpretation
of Dreams,* 185 n.44; on Medusa figure, 37; on permanent traces, 33, 185
nn.44–45; "The Uncanny," 123, 182
n.36

Garrison, William Lloyd, 70
Garrow, David: *FBI and Martin Luther
King, Jr., The,* 139
Gates, Henry Louis, 116, 150, 163, 166;
"Binary Oppositions in Chapter One
of *Narrative of Frederick Douglass,*"
85; on the Talking Book, 209 n.21
Gay and lesbian activism, 14
Gaze: "the assertoric gaze," 172, 173;

Jacobs, Harriet: *Incidents in the Life of Slave Girl*, 89–90

Jazz (Morrison), 150, 209 n.21

Johnson, Charles: on black cultural history, 58; experience of spectragraphic misrecognition, 31–32; "A Phenomenology of the Black Body," 9, 31

Jones, Bill T., 146, 167–68; black dance traditions and, 163; black gay identity and, 163; fetishism and, 164–66; the gaze subverted by, 166; *Last Night on Earth*, 14, 162–66; "Last Night on Earth", 164–66; physical allure of, 163–64; resistant look of, 164, 166; solo performances, 163, 164; and Arnie Zane 162–63

Jordan, Winthrop: *White Over Black: American Attitudes toward the Negro*, 96, 97

Journal of African American Men (*JAAM*), 4, 181 n.13

"Kabnis" (Toomer): architextuality in, 124, 126–30

Kaplan, Sidney, 55–56, 58; *Black Presence in the Era of the American Revolution*, 58

Kennedy, Robert, 138

Lacan, Jacques, 2, 129, 149, 197–98 n.21

Lane, William Henry (Juba), 147–48

"Last Night on Earth" (choreography), 164–66.

Last Night on Earth (Jones), 14, 162–66; compared to *Vanishing Rooms*, 162; fetishism and, 162

Levin, Michael, 171, 172; *Modernity and the Hegemony of Vision*, 170

Levine, Lawrence, 77, 116

Literacy, history of black, 196–97 n.15

Lodge-room, Masonic: architecture of, 10, 67, 76–78; and cultural memory,

67–69; as figure for self, 10, 76–78, 80; sex and gender symbolized in, 80

Look: versus the gaze, 6, 182 n.19; resistant: 12–13, 141; James Baldwin and, 141–43, 145

Louima, Abner, 5

Louis, Joe, 150

Mackey, Albert, 67, 77–80; *Encyclopedia of Freemasonry and Its Kindred Science*, 78; *The Symbolism of Freemasonry*, 80

Mapplethorpe, Robert, 7, 25, 45

March on Washington (1963), 5

Masculinity, race and, 1, 149

Masculinity studies: black, 4–5; b(l)ackside of, 4, 180 n.10; crisis theory in, 6; current state of, 2; firstwave, 3; maleness of, challenged, 49; origins of, 179 n.7; second-wave, 3–4; whiteness of, 2–4

Mask, 116. *See also* Passing, racial; Minstrel mask

Masonic lodge-room. *See* Lodge-room, Masonic

Masonry. *See* Freemasonry

Master Mason, 67, 78, 80. *See also* Freemasonry: important posts in

Memory-trace. *See* Freud, Sigmund: on permanent traces

Mercer, Kobena, 6, 25, 34, 45, 180 n.9; *Welcome to the Jungle*, 3

Metapicture, 21, 30

Military masculinism: in colonial period, 55–56; Martin Delany and, 71–72; Booker T. Washington and, 104–5

Miller, D. A., 117; "Secret Subjects, Open Secrets," 118

Million Man March, 5

Mimicry, 48; Roland Barthes on, 47; ocular, 171; Albert Watson and, 46

Minstrel mask: *Up from Slavery* and, 98;

Photography (*cont.*)
versus photo-graphic, 207 n.9;
Wright and, 134. *See also* Watson,
Albert
Polymorphous perverse, 84, 90–91, 95
Pose: cool, 46–47; Martin Delany's pictorial, 75, 83; Disdérian protocols
and, 75; Prince Hall's pictorial, 61,
83; in "Last Night on Earth," 165–
66; linguistic, in *Native Son,* 46;
photographic, 10, 46–47
Prince Hall Freemasonry. *See* Freemasonry: black
Prince, Nero, 59, 61
Psychoanalysis: first-person narrative
and, 83–84; race and, 195–96 n.9

Racist (mis)representation, 13, 62, 142,
158, 175. *See also* Spectragraphia
Radway, Jan, 93, 94
Rampersad, Arnold, 158–59
Rape, female: in *Narrative* of 1845, 86–
87; slavery and, 87–88, 198 n.23. *See
also* Slavery: gender and
Rape, male: slavery and, 88; threat in
Narrative of 1845, 87–95; threat in
Native Son, 187 n.66
Realist tautology, 66, 82; Freemasonry
and, 66
Regimentalism: *Up from Slavery* and,
100; Samuel C. Armstrong and, 102–
4; Booker T. Washington and, 104–6
Reid-Pharr, Robert: *Conjugal Union:
The Body, the House, and the Black
American,* 190 n.27, 200 n.69
Representation: arrested, 28; artifactual,
60–61, 63, 106
Representation, black male: ekphrastic
threat in, 34, 43; in *Native Son,* 43;
fugitive, 61–62, 103; narrow economy of, 6; photographic effect on,
7, 31, 32. *See also* Racist (mis)repre-
sentation

Representation, racial: camerical roots
of, 26–28
Robins, Natalie, 207 n.18; *Alien Ink:
The FBI's War on Freedom of Expres-
sion,* 206–7 n.6
Romance narrative, 93–94, 98, 99
Romantic racialism, 99, 200 n.65

Saint-Aubin, Arthur Flannigan, 111;
"Testeria: The Dis-ease of Black Men
in White Supremacist, Patriarchal
Culture," 2, 3
Screen. *See* Representation, black male:
narrow economy of
Secrecy: in *Narrative* of 1845, 118; space
and, 113; as spiritual exercise. *See also*
Silence
Sedgwick, Eve: architecture and, 12; *Between Men,* 1–2, 149; *Epistemology of
the Closet,* 111–14, 197–98 n.21, 204
n.17. *See also* Speech acts
Seltzer, Mark, 54, 56, 60–63, 66, 69,
103, 106, 127; *Bodies and Machines,* 69
Shakur, Tupac, 21
Silence: in *Cane,* 130; the closet and,
113; in *Native Son,* 45–46; space and,
113, 117; subaltern, 7–8, 117. *See also*
Secrecy
Silverman, Kaja, 127; on the gaze, 41;
heteropathic identification and, 32;
on the look, 6; on the photographic
pose, 47, 103; and screens, 6; on
traces, 39–41
Slave: advertisements, runaway, 61–62,
190–91 n.33; literacy, 191 n.33; narratives, 83; self-censoring in, 89–90.
See also Slavery: male-male sexual violence in
Slavery: labor versus work in, 192 n.51;
gender and, 85–86; homosexuality
in, 199 n.34; male-male sexual violence in, 87–95; sentiment and, 99
Soldier: as icon of manliness, 71

Maurice O. Wallace is Assistant Professor of English and African-American Studies at Duke University.

Library of Congress Cataloging-in-Publication Data
Wallace, Maurice O.
Constructing the Black masculine : identity and ideality
in African American men's literature and culture, 1775–1995 /
Maurice O. Wallace.
p. cm. — (A John Hope Franklin Center book)
Includes bibliographical references and index.
ISBN 0-8223-2854-2 (cloth : alk. paper)
ISBN 0-8223-2869-0 (pbk. : alk. paper)
1. African American men — Race identity. 2. African
American men — Psychology. 3. Masculinity — United States.
4. Ideals (Psychology). 5. African American men —
Intellectual life. 6. African American intellectuals — History.
7. African American men in literature. 8. American
literature — African American authors. I. Title.
B185.625 .W355 2002   305.38′896073-dc21   2001006934